# USING COMPUTER BULLETIN BOARDS

**JOHN V. HEDTKE**

PUBLISHING
FOR THE
TWENTY-FIRST
CENTURY

MIS:
PRESS

P.O. Box 5277
Portland, Oregon 97208-5277
(503) 282-5215

**Second Printing**

**ISBN** 1-55828-020-2

Printed in the United States of America

Amiga is a registered trademark of Commodore Business Machines, Inc.

Apple IIgs and Macintosh are registered trademarks of Apple Computer, Inc.

Atari is a registered trademark of Atari, Inc.

BT TYMNET is a registered trademark of BT Tymnet, Inc.

Commodore, Commodore 64 and Commodore 128 are trademarks of Commodore Business Machines, Inc.

CompuServe is a registered trademark of CompuServe Information Service (CIS and EIS are not CompuServe
    Information Service trademarks).

CP/M is a trademark of Digital Research, Inc.

DataPac is a trademark of Bell of Canada.

Delphi is a registered trademark of General Videotex Corporation.

DIALOG is a registered service mark of DIALOG Information Services, Inc.

Dow Jones News/Retrieval is a registered trademark of Dow Jones & Company.

EAASY SABRE is a service mark of American Airlines, Inc., and a product of the SABRE Travel Information
    Network of American Airlines, Inc.

EasyLink is a service mark of Western Union Telegraph Co.

The Economic Bulletin Board is a registered trademark of the U.S. Department of Commerce.

Fido, the dog-with-diskette, and FidoNet are registered trademarks of Tom Jennings. Fido, FidoNet, and all support
    programs are copyright 1987, 1989 by Tom Jennings.

Galactic Empire is copyright 1988 by M.B. Murdock & Associates.

GEnie, RoundTable, and LiveWire are trademarks of General Electric Company, U.S.A.

Hamrbi and King are copyright 1977 by People's Computer Company, Menlo Park, CA.

Hayes Smartmodem is a registered trademark of Hayes Microcomputer Products, Inc.

# DEDICATION

To my father, **Dr. Charles Herman Hedtke,** from whom I learned to write. When I was a child, he showed me how to look things up and taught me the value of having an extensive library of research materials. I am pleased that I have modeled my working habits after his. This book is dedicated to him.

# ACKNOWLEDGMENTS

There are two books for every book that is written. The first is the book that the author envisioned. The second is the book as it actually turned out. With any kind of luck, the two books bear some resemblance to each other.

I want to take a moment to acknowledge the support and many contributions of the following people and companies without whose efforts the book that you hold in your hand would not be nearly as close to the book I envisioned several years ago.

First and foremost, I want to acknowledge the (reasonably) patient efforts of my wife and partner, **Patricia Callander Hedtke,** who first suggested that I write a book on BBSing, and who is a continual inspiration to me on what to say and how to say it better. Patricia has reviewed chapters for their flow and consistency, emphasized where I could improve, and made hundreds of invaluable suggestions that are incorporated in the final text. Without her efforts, this book would not be half as good as it is.

**Bob Williams,** president of MIS: Press, for wanting to do a book on bulletin boards.

**Bill Gladstone,** Waterside Publications, for putting me and Bob Williams in touch with each other and for negotiating the contract.

**Kim Anne Thomas, Ronda Cole, Milan Moncilovich,** and **Doug Snyder,** my editors at MIS: Press, for patience and clear explanations.

**The Flying Kiwi,** sysop of The Library, for helping me in my research efforts and for providing a consistently superior bulletin board to the Greater Puget Sound.

**K. C. Coldbrook,** for taking time out of his already busy schedule to review the first half of the book and to point out where I could say more.

**Mike Coombs,** for providing copies of the many shareware bulletin board systems and communications packages featured in this book.

**Ken Kaplan,** co-founder of the International FidoNet Association, for his time and knowledge about FidoNet and networking in general.

**Bob Donnell,** KD7NM, who has been telling me about the wonders of packet radio for years now, for showing me how packet radio works.

**Tim Pozar,** Late Night Software, for his extensive and generous help on ARPANET, Usenet, and FidoNet.

**Jon Singer** (yes, folks, I know Jon too), for providing technical information on network addressing.

**Lisa Gronke,** for her time reviewing and discussing the section on UUCP and Usenet.

**Bob Dinse,** sysop of Eskimo North, for his advice and comments on being a sysop.

**Jack Rickard,** editor of the *Boardwatch Magazine,* for his time, expertise, and advice.

**Van Van Horn,** for FidoNet information and setting me up with a FidoNet account on credit.

**Mike Zakharoff,** sysop of the Interstate BBS, for providing extensive information about FidoNet and for giving permission to reprint his policy statement.

**Steve York,** for information on the development of Citadel and room BBSes.

**Dave Dodell,** for his comments on the direction of BBSing.

**Robert and Debi Michnick,** sysops of ProStar Plus, for information about doors and online games.

**Sharma,** for her support and "background" work at Art's.

**Grant Fjermedal,** a superior author in his own right, for advice on the publishing process.

**Kalen Bonn and Beowulf,** for information on the early history of BBSing in Seattle and for their suggestions and feedback on the first few chapters.

**Doc Sherrell,** for last-minute help fixing one of my computers.

**Heather R. Scott, Jeremiah Johnson, Steve Petersen, The Dragon, John, Penny Priddy, Pink, Zen Master, Maher Maso,** and the other sysops on the DragCit network for their strong and active support, advice, helping me gather information and opinions.

The following individuals and companies have also been very gracious in extending me help, support, and time, and are strongly deserving of recognition and your patronage:

**Philip L. Becker,** president of eSoft, Inc., creator of The Bread Board System (TBBS).

**Jim Harrer** and **Rick Heming** of Mustang Software, Inc., creators of WILDCAT!

**Fred Clark** of Clark Development Company, Inc., creator of PCBoard.

**Tom Jennings** of Fido Software, creator of Fido.

**A. J. Chitoff,** marketing communications manager for Delphi/General Videotex.

**Stephen R. Haracznak,** manager of press relations for GE Information Services and its GEnie service.

**Hayes Microcomputer Products, Inc.**

**Kitty Munger Thomas,** public relations specialist for CompuServe, Inc.

**Denise Greene,** BIX customer service representative, and **Tony Lockwood,** BIX managing editor.

**Robin Gail Ramsey** of The WELL.

**Prodigy Information Services, Inc.**

**Robin Carlson,** manager, public relations, US Sprint Communications Co.

**Rick Brandt,** public relations coordinator for BT Tymnet, Inc.

Finally, to the many contributors to BBSing forums on The Library and on Memory Alpha, Eighth Dimension, The Log Cabin, C Hacker's Forum, Challenger 51-L, Age of Aquarius, The Fifth Dimension, Pinxit, and all the other members of the DragCit network, my warmest thanks for your advice, help, and suggestions.

# TABLE OF CONTENTS

# INTRODUCTION

Welcome to *Using Computer Bulletin Boards*. This book introduces you to computer bulletin board systems (BBSes): what they are and how to use them. You can use BBSes to exchange messages with people, send and receive files and programs, play games, and get information.

## Who Should Use This Book?

This book introduces beginners to BBSes and basic telecommunication concepts and helps intermediate and advanced bulletin board users to use BBSes more effectively. This book is for you if you want to:

- have fun with BBSes
- use BBSes and online information services to get information on a subject
- make money with BBSes
- set up a BBS of your own

This book will teach you how to use BBSes of all kinds. It starts by discussing basic telecommunications concepts and shows you what equipment to use. The book then demonstrates using a BBS. Next, the book introduces you to a wide variety of popular BBSes. It shows you how to set up your own BBS—how to choose software, a computer, and a modem—and how to make money with your BBS. The book concludes by showing ways in which businesses, school systems, and the government use BBSes.

## Conventions

This section shows you how the various typestyles are used to present information.

Information you type as input appears in *italics*.

Terms being defined are also displayed in *italics*.

Prompts and information that appears on the computer screen is displayed in the `courier` typeface.

Keynames, the names appearing on the keys of a standard IBM keyboard, appear in brackets (for example, [ENTER], [ESC], and [SHIFT]. If you need to press several keys at once, the keys are joined with a hyphen (-). For example, [ALT-T] means that you should hold down the [Alt] key and press the letter T. Similarly, [CTRL-W-S] means that you should hold down the the control key [CTRL] and press W and S.

## Screens and Figures

The screens appearing in this book are depicted as they appear on an IBM Personal Computer using an EGA monitor. What you see on your screen may be slightly different, depending on the configuration of your hardware.

# How to Use this Book

If you are new to BBSes, start by reading Chapters 1 and 2 to learn about telecommunications and how to log on to a BBS. You can then try some of the BBSes in your area (numbers for nationwide BBSes are listed in Appendix B).

After getting your feet wet, read Chapters 3, 4, and 5 to round out your understanding of how to use basic BBS features. You can then use Chapters 6 and 7 to expand your knowledge of specific BBSes. Chapters 8 and 9 show ways to exchange information with BBS users outside your local area.

Chapters 10 and 11 are invaluable for people interested in getting the most out of BBSes and in setting up a BBS of their own. Chapter 12 gives you a glimpse of the future of BBSing.

Each chapter concludes with a section entitled "Becoming an Expert," that summarizes the chapter and may add additional information you will find helpful as your experience with BBSes grows.

# How This Book Is Organized

Chapter 1, "Basic Concepts," describes some essential telecommunications concepts and shows you what equipment and software you need to use BBSes.

Chapter 2, "Getting Started," shows you how to log on to and use a typical BBS. Sample screens demonstrate how to set up your own user identification, get help on the BBS's features, and log out.

Chapter 3, "Reading and Entering Messages," builds on the techniques you learned in Chapter 2. In this chapter, you learn how to exchange messages with other BBS users.

Chapter 4, "Sending and Receiving Files," teaches you to send and receive files and programs. This chapter also contains valuable information on viruses and how to avoid them.

Chapter 5, "Chatting and Playing Games," introduces you to some of the more unusual features of BBSes, such as chatting with the sysop and with other users, and running programs such as online games.

When you are comfortable with the material in the first half of the book, you can start broadening your horizons. The second half of the book addresses topics of interest to the intermediate BBS user.

Chapter 6, "Linear BBSes," describes how to use six of the most popular linear BBSes: RBBS-PC, Fido, OPUS, PCBoard, WILDCAT!, and TBBS. The chapter also presents a brief history and sample screens for each BBS.

Chapter 7, "Room BBSes," introduces you to room BBSes and how they work. The chapter examines TurboCit, a popular room BBS, in detail.

Chapter 8, "Extending Your Reach," focuses on ways to interact with BBS users outside of your local calling area around the country and the world. The chapter talks about using long-distance phone services, networks, and BBSing over amateur radio.

Chapter 9, "Online Information Services," presents information about a variety of online information services such as CompuServe, GEnie, Delphi, and BIX.

Chapter 10, "Setting Up Your Own BBS," shows you how to start your own BBS. The chapter discusses selecting hardware and software, arranging for phone service, establishing policies, dealing with problem users, and keeping your BBS exciting. It concludes with a section on how to make money with your BBS.

Chapter 11, "Ways You Can Use BBSes" discusses how different organizations can use BBSes to advertise services, increase communication with customers, and make their organization more efficient. The chapter also shows some of the ways BBSes are used in school systems and government.

Chapter 12, "Epilogue: The Future of BBSing" is a look at the what's ahead according to some noted BBS developers and sysops.

The four appendices present additional information of special interest.

Appendix A, "Communications Software," lists a number of inexpensive and easy-to-use communications programs for various computers.

Appendix B, "BBS Numbers," lists some BBS numbers around the country and tells you how to find BBSes in your area.

Appendix C, "BBS Software," gives sources for BBS software.

Appendix D, "Troubleshooting," describes how to interpret your modem's indicator lights.

The glossary defines many of the terms covered in the book.

The bibliography lists books and articles on related subjects for further reading.

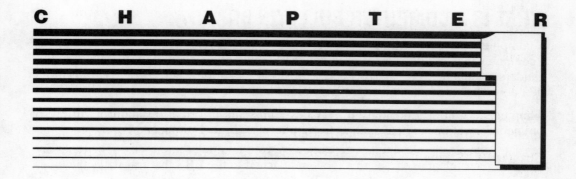

C H A P T E R

1

# BASIC CONCEPTS

This chapter gives the definition of computer bulletin boards and an overview of how they work. It describes some basic telecommunications concepts, shows what equipment and software you need to use a bulletin board system, and explains how to set up the equipment.

# WHAT IS A COMPUTER BULLETIN BOARD?

A computer bulletin board (also known as a *bulletin board system*, or *BBS* for short) is a computer that uses a special program that allows other computers to call it over a standard telephone line. A BBS acts as a storage facility, where people calling from their computers can post messages and upload and download programs.

*Modems* (short for <u>mo</u>dulator-<u>dem</u>odulator) make communication between BBSes and computers possible. When you call a BBS, the modem attached to your computer translates the electrical impulses generated by your computer into tones. The tones are then sent over telephone lines to a modem attached to the BBS that translates the tones back into electrical impulses that the BBS computer can understand.

## Uses of BBSes

BBSes are used in many different ways. Like a cork bulletin board, they can be used to post pieces of news, humor, and notices. Many BBSes are like CB or ham radio; you can have a conversation with one or more persons by typing messages back and forth to each other. BBSes are also used to send and receive private messages quickly and easily. They can also be used to obtain information about a given topic and even to ask other people to help you do research. BBSes let people exchange files and programs, play games, buy and sell things, and meet and talk to other people in different parts of the country.

BBSes frequently focus on a specific topic or set of interests. There are BBSes specializing in virtually any topic imaginable. Just a few of the topics BBSes specialize in are:

| | | |
|---|---|---|
| adult conversation | engineering | matchmaking |
| Amigas | farming | music |
| astrology | folk music | painting |
| auto repair | games | parenting |
| Commodores | geology | philosophy |
| computers | ham radio | physics |
| dancing | human rights | programming |
| ecology | job seeking | rock music |
| electronics | Macintoshes | sports |

Many businesses also use BBSes for simple electronic mail and information distribution networks. BBSes can be used to collect large amounts of data from a variety of remote sites quickly. Some of the businesses that are now using BBSes include:

| | | |
|---|---|---|
| auto mechanics | engineering firms | sales organizations |
| banks | film studios | software companies |
| construction firms | government offices | travel agencies |

## A Short History of BBSes

Ward Christensen and Randy Suess wrote the first BBS software, known as CBBS (for Computer Bulletin Board System), in 1978. Designed to look something like an actual cork bulletin board found on a school or office wall, CBBS was to act as a local message center that computer users could dial up over the phone lines. The idea of computer bulletin boards caught on rapidly and a number of other BBS programs were developed.

Since 1978, the number of BBSes has grown from a handful to over a half a million. The number of BBSes and BBS users continues to grow rapidly, particularly in metropolitan areas. It has been predicted that by the year 2000, there will be between 15 and 20 million BBS users in the United States.

# UNDERSTANDING COMMUNICATIONS

This section tells about the *ASCII character set,* a standard system of storing and transferring information. It will also show how computers send and receive ASCII characters using *bits,* electrical pulses used to store information.

## The ASCII Character Set

Every character the computer receives, processes, or sends is stored as a number. To make this process easier, computers use the American Standard Code for Information Interchange, commonly known as the *ASCII code* or the ASCII character set. (ASCII is pronounced "ask-ee.") The ASCII code assigns a unique numeric value (known as an *ASCII value)* to every number, character, and symbol that appears on a computer screen.

ASCII values are very much like ciphers you may have used when you were younger, substituting 1 for A, 2 for B, and so on up to 26 for Z. In this case, though, the ASCII value for a capital *A* is 65, a capital *B* is 66, and so on. Because capital and lowercase letters need to be differentiated, there is a separate set of ASCII values for lowercase letters. For example, the ASCII value for *a* is 97, for *b* it is 98, and for *z* it is 122. Numbers and punctuation also have unique ASCII values. Even a space has an ASCII value, 32. Figure 1-1 shows a table of characters and their ASCII values.

| | | | | | | | | | | |
|---|---|---|---|---|---|---|---|---|---|---|
| 0 | null | 22 | ▬ | 44 | , | 66 | B | 88 | X | 110 | n |
| 1 | ☺ | 23 | ↕ | 45 | - | 67 | C | 89 | Y | 111 | o |
| 2 | ● | 24 | ↑ | 46 | . | 68 | D | 90 | Z | 112 | p |
| 3 | ♥ | 25 | ↓ | 47 | / | 69 | E | 91 | [ | 113 | q |
| 4 | ♦ | 26 | → | 48 | 0 | 70 | F | 92 | \ | 114 | r |
| 5 | ♣ | 27 | escape | 49 | 1 | 71 | G | 93 | ] | 115 | s |
| 6 | ♠ | 28 | right | 50 | 2 | 72 | H | 94 | | 116 | t |
| 7 | beep | 29 | left | 51 | 3 | 73 | I | 95 | _ | 117 | u |
| 8 | backspace | 30 | up | 52 | 4 | 74 | J | 96 | | 118 | v |
| 9 | tab | 31 | down | 53 | 5 | 75 | K | 97 | a | 119 | w |
| 10 | linefeed | 32 | space | 54 | 6 | 76 | L | 98 | b | 120 | x |
| 11 | home | 33 | ! | 55 | 7 | 77 | M | 99 | c | 121 | y |
| 12 | formfeed | 34 | " | 56 | 8 | 78 | N | 100 | d | 122 | z |
| 13 | enter | 35 | # | 57 | 9 | 79 | O | 101 | e | 123 | { |
| 14 | ♫ | 36 | $ | 58 | : | 80 | P | 102 | f | 124 | | |
| 15 | ☼ | 37 | % | 59 | ; | 81 | Q | 103 | g | 125 | } |
| 16 | ► | 38 | & | 60 | < | 82 | R | 104 | h | 126 | ~ |
| 17 | ◄ | 39 | ' | 61 | = | 83 | S | 105 | i | 127 | ⌂ |
| 18 | ↕ | 40 | ( | 62 | > | 84 | T | 106 | j | | |
| 19 | ‼ | 41 | ) | 63 | ? | 85 | U | 107 | k | | |
| 20 | ¶ | 42 | * | 64 | @ | 86 | V | 108 | l | | |
| 21 | § | 43 | + | 65 | A | 87 | W | 109 | m | | |

*Figure 1-1. Table of ASCII Characters*

The first 32 ASCII characters, from 0 to 31, are *control characters*. These characters don't normally show up on your screen, but they do tell the computer to do something, such as enter, backspace, tab, and form feed. The ASCII values for control characters, letters, numbers, and punctuation use the values from 0 to 127.

The ASCII character set lets computers communicate with each other with an accepted standard. When a computer sees an ASCII value of 84, the computer will always interpret that as a capital *T*.

## How Computers Store Information

A computer stores the value representing an ASCII character using electrical pulses or *bits*. The term "bit" is short for *binary digit*. There are only two binary digits, 0 and 1.

If the computer used only a single 0 and a single 1 to represent each value, this would limit the values the computer could store to either 0 or 1. The computer uses a combination of bits, that is, combinations of 0's and 1's, to represent values greater than 0 and 1.

For example, suppose a computer used a combination of two bits to represent values. Different combinations of the two bits can represent four values, from 0 to 3, as shown in Figure 1-2.

```
00          01          10          11
 0           1           2           3
```

*Figure 1-2. Numbers with Two Binary Digits*

Similarly, with three bits, the computer could store up to eight different values from 0 to 7, as shown in Figure 1-3.

```
000    001    010    011    100    101    110    111
 0      1      2      3      4      5      6      7
```

*Figure 1-3. Numbers with Three Binary Digits*

As these figures show, each time another bit is added, twice as many values can be stored. With four bits, the values for 16 different characters can be stored, with five bits, 32, and so on. To store values from 0 to 127, the number of characters in the ASCII table, seven bits are needed. Figure 1-4 shows several ASCII characters, their ASCII values, and the seven-bit representation of the same value.

```
  1      ☺       0000001        8    backspace   0001000
 13    enter     0001101       32    space       0100000
 48      0       0110000       49    1           0110001
 55      7       0110111       56    8           0111000
 65      A       1000001       90    Z           1011010
 97      a       1100001       98    b           1100010
122      z       1111010      127    ⌂           1111111
```

*Figure 1-4. ASCII Characters and Their Binary Values*

There are an additional 128 ASCII codes with values from 128 to 255 that are used for line drawing characters, characters from foreign alphabets, and special math symbols. By adding one more bit to seven-bit groups, a computer is able to store these 128 additional characters.

A group of seven or eight bits that represents a single character is known as a *byte*. You have doubtless heard this term before in reference to the storage capacity of a computer, probably as "kilobytes" or "megabytes." A diskette that is rated at "360 kilobytes" is able to hold approximately 360,000 characters, about one character per byte. To give an example about how much text this is, this book contains about 360,000 characters. Similarly, a 40-megabyte hard disk could hold approximately 40,000,000 characters, roughly equal to the number of characters in 111 copies of this book.

## How Computers Talk to Each Other

When people talk on the telephone, they are sending and receiving information in the form of sound waves. What one person says at one end is translated into electrical signals, transmitted along the telephone wires, and turned back into sound waves at the other end.

Computers talk over the telephone lines in much the same way, but instead of sound waves they communicate with electrical pulses representing bits. A modem converts the electrical pulse for each bit into a specific tone depending on whether the bit is a 1 or a 0. The tone for the bit is then transmitted over the phone lines. Another modem at the other end of the line receives the tone and converts it back into an electrical pulse its computer can understand. Figure 1-5 shows how two computers communicate.

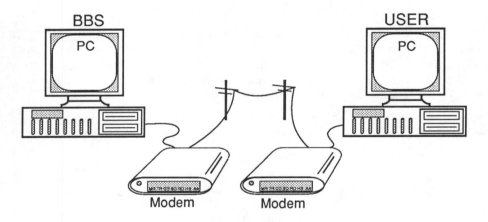

*Figure 1-5. Basic Computer Communications*

### Parity

*Parity* is a simple form of error checking used to show if a byte was received correctly. Noise on the line can garble information sent between computers, just as it can garble voices when you are talking on the phone. When computers communicate over the phone lines, the tones for the bits may be distorted so that the modem interprets them incorrectly.

In an attempt to prevent transmission errors, a computer adds an extra bit, known as the *parity bit,* to a seven-bit byte. The computer then adds the bits in the byte together to see if the total (including the parity bit) is odd or even. If the computer is checking for *even parity,* all the bits in the byte must add up to an even number. If the computer is checking for *odd parity,* all the bits in the byte must add up to an odd number.

For example, suppose the computer is checking the parity of the letter *G,* which has an ASCII value of 71. The binary representation of 71 is 1000111. The digits add up to 4 (1+0+0+0+1+1+1). If the parity is even, the parity bit would be 0. If the parity is odd, the parity would be set to 1, making the total of the digits 5, an odd number.

Although checking the parity is helpful, it is not foolproof. Under certain conditions, mistakes can slip through. For example, if the bits for the character *G* (1000111) were being sent with even parity and two of the bits were changed, the character could become 1000<u>00</u>1, or the letter *A*. Because the digits still add up to be even (1+0+0+0+0+0+1 = 2), the receiving computer won't know that anything is wrong. Parity checking is used by itself only when an occasional mistake won't be critical. Chapter 3 discusses several other ways of checking for errors that are more reliable.

Most computers and modems only check for parity if you are using seven-bit bytes. If you are using eight-bit bytes, parity is not checked. Most BBSes use either seven data bits with even parity, or eight data bits with no parity.

### Start and Stop Bits

When you ask someone to copy an address over the phone, you don't usually blurt out the information all at once. You first ask, "Have you got a pencil?" followed by "Okay, here goes" as a way of letting the other person know when you are about to start.

Similarly, before one computer sends a byte of information to another, it sends a *start bit* before each byte to let the receiving computer know that it's about to receive information. The start bit always has a value of 0. The receiving computer then starts copying seven or eight bits depending on what it has been told to expect. To signal the end of the byte, the sending computer adds a *stop bit* (some large computers use two stop bits, but virtually all BBSes use just one). The stop bit always has a value of 1. Start and stop bits are not included in the parity check.

Modems that send bits and bytes at random intervals depend on start and stop bits to know where one byte of information ends and the next one begins. The technical name for this kind of information interchange is *asynchronous.*

By contrast, some modems are *synchronous;* that is, they send and receive information at a specific time. Synchronous modems send special signals that are different from start bits to each other when they first connect so they can synchronize their internal clocks. Each modem is then able to send and receive data without having to send start and stop bits.

Synchronous modems are faster than asynchronous modems. However, the higher-precision equipment necessary for synchronous communication is more expensive than asynchronous equipment. Because of this price difference, virtually all BBSes use asynchronous communications.

### Modem Speed

Modems need to communicate at the same speed. If one modem is talking faster or slower than the other, no communication is possible. Therefore, the speed of each modem is rated in *baud* or in *bits per second*.

Baud is a technical term, named after Emile Baudot, a pioneer in early telegraphy. Although "baud" is related to how fast your modem can change its tone to indicate a bit, which is not precisely the same thing as "bits per second (bps)," everyone uses the two terms interchangeably.

Standard modems operate at speeds of 300, 1200, 2400, and 9600 bps. Most modems sold today are able to match the speed of slower modems. For example, if your modem is able to run at 2400 bps, it can also run at 1200 and 300 bps, but not at 9600 bps.

A 2400-bps modem sending eight-bit bytes with no parity bit, and a start and stop bit, can transmit 240 characters every second, or the approximate equivalent of ten 8-1/2-by-11-inch typed, single-spaced pages every minute.

### Full- and Half-duplex

Electronic equipment that communicates in *full-duplex* mode is able to send and receive information at the same time. Telephones are full duplex, because you can both talk and listen at the same time. Almost all modems are able to do this also. *Half-duplex* equipment, on the other hand, can only do one thing at a time, talk or listen. Ham and CB radio conversations are in half-duplex mode: first one person talks, then the other person talks. If both people are talking, then neither can hear what's going on.

Virtually all BBSes run in full-duplex mode. You will use half-duplex mode only if you are transmitting information "modem-to-modem" over the phone lines directly to someone else's computer (rather than to a BBS).

## CHOOSING EQUIPMENT

Choosing the hardware and software you want to use may be the most difficult decision you have to make about BBSes. Ask friends, computer dealers, and users' groups for advice on the kinds of equipment available. Also, try using some of the hardware and software before actually spending money on it. Special-interest groups (SIGs) and users groups for your brand of computer are good places to experiment with various types of equipment.

To call a BBS, you will need the following:

- a computer
- a modem
- a communications program for your computer
- a telephone line

This section tells you what to look for in each of these categories and describes things that you must have and things that you may want to have.

## Computers and Terminals

Obviously, the first thing you need is a computer with a keyboard, a display screen, and a diskette drive (or a cassette tape drive) for entering and storing programs. The computer may also have a hard disk drive for storing programs. You can use almost any computer for telecommunications, including Commodore 64s and 128s, Apples, IBMs, and Macintoshes.

**Note:** If you don't have a computer, you can also use a *terminal* (also known as a *CRT*). A terminal is simply a keyboard and a display without the central processing unit, which is the part of the computer that actually "thinks." Terminals can be had very inexpensively at many electronics second-hand stores and swap meets, but they may require some know-how on your part to hook them up. Since terminals have no memory, you cannot store any information displayed on the screen. Terminals are certainly inexpensive, but the low cost of an entry-level computer system makes terminals a poor bargain.

Your computer must have a *serial port* (on some computers, this may be identified as a *modem port*). A *port* is a connector on the back of the computer into which cables can be plugged. A serial port accepts data a bit at a time; that is, serially. When all the bits of data in a byte have been assembled, the serial port passes the assembled byte to the rest of the computer for processing. You can think of the way a serial port assembles data as something like assembling a train: first the locomotive (the start bit), then the cars (the data), and finally the caboose (the stop bit). When the caboose is added, the train is complete and it can pull away.

Your computer probably also has a *parallel port*. Where a serial port accepts data a bit at a time through a single set of wires, a parallel port accepts all the bits in a byte at the same time with multiple sets of wires.

Parallel ports have an advantage over serial ports in that they tend to be faster. Since the data doesn't have to be assembled a bit at a time, there is a small, but significant, time savings. Moreover, the parallel port, unlike the serial port, does not have to process the start and stop bits.

Unfortunately, most modems cannot take advantage of parallel ports' transmission speed; modems cannot send all the bits of information in a byte at the same time (some of the high-speed modems used by large computers do, but the modems currently used for BBSing do not). In other words, modems slow the transmission of data received from parallel ports because they only send and receive bits serially.

You may know that there are chips on the market that do "serial-to-parallel" conversion. These chips build the bytes serially from separate bits and then retransmit the data in parallel form, all eight bits at once on eight separate wires in the cable.

Unfortunately, there is no advantage in this. When information is transmitted over a parallel cable, a pulse for each bit is sent down eight separate wires. The parallel port receives the pulses and assumes that the information will all arrive at the same time. If one of the bit pulses arrives too late or is substantially weaker than the others, the byte will be incomplete. The parallel port will then tell the computer that there has been an error reading the information. Bit pulses in cables longer than about ten feet become unreliable because of the resistance of the wire and will arrive later or weaker than the other pulses, causing data transmission errors. For these reasons, parallel ports on microcomputers are usually used for relatively high-speed transmission of data to printers.

To summarize, your computer needs to have a serial port available for an external modem to be connected, or have room for an internal modem with its own serial port.

## Modems

A modem *modulates* or translates the electrical pulses representing bits into tones that can be sent over a telephone wire. The modem then sends the bytes serially (a bit at a time) over the phone wire to another modem that *demodulates* or translates the tones back into bits, which are then passed on to the serial port of the computer for reassembling into bytes.

### Compatibility

There are many ways in which modems can send and receive the tones that represent bits. All of them can be effective, but in order to understand anyone else's modem, both modems must use the same set of tones.

In the early 1960's, AT&T only allowed Bell System modems to be connected to the phone lines. One of the modems developed by the Bell System for 1200-bps operation was the Bell 212. The frequencies and timing of the modem tones became an industry standard for 1200-bps operation, and any modem that uses these frequencies and the timing is said to be *Bell 212-compatible*. Any modem that you buy for BBSing must be Bell 212-compatible.

The phrase *Hayes-compatible* is frequently used to imply Bell 212-compatible, but it actually is something different. Hayes Microcomputer Products, Inc., manufactures a series of high-quality modems that have a number of features such as automatic dialing, automatic baud-rate sensing, and automatic answering. Part of the programming for the modem allows you to send commands directly to the modem to tell it to turn on or off certain features, and to change the way it handles information. It is the ability to understand these commands that makes a modem Hayes-compatible. In general, though, if a 1200- or 2400-bps modem is advertised as Hayes-compatible, you can safely assume that it is also Bell 212-compatible.

**Note:** Some modems, particularly older, *acoustically coupled* modems, are Bell 212-compatible but not Hayes-compatible. Acoustically coupled modems have rubber cups that you plug a telephone handset into. The modem actually generates the tones through a little speaker set next to the mouthpiece of the phone handset. Acoustically coupled modems are not used much anymore, having been replaced by *direct-connect* modems that simply plug into the phone line with a standard phone cord. Although acoustically coupled modems will talk to other Bell 212-compatible modems, most of the features in your communications program will depend on being able to send Hayes-compatible commands to the modem. If you are using an acoustically coupled modem, you will probably have to dial the BBS number yourself instead of letting the computer do it for you.

## *Speed*

Decide how fast a modem you want to buy. 1200-bps modems are currently going for about $50, and 2400-bps modems are about $80. 9600-bps modems still cost at least $300, but it's almost certain that they'll become cheaper as time goes on; modems rated 2400 bps were at least $300 in 1987, and 1200-bps modems were at least $300 in 1985.

When buying a modem, consider what you're likely to use it for. Most people can't read message text as fast as a 1200-bps modem can display it on the screen, so a 1200-bps modem is probably fast enough for plain message reading and an occasional file transfer.

If you want to mix reading messages and sending and receiving files, a 2400-bps modem is better. Twice as fast as a 1200-bps modem, a 2400-bps modem takes only a few moments to transfer all but the biggest files.

If you intend to do a lot of file transferring, particularly from online information services that charge you for the amount of time you spend online, give serious thought to
a 9600-bps modem. The initial extra expense will rapidly be repaid with lower access
fees and faster file transfers. A file that takes eight minutes to transfer at 1200 bps will
take four minutes to transfer at 2400 bps and one minute to transfer at 9600 bps.

Unfortunately, the communications standards for 9600 bps modems are still being
determined at this time. There is no universal "Bell 212-type" standard for 9600-bps
modems yet, but there are two potential standards in use by various modem manufacturers. Many 9600-bps modems are currently available that use one of these potential
standards. There are also some modems that can talk in both forms with the flip of a
switch. These are much more expensive, though, because you're really buying two
modems in the same box.

The current lack of a standard has kept many people from buying an otherwise afford-
able 9600 bps modem. They don't want to get stuck with a modem that doesn't communicate using the accepted standard—after the standard is established, a large number
of 9600-bps modems will be obsolete. Check with a reputable dealer for the latest
news on a standard for 9600-bps modems.

Another thing to be aware of before buying a 9600-bps modem is that many older
phone lines and phone circuits may not be "clean" enough to support modems above
1200 or 2400 bps. Any extraneous static or noise on the telephone line can inject spurious information into the signals to and from a BBS. This can cause strange characters to appear on your screen, or, in the case of sending or receiving a file, errors in the
file transfer. If you suspect that your phone service is not the best, see if you can try a
modem before you buy one. There's no point in owning a fast modem if it won't go at
its top speed on your phone lines.

### External Modems

Most modems are *external;* that is, they have a chassis and a power supply all their
own. They sit outside the computer and connect to a serial port with a cable that runs
from the back of the modem to the back of the computer.

External modems almost always have a set of status display lights to show the status of
various items. The status display is discussed in Appendix D, "Troubleshooting," if
you want to know more about it.

External modems have the following general advantages:

• *They can work with almost any computer.*
  All you need to do is connect a cable from the back of the modem to the computer
  you want to use it with.

- *They are portable.*
  If you want to use the modem with a different computer, you just unplug the cable and the power cord and move it. You don't have to take the computer apart to get to the modem.

- *You can see the status display lights.*
  Because the modem is not hidden inside the computer, you can easily read the status display lights.

- *They don't use up a slot in your computer.*
  If slots for cards are at a premium in your computer, you don't have to rearrange cards or make choices about which card not to use in order to install the modem.

## Internal Modems

*Internal modems* are a printed circuit board with the modem and a built-in serial port. This board goes into your computer, where it is powered by the computer's power supply. An internal modem does not have a chassis of its own. It probably doesn't have status display lights either, as they are very difficult to see inside the computer.

Internal modems have these general advantages:

- *They don't take up extra room on the desk.*
  External modems, though small, have to go somewhere. Finding space on your desk for one more thing can be difficult. By the same token, since internal modems don't have a separate power supply, you don't have to look for another available plug in your power strip.

- *They come with their own serial port.*
  Having an external modem requires you to have an available serial port in your computer. If you already are using the one you have, you might have to buy another serial card, which would take up the slot you saved by buying an external modem in the first place.

- *They are frequently cheaper.*
  Because you aren't paying for the chassis and extra power supply, internal modems tend to cost less than external modems.

- *They are designed to be used in one type of computer.*
  Internal modems can be optimized for a particular type of computer.

If all the other factors are equal, you should probably buy an external modem. The status display lights can tell you a great deal about what is happening in the communications process and can be very helpful to you when tracking down problems.

### Modem Features

There are a number of features that are more or less standard on modems these days. Buy a modem with as many of the following features as you can get:

*Autodial* (automatic dialing) is the ability to have the modem dial a number by sending it a command from your communications program.

*Automatic speed sensing* (also known as *automatic baud-rate sensing*) is the ability of your modem to detect another modem's speed. When you dial a BBS, this feature lets you set your modem to its highest speed. Your modem will then try to establish communications with the other modem at the highest speed, then at the next highest, and so on until the two modems reach agreement. For example, if you have a 2400-bps modem, and you phone a BBS that can only run at 1200 bps, your modem will sense this and automatically adjust its speed to 1200 bps.

*Autoanswer* (automatic answering) is the ability of your modem to answer incoming phone calls. Modems on BBSes are all autoanswer. Having autoanswer capability is useful both if you want to set up your own BBS at some time and for doing direct modem-to-modem file transfers.

A *speaker* is a surprisingly essential item. When the modem first dials the number, listening to the speaker will tell you that the modem has been able to get a dial tone, that the program has told the modem to dial the number, and that the number is either ringing, busy, out of service, or even wrong. If your modem does not have a speaker, you have to pick up the phone and listen to find out why the modem isn't connecting.

Other common features include a *test mode* that lets the modem check itself, an *internal help file* that lets you ask the modem to display a list of its commands with a brief explanation, and *automatic voice/data switching,* which lets you break into the middle of a data call and actually talk on the phone. This last feature is useful if you are trying to communicate directly with another user and you need to talk to them for a moment.

One final thing to look for is an *FCC registration*. The Federal Communications Commission has to approve all equipment that is designed to be connected to a phone line. The modem should have a registration label on it somewhere. Your chances of finding a modem that is not registered are small, but you could get into trouble with the telephone company if you hook any unregistered device to the line and it causes problems with the phone lines.

## Communications Software

When microcomputers first appeared, just getting the computer to talk to a modem and see what was coming in was an accomplishment. The number of features in communications software were few and relatively straightforward. But as is the case with all software, programs started getting bigger and better. More features were added to communications programs. Fortunately, despite these extra features, communications software prices have remained steady.

These days, there are a lot of features that you should look for in communications software including screen capture, autodial, multiple phone directories, and macros. This section tells you what these features are and how to identify them.

*Under no circumstances should you rush out and spend several hundred dollars on a commercial communications program.* Almost always, if you spend even a hundred dollars for a communications program, you will be wasting your money. There are dozens of excellent communications programs for every kind of computer that are available free or very inexpensively. Appendix A, "Communications Software," lists a number of suggestions for places to obtain communications programs.

As a matter of fact, you may have a communications program on your computer already. For example, Microsoft Windows comes with a simple communications program called TERMINAL that runs under Windows. Microsoft Works (for both the IBM and the Macintosh) has a good communications program as one of the four main features. Many other software products also have communications programs. Check your computer's software or ask your dealer for more information.

The first thing you should look for in communications software is *compatibility*. The software must be compatible with your computer and modem, as well as with the other software you are using. If your software is not able to send the right command codes to your modem, you won't be able to use all of the features of the software or the modem. However, if your modem and software are not compatible (for example, if your modem is not completely Hayes-compatible), you may be able to tell the software how to talk to the modem.

There is another kind of compatibility that you should consider. Is the software compatible with different BBSes and online services? Some software runs exclusively with online information services such as CompuServe and Western Union's EasyLink Instant Mail Service. Therefore, you need to look for a general-purpose communications program. By the way, it is perfectly all right to have more than one communications program on your computer.

### Required Features

A communications program should, at the very least, be able to:

- *Change communications parameters quickly.*
  Communications parameters—such as the speed, parity, and the number of start, stop, and data bits—can be different depending on the BBS or online service you are using. Your software should let you change the parameters quickly and easily.

- *Capture (save) screen information to a disk file or the printer.*
  When you log on to a new BBS for the first time, a lot of valuable information about the type of BBS software, the focus of the BBS, and how to use the BBS appears on the screen. You can use the screen capture feature to save this information and examine it at your leisure later. Screen capture is also useful for copying help files, messages, and file lists.

- *Send and receive files using one of several transfer protocols.*
  Transfer protocols are a set of rules for establishing communications between two computers. The two essential protocols are ASCII and XMODEM, but other protocols such as XMODEM-CRC, YMODEM, and ZMODEM are also very good to have. Transfer protocols and how to use them are discussed in detail in Chapter 4, "Sending and Receiving Files."

- *Use a dialing directory.*
  A dialing directory is a list of the phone numbers you dial frequently, together with specific communications parameters for that BBS. Dialing directories allow you to dial a number or a group of numbers by entering the number for the directory entry. The software then looks up the phone number and the communications parameters in the directory. Dialing directories also keep track of things like the last time you phoned and how many times you have called the number and gotten through.

### General Features

There are many other features that are worth having in a communications program. A *text buffer* automatically captures the information displayed on the screen. Unlike the screen capture feature mentioned earlier, a text buffer does not automatically save information to disk. Instead, you can scroll through the information at any time to see what appeared on your screen and has just scrolled off. This is very handy for taking a quick look at the menu of commands that just rolled off the top of the screen rather than having to display it again. Some communications programs also allow you to search the buffer for a specific item and to save the buffer to disk for later use.

*Macros* are text assigned to a key on the keyboard, typically a function key. When you press the key, the communications program transmits the text you have stored. For example, you could store your name as a macro assigned to the [F1] key. Then, whenever you needed to enter your name, you simply press [F1] .

As you become familiar with a BBS, it may be convenient to automate sets of commands you use frequently. You can set up *scripts* (collections of commands, text, and instructions) that will automate many procedures. The most common example of a script is one that logs you on to a BBS. The script does everything that you would do: enters your name or user ID, enters your password, and possibly navigates a couple of menus or bulletin listings.

Another example of a common script is one that logs on to a BBS, goes to the message area, turns on screen capture, reads all the messages addressed to you, and then logs off of the BBS. The program can watch the clock on your computer and performs a script at the specified time. This lets you log on to a BBS when it's easy to get in or when the long-distance rates are low.

Scripts are very powerful tools. Most BBS users don't use them because scripts can look like they're difficult to understand, but anything that you can tell another BBS user how to do, you can set up a script for. Check your communications software for sample scripts and basic scripting procedures.

You can also combine keyboard macros with scripts. For example, you could assign the text instruction to load and run a logon script to a key. You would then be able to press a single key to automatically dial a BBS and go through the BBS's logon procedure.

Any communications program with a lot of powerful features should be well documented. The documentation should tell you how to use each feature and should also give you hints about shortcuts and ways to use the program better. The program should also have some kind of online help that is easy to display and use.

One thing to look for in judging ease of use is whether the software uses *menus* or *commands*. A menu is a list of options that appears at the top of the screen most or all of the time. You then select an option from the menu, usually by entering the number of the option. Software that uses commands does not have a list of options constantly on the screen. Instead, you enter a command by pressing a combination of keys (usually the [ALT] or [CTRL] key with a letter or a number). Help is usually available at any time by pressing a single key such as [HOME]. The program then displays one or several screens of command help.

The advantage to software that uses menus is that you always know what you can do. This is very helpful when you are just starting out; however, as you develop your skills as a BBS user, you may want to use software that lets you enter a couple of quick keystrokes to start a process. The majority of communications programs for the IBM use commands instead of menus.

Not many communications programs for the IBM have a word processor actually built in, but most allow you to temporarily exit the communications program, run the editor or word processor of your choice, and then return to the communications program with the BBS still online. You can use this feature to quickly create and edit message text. Programs for other computers such as the Macintosh allow you to use system features such as the clipboard or the note pad to edit text quickly.

## Special Features

In addition to the features already discussed, the following features are convenient, but not absolutely necessary:

- *The ability to emulate different types of terminals.*
  This feature is convenient if you are logging on to BBSes or large computer systems that expect you to have a specific type of terminal. The information they send to you is translated and displayed on your computer as if you were using that kind of terminal.

- *A filter.*
  If your communications program has a *filter* (also known as a *character translation table*), you can tell it to change or suppress characters before displaying them on your screen. For example, if you need to translate the extended ASCII characters (values from 128 to 255) to something that your computer could display, you could set up characters for the software to translate each of the ASCII characters into. Filters are occasionally useful, but you probably won't use one very often.

- *The ability to split the screen.*
  When you are chatting with the BBS's system operator (or *sysop* for short) or another user, you can split the screen so that you can see what is being typed to you while at the same time start typing your reply. When you press [ENTER], the program sends the information you typed to the BBS.

- *The ability to run as a RAM-resident program.*
  *RAM-resident programs* (also known as a *memory resident,* or a *terminate and stay resident* program) stay in memory. This means that you can pull up the communications program in the middle of another program. Some communications programs that can stay in memory use this feature to do complex tasks while you are doing something else at the same time. For example, you could download a large file to the communications program in memory while you are working on a spreadsheet at the keyboard.

**Note:** RAM-resident software can occasionally cause compatibility problems with other software you may want to run. Some large or complex programs use much or all of your computer's available memory. RAM-resident software may take up enough memory to prevent such a program from loading.

## Making Your Choice

Take a look at several different communications programs, particularly shareware. *Shareware* are programs that are distributed by users rather than dealers and can be used free-of-charge on a trial basis. If you can, talk to BBS users and sysops and ask them what they use and why. Check with local users' groups and computer dealers as well. If you're still not sure of which program to get, go with a shareware program. If you find that you like it, you can register and pay for it. If you don't like it and don't use it, you don't have to pay for it.

# SETTING UP YOUR HARDWARE AND SOFTWARE

If you are not already familiar with microcomputers and modems, you may want to have someone help you set up your computer and modem. Doing it yourself is not difficult, but it can be reassuring to have someone who is familiar with the process point out the specifics of working with your particular computer and modem. If you bought the equipment directly from a computer dealer, you may be able to enlist the dealer's help in setting your system up.

## Setting Up the Modem

The first thing to do when setting up your modem is to read the manual. Each modem is different, and the manual is the first place to look to learn about how to use the modem.

*DIP (Dual Inline Package) switches* are very small switches that you set with the tip of a pen or a screwdriver. If your modem uses DIP switches, make a small chart of the positions of all the switches as they are when the modem is fresh out of the box. Compare these settings against the various settings listed in the manual to see what the *factory defaults* are (the settings made at the factory). You'll probably find that these settings are close to what you want, if not exactly right. Tape the list of switch settings to the bottom of the modem. If you change any of the switch settings, make a note of what you changed on the chart. If you ever need to get back to the factory default settings, this chart will be invaluable.

**Note:** Whenever you change the setting of a DIP switch, be very careful not to press too hard. DIP switches can be fragile. Furthermore, if the DIP switch is mounted on a printed circuit board, too much pressure can crack the board, a connection between components, or the soldered joints of the switch itself. Repairing this kind of damage is not covered by your warranty.

You will usually want to set the modem for its highest asynchronous communications speed. For example, if you have a 2400-bps modem, it should be set for 2400-bps asynchronous operation. In addition, you should set the following features as shown here:

| Feature | Setting | What This Means |
|---|---|---|
| Autoanswer | no | don't answer the phone |
| Hayes compatibility | yes | use Hayes-style commands |
| Tone dialing | yes | use tones, not pulses |
| Half/full duplex | full | use full-duplex |
| 7/8 data bits | 8 | use 8 data bits in a byte |
| Parity | none | don't check parity |

Your modem may not have all of these options available for changing with switch settings, and it will probably have other default settings not listed here. For example, you may need to set the speaker's volume with a small control on the back of the modem. See your manual for more details on your modem's specific options.

## Connecting an External Modem

Once you have set the switches on the modem, you can connect a cable from the back of the modem to the serial port in the back of the computer. The modem will have a 25-pin *female connector* (a socket, versus a *male connector,* a plug) known as a *DB-25* connector. The serial port on the back of your computer is probably one of three types:

- a DB-25 female connector like the one on the back of the modem
- a 9-pin female connector
- a DB-25 male connector (only if you have an older serial port made by IBM)

Your cable provides a connection from the modem to the serial port in the computer. If you are not sure you have the right cable, check with the dealer from whom you purchased the modem. There are custom cables to connect DB-25 connectors to virtually any other connector used on microcomputers.

When the cable is plugged in, position the modem where the front lights are easy to see. Connect your phone line to the modem. Depending on the modem, you may be able to connect a second phone cable from the back of the modem to your phone. Other modems only have one socket for phone lines. To connect the phone and the modem simultaneously, you need to use a "Y" connector (available for about a dollar) that lets you clip two phone lines into the same socket. You are now ready to install the communications software and test your installation.

## Installing an Internal Modem

If you have an internal modem, it is critical that you follow the directions in the modem manual for installing the modem safely and correctly. You should read and understand all the instructions before you remove the modem from its protective anti-static wrapping.

If you are uncomfortable with the idea of opening your computer and installing a card yourself, consider taking the computer and modem in to a computer dealer for installation. The whole process should take only a few minutes, particularly if you have already installed the communications software on the computer. This will let the dealer help you configure your communications software and test the installation. You should also be aware that many computer manufacturers require you to have an authorized dealer service the computer. Removing the cover of your computer may void the warranty.

When you install the modem, be sure to follow all the directions for preventing static electricity. A single spark of static can easily destroy the modem's chips. Worse, the damage caused by a spark may take a while to surface, long after the warranty has expired.

The computer identifies each serial port in the computer with a different name. The names for the serial ports on an IBM are COM1 and COM2, and the names for the parallel ports are LPT1 and LPT2. You need to set the switches on the modem so that the computer knows which serial port the modem is identified as. Depending on the type of computer you have, you may also need to set a switch in the computer itself to tell it that you now have another serial port.

## Setting Up Your Software

Once you have connected your modem to your computer, you can install your communications software and set up your communications parameters. One of the best things about setting up a communications system is that once you have it up and running, you probably won't need to change anything until you decide to buy a faster modem.

As with setting up the modem, you should read the manual for your communications software before doing anything else. Look for a "Quick Start" section, a guide to getting the program installed, or an introductory tutorial to the software. Most communications programs are already set up for a Hayes-compatible modem, but you will have to provide some additional information during the installation process, such as the name of the serial port.

The following list shows suggested entries for various options and communications parameters commonly found in communications software. Remember that not all communications programs support all of the options in this list. The documentation that comes with your communications program should tell you how to set each of these options.

| | |
|---|---|
| modem speed: | set to your modem's highest speed |
| data bits: | 8 |
| stop bits: | 1 |
| parity: | "N" or "NONE" |
| time to wait before cancelling a call: | 45 seconds |
| time between redials: | 5 seconds |
| terminal emulation: | ANSI |
| local echo: | off |

If your communications program already has a default for an option, you can probably start by trying the default and then changing it later on if you need to.

When you complete the communications software's installation procedure, your system is complete. You are now ready to test it. The best way to test your installation is to try logging on to a BBS. Chapter 2, "Getting Started," shows you how to do just that.

# BECOMING AN EXPERT

Choosing and setting up hardware and software is the most technically demanding part of using BBSes. Talk to a friend, a computer dealer you trust, or someone from a local computer users' group who has experience in setting up modems and communications software. Get their advice on what to buy, enlist their help in setting up your equipment and software, and have them help you learn how to use it.

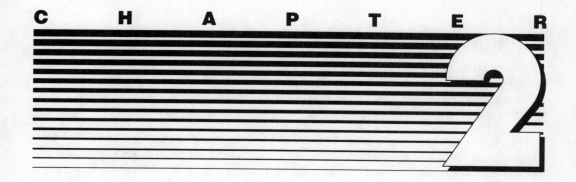

C H A P T E R

2

# GETTING STARTED

This chapter shows you how to log on to a typical bulletin board system. Sample screens demonstrate how to set up your own user identification, take a look around, use the BBS's bulletin and help features, and log off.

# FINDING A BBS TO CALL

The first BBS you call should be local, so you don't have to pay for long-distance charges. Beyond that, it doesn't much matter which BBS you call the first time. It is more important to learn how to log on to a BBS and explore it. As you develop your skills as a BBS user, you look for BBSes that you particularly like.

If you have friends who are BBS users, ask them to recommend several BBSes they like. If you don't know anyone in your area that can recommend a BBS, you can frequently get BBS numbers from local computer stores. Stop in and ask if they have a list of local BBSes. While you're at the store, look for a monthly magazine called the *Computer Shopper.* This magazine comes out monthly and lists the numbers and profiles of bulletin boards across the country in order of area code. You can also find BBS numbers through local computer users' groups. Appendix B, "BBS Numbers," lists several sources for BBS numbers.

Before you dial the BBS, you also need to know the baud rate, the number of stop bits, and the parity. If you are working from a list of BBSes, this information will probably look something like 3/12/2400-8-1-N. This means that the board will run either 300, 1200, or 2400 baud with 8 bits, 1 stop bit, and no parity. Most BBSes are currently running at 1200 or 2400. Very few BBSes run at 300 baud anymore.

# CALLING A BBS FOR THE FIRST TIME

Once you have picked a BBS, you're ready to begin. Start your communications program and enter the phone number, baud rate, stop bits, and parity for the BBS you are calling. See your communications program's help screens or manual for directions on how to do this.

If you don't have any communications parameters with the phone number, try setting your parameters at 1200 baud, 8 bits, 1 stop bit, and no parity. If this doesn't work, try 1200 baud, 7 bits, 1 stop bit, and even parity. If neither of these work, try the same settings at 300 baud. If all else fails, see Appendix D, "Troubleshooting," for more information.

**Note:** Most communications packages have a *screen capture* feature. This feature captures the information as it appears on your screen and saves it to a file. If your communications package has this feature, turn it on before you start dialing. This will let you review the information in detail after you log off.

Next, use the communications program to dial the BBS number. Many BBSes are busy most of the time, so it may take you a little while to connect. If your modem has a speaker, you'll be able to hear the busy signal. When the BBS answers the phone, you'll hear a high-pitched tone in the modem's speaker. This is the BBS's modem and your modem telling each other what speed they can talk at. As soon as they agree on a speed, the speaker will shut off. Depending on your communications program, you may also hear tones indicating that you have connected with the BBS or see a CON-NECT message on your screen.

The BBS will probably start displaying information on your screen almost immediately. If not, press [ENTER] a couple of times.

If nothing happens after about 15 seconds, or if gibberish appears on the screen, see the "If You Have Trouble" section later in this chapter. Otherwise, you're ready to set up your user identification on the BBS.

## Logging On

The first time you call any BBS, you must set up information that tells the BBS who you are and how it should send you information. This process is known as *logging on*. This section takes you through a sample logon procedure and shows you how to set yourself up as a new user.

**Note:** The sample screens shown in this chapter are representative of the majority of BBSes. Although you will probably see some differences between the these figures and those displayed by the BBSes you call, the principles of logging on and using a BBS are the same for all BBSes. If the BBS you are calling looks completely different from the examples in this chapter, use your communications program to capture the information to disk or paper, then compare it to the sample screens for specific types of bulletin boards described in Chapters 6 and 7.

When you first connect with the BBS, press [ENTER] a couple of times (many BBSes wait for you to press [ENTER] or [ESC] before sending you information). You will then see some information about the BBS, then a prompt. Figure 2-1 shows a sample opening screen for a fictitious BBS, Grotto de Blotto.

# 2 Getting Started

```
CONNECT 555-9492

August 9, 1990

        Welcome to Grotto de Blotto!
              206-555-9492
      Operating at 300, 1200, and 2400 baud

Grotto de Blotto is a verified-access BBS,
running 24 hours a day (we never sleep) in
beautiful downtown Wallingford, gateway to
Ballard!

New users are always welcome.  Please be sure
to read the logon bulletin for information on
the policies and procedures for this system.

Press [ENTER] to continue...
```

*Figure 2-1. Sample Opening Screen*

Before continuing, take a look at the opening screen.  It tells you the name of the BBS, the BBS's phone number, baud rate, hours of operation, location, and where to get help on using the BBS.

When you press [ENTER], the BBS prompts you for your first name:

```
What is your FIRST Name?
```

Enter the first name you want to be known by.  You can enter your real name or some BBSes allow you to use a pseudonym.  The BBS will then prompt you for your last name.  Prompts and sample responses are:

```
What is your FIRST Name? Sam
What is your LAST Name? Spade
Please wait a moment while I check the userlog...
```

When you first start out using BBSes, it's a good idea to use your real name rather than a pseudonym.  If you have friends that are using the BBS, they'll be able to identify you easily.  Many BBSes also will not allow you to use pseudonyms to ensure some measure of user accountability.  As you become more proficient, you can use a pseudonym (or "nym" for short) to build up a persona that might not have anything to do with you.  Pseudonyms also ensure you a layer of privacy.

The BBS looks for your name in the *userlog,* the list of current users. It will then ask for your location:

```
What is your CITY and STATE? Seattle, WA

I don't find you in the userlog.

Do you want to set up a new user ID?
```

The BBS didn't find a listing in the userlog for a user with your name and location. It asks if you're a new user in case you mistyped an existing name.

**Note:**   Always enter your name and city the same way. This will save you having to remember in the future whether you're logged on to this BBS as *Sam Spade, Samuel Spade,* or *S. Spade.*

Enter *Y* to set up a new user ID. If you enter *N,* the BBS will prompt you again for your first name and location:

```
Enter a password:
```

Enter a password at the prompt. Your password prevents somebody else from logging on to the system with your name. Most BBSes will accept passwords of three to eight characters, but some will accept passwords as long as twelve characters. Passwords should be easy for you to remember without being obvious.

Don't use the same password for all the BBSes you call. If someone finds out your password for one BBS, they may try to use it on any BBS you use. Keep your passwords written down in a safe place.

When you enter your password, the BBS will ask you to enter the password again to make sure that you typed it correctly. The BBS may only display dots or asterisks the second time.

Some BBSes will also ask for a telephone number, a mailing address, or other information for verification of your identity. There is an implicit understanding that personal information will be held in confidence by the sysop.

## Setting Display Options

Choosing and verifying your password usually completes the new user logon procedure. Many BBSes, however, will ask you for more detailed information about your computer in order to display information faster or more attractively. Don't worry if you make a mistake as you answer questions. You can always change your answers later.

```
How many characters can your screen display?
```

Enter the number of characters your computer can display on a line. Commodore 64 and early Apple computers can only display 40 characters per line; most other computers, including IBM and Macintosh, can display 80 characters.

```
How many nulls?
```

*Nulls* are delays the BBS sends to your computer to give it time to skip to the next line. Enter *0,* or, if you're using a 2400-baud or faster modem, enter *2.* If you discover that you miss the first few characters on each line, try increasing the number of nulls by 1 or 2.

```
Can your terminal display lower case?
```

This option lets you set the display either for all uppercase or uppercase and lowercase display. If you can see uppercase and lowercase letters on your screen, enter *Y;* otherwise, enter *N*.

```
Do you want linefeeds?
```

*Linefeeds* tell the computer whether or not to move the cursor down a line at the end of each line. If the computer doesn't do it automatically, the BBS needs to tell the computer to do it, or else each line will write over the previous line. Enter *Y* so the BBS inserts linefeeds. Then, if both the BBS and the computer move the cursor down a line, everything will be double-spaced.

```
Do you want tabs?
```

This tells the BBS if your computer and communications software can handle tab characters. IBM and Macintosh computers can handle tabs. If you're not sure, enter *N* and the BBS will send spaces instead. This is a little slower than using tabs but will look the same on your screen.

```
What kind of graphics do you want: [N]one, [A]scii, or [C]olor?
```

Some BBSes have very attractive graphics capabilities and will create positively baroque menus for you.

- *None* means that you only want to display text you could type on a typewriter, with no special characters. All computers can use this display option.

- *ASCII* graphics use all 255 characters in the IBM character set. Most IBM PCs and IBM clones can properly receive ASCII graphics.

- *Color* graphics use all 255 IBM characters as well as the ANSI screen commands to provide color. Both your computer and your communications package must support ANSI screen commands (for example, QMODEM and ProComm support ANSI screen commands; Hayes Smartcom does not).

Figures 2-2 and 2-3 show several examples of graphics.

*Figure 2-2. Sample Graphics Display*

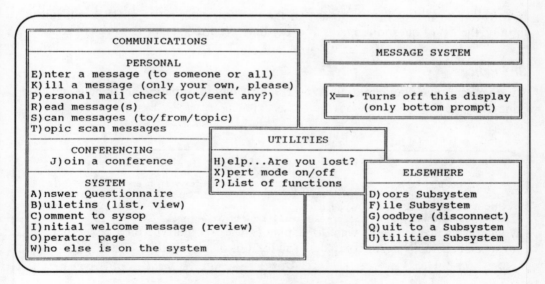

*Figure 2-3. Sample Graphics Display*

Be aware that the fancier your screens are, the longer it will take for the computer to display them. If you're not sure about the level of graphics to ask for, enter *N*. You can ask the sysop later about what options to choose.

```
FILE transfer default type <A>scii, <X>modem, <C>Xmodem/CRC?
```

Choose the default file transfer method. Your communications package must be able to use the file transfer protocol you select. File transfer protocols are discussed in Chapter 4, "Sending and Receiving Files." For now, enter *X* for XMODEM, the most widely supported file transfer protocol.

After you have entered all your choices, the BBS asks you to approve your choices, as shown in Figure 2-4.

```
Screen width: 79
Nulls: 0
Lowercase: YES
Linefeeds: YES
Tabs: YES
Graphics: NONE
File transfer protocol: XMODEM
Is everything correct?
```

*Figure 2-4. Selected Options*

If you want to make changes to any of the options, enter *N*. The BBS will run you through the list of questions again. If everything is correct, enter *Y*.

### BBS Policy

After you approve your choices, most BBSes display information about general system policy.

```
                    N E W    U S E R    I N F O:

Grotto de Blotto is a BBS for swapping technical information and having adult
discussions on a wide variety of topics.  Use of this board is a privilege,
not a right.  Users are expected to act in a reasonably civil fashion.  Anyone
who cannot comply with these rules will be denied access.

I cannot guarantee the accuracy of any information posted on this bulletin
board, nor can I guarantee the results of using software from this system on
any computer.  Please be careful.  If you have a problem, let me know, and I
will take whatever steps seem appropriate.

Cash contributions for the maintenance of this BBS are always welcome, but are
not necessary.  The best way to support this BBS is to use it.  Thank you.

                    Your Sysop, Michael Dispater

Press any key to continue...
```

*Figure 2-5. Policy Message*

You are now logged in as a new user.

### User Verification

Many BBSes do not grant you full access to the features of the BBS until you have been *verified;* that is, until the sysop has phoned you to make sure that you are who you say you are. This is to prevent people from logging on under several different names and using the BBS several hours a day. If you are on a restricted access until you have been verified, you will probably be able to read and enter messages, but you may not be able to *download* (transfer) files from the BBS to your computer.

Most sysops that require verification will probably phone you within the next day or so.

### Making Donations

Sysops frequently solicit donations for their BBS. If you become a regular user of a BBS, give serious consideration to making a donation. BBSes cost money to set up and more money each month to run, as well as about an hour a day of the sysop's own time. Many BBSes are taken down by sysops who can't afford the monthly expenses; making an occasional donation to the BBS ensures that it will continue to operate.

The sysop may also solicit donations for specific projects, such as more disk space for files and messages, faster modems, and so on, all of which will benefit you and the other BBS users directly. In return for your donation, you may receive more time on the BBS, "aide" status (a sort of "assistant to the sysop" position), public thanks in the bulletins, and the reasonably undying thanks of the sysop.

### Paying for Access Privileges

About 10% of all BBSes require you to pay an access fee of some kind to get full privileges on the BBS. These BBSes almost always cater to a very specific set of interests, or have a wide variety of features not normally available to other BBSes. For example, many BBSes that charge for access privileges have several hundred megabytes of files online that you can download to your computer. Other BBSes will have almost no files but will have 8 to 32 lines coming in to the BBS, so you can "talk" to other BBS users directly.

BBSes such as these usually charge fees to help recoup the fairly substantial costs for setting up and running the BBS. If the basic monthly phone service for one line costs $15, an 8-line BBS costs $120 a month just for the phone. Unless the BBS is being run as an actual business, it is extremely rare for the sysop to break even, let alone make a profit.

When you are just starting out, you should probably not pay for privileges on a BBS. Most pay systems offer a free trial period to give you a chance to explore the BBS and find out if it's worth the membership fee. Just because a BBS charges a fee for access doesn't mean that there is anything of interest to you on the BBS.

You should not pay for BBS access privileges until you are able to log on and off of BBSes with ease and can use most of the features of the message and file systems comfortably. By the time your BBS skills have reached this level, you will have discovered most of the things you want in a BBS and will be able to make an informed decision about whether a BBS is worth a membership fee.

## If You Have Trouble

This section gives some hints about what you can do if you have trouble communicating with a BBS.

### If the BBS you're calling is busy.

Use the autodial feature of your communications package to keep trying the BBS. The average call is about 10-20 minutes. You should also remember that 5:00 P.M. to midnight on weekdays is prime time for BBS usage. Adjusting your schedule so that you phone earlier or later may make it easier to get through on the first try.

### If you don't seem to be connecting to the BBS.

Listen carefully to the modem's speaker, or try dialing the BBS number yourself to see what happens. You could be getting a busy signal, a disconnect recording, or even a rather annoyed person.

**Note:** If you get a person rather than a BBS when you dial a new number, pick up your phone and ask if there is a BBS operating at that number. If not, apologize, hang up, and contact the person you got the number from to let them know that the number is not a BBS.

### If the BBS answers but nothing happens immediately.

Press [ENTER] several times and wait about five seconds. If nothing has happened yet, try pressing the [ESC] key several times. Again, allow a few seconds for the BBS to respond. You can also try entering [CTRL-F] (hold down the [CTRL] key and press F) several times. Pressing [CTRL-F] sends an ASCII value that tells the modem on the other end you are listening.

If there is still no response, remove the handset on your phone briefly and listen. If you don't hear the high-pitched tone, the modem on the other end has already gotten disgusted and hung up. This means that you may have been doing the right things, but not quickly enough (many modems have short attention spans). Try dialing the BBS again.

**Note:** The amount of time BBSes take to respond when you first connect varies considerably depending on the software and hardware the BBS uses. Some of the BBSes that run on Commodore 64s or some CP/M computers can take up to 10 seconds to respond, which can seem like forever when you are first logging on. Leave room in your expectations for a slow BBS.

**If the BBS isn't responding but you still hear the high-pitched tone when you remove the handset, or nothing but strange characters are appearing on your screen.**

Your communications settings are probably not quite right. For example, if the BBS's modem is expecting no parity and you are using even parity, or if the two modems are set to different baud rates, you will see lots of strange characters on the screen, looking something like the display shown in Figure 2-6. Hang up the phone, reset your communications parameters as necessary, and try again.

```
Eq!!◄8 ñäbbääiá-ñDñ├—çä♠☺âí║d┤äΣf•┤äéâà├—d║°τ♦♦âD≤r
≤ñµDçü├äµ$çUÄβäú└ê3=êh.=ŸÀBËÊðéÏðíÓúéðÓDµb4«H
ÚéÀú$ÌéF
òÒÊÊBµ2        ÌBãó-Êð--úDµ·■À
tGÜANÇ+!îàáç°
ôL- │à%´J´ÿíB½óv¼'±b5gÙAN-¡àÕ!yCÀúdp!g¥áðÓËâÔËÏÊéÏb-ÌtbÀ-
éÊí5àÿ ót8-sµÊb$ÓÌÍÌíÂÌ-Êð8Dµ·½À¶C
ÙANËÀúdÌéÇ(þübRàþìB1 ðÕódDWöÃäb4  üBCéË
ÀúdÌé$ÑüÊ$ÀwÀÌé4k11+Õk!¢ÌË¼?g)!är¤Ã¼öeëÊðDµ
¶k!š!k!ßb
```

*Figure 2-6. Example of Incorrect Communications Parameters*

**If strange characters or mangled screens or text are *occasionally* appearing.**

Occasional problems are usually caused by *line noise*. Line noise is a generic term for static, spikes, or anything else that interferes with the modem signal as it passes through the phone lines. (You can also see a good example of line noise if someone picks up another extension of the same phone while you're talking to a BBS.) Figure 2-7 shows what line noise looks like when you're talking to a BBS.

```
      Saturday 08Feb90 17:50 (PST) From *ÛŠùZÔæWRjÝìË n m Spade
 Well, I'm finally here.

      Sunday 08Feb09 18:03 (PST) From Chanterelle
 Nice to see yo[nëwD¢].+¨¨2«] Sam.

      WednesdÂy'12À¯¿ö 3:01 (¯ST) From  Moreta
 Gee, I must be seeing things.
```

*Figure 2-7. Example of Line Noise*

If there is a lot of line noise, try hanging up and dialing in again. Line noise is frequently the result of going through a noisy circuit at the telephone company's switching office. Dialing in again will probably give you a different circuit.

Some telephone companies with older equipment have difficulty with 2400 baud, particularly in outlying areas. If you think that this may be the cause of your problem, try hanging up and dialing back in at 1200 baud. Some long-distance services also make special provisions for data calls by dedicating a group of "clean" circuits primarily for data rather than voice. Check with your service representative to find out if you have this option.

*Above all, never use a BBS on a party line.*

**If everything is working and then suddenly you get no response from the BBS (possibly accompanied by a few strange characters).**

One of several things can cause this problem. First, the BBS you were calling may have *crashed*. BBSes most often will crash from power flickers that cause the computer they are running on to reboot. Some BBSes are set up to restart automatically when this happens, but even so, you will have to hang up and dial in again.

A "call waiting" feature on your phone can also disconnect you from the BBS. The one-second beep that indicates there is a second call on the line is interpreted by the BBS modem to mean that you have hung up, and it hangs up also. If you have call waiting, see if you can enter a code on your phone pad to disable it while you are dialing out. Call your telephone company business office for information on how to do this. You can also call BBSes late at night or early in the morning, when you're not as likely to get incoming calls.

Telecommunications problems can be difficult to track down. If something isn't working, it can be hard to point to the problem immediately. Many modems have a set of indicator lights on the front panel that tell when data is passing through, and what the modem is sending and receiving. If you need more assistance, Appendix D, "Troubleshooting," has some tips on how to identify possible problems.

Chapter 3, "Reading and Entering Messages," discusses the message system in detail.

## LOOKING AROUND THE BBS

After logging on to the BBS and reading the system policy, start looking around the BBS to see what's there. Most BBSes have a *main menu* of some kind. The main menu is the starting point for almost everything on the BBS. Figure 2-8 shows you the main menu for Grotto de Blotto.

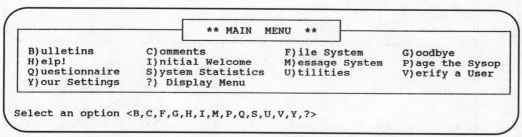

```
                        ** MAIN  MENU  **

    B)ulletins        C)omments           F)ile System        G)oodbye
    H)elp!            I)nitial Welcome    M)essage System     P)age the Sysop
    Q)uestionnaire    S)ystem Statistics  U)tilities          V)erify a User
    Y)our Settings    ?) Display Menu

  Select an option <B,C,F,G,H,I,M,P,Q,S,U,V,Y,?>
```

*Figure 2-8. Sample Main Menu*

Because commands are designed to be reasonably intuitive, you can count on most of the commands you learn on one BBS working about the same on another BBS. For example, *E* usually stands for *Enter message* and *G* usually stands for *Goodbye*. However, you should also remember that each BBS can be a little different from any other BBS. For example, the command to log off from a BBS can be *G* for *Goodbye*, *E* or *X* for *Exit*, *T* for *Terminate*, *Q* for *Quit*, or even *H* for *Hang up!*

As a new user, you may not be able to use some of the functions shown on the main menu. Many sysops prefer to validate the users before granting extensive privileges. If this is the case, you may see only a portion of the options shown in Figure 2-8, or you may not be able to get the BBS to recognize commands that are on the main menu.

Remember that BBSes are designed for new users. It's almost impossible for you to do something that will damage the BBS by entering the wrong command. In the unlikely circumstance that you think you may have caused a problem, leave a courtesy note to the sysop to say that you know you entered the wrong command. (See Chapter 3, "Reading and Entering Messages," for information on sending a message to the sysop.) Sysops are used to new users making mistakes, and will appreciate your courtesy.

## Checking the Bulletins

The first thing you should do is find out more about the system. Enter the command for *Bulletins* or *Info* (usually *B* or *I*). The bulletin menu will appear, as shown in Figure 2-9.

```
    BULLETIN        DESCRIPTION
    --------        -----------
       1            System Policy (READ ME!)
       2            General Information
       3            New User Information
       4            What's Happening (Event Calendar)
       5            Viruses and Files
       6            Validation and Access Levels
       7            Contributions
       8            New Files
       9            Archive Formats (ARC, ZIP, and PAK)
    Enter a bulletin number, or press [ENTER] to return to the main menu.
```

*Figure 2-9. Bulletin Menu*

The bulletins listed in the bulletin menu contain information about the system and how to use it, as well as any changes to the policy. Bulletin 2, shown in Figure 2-10, contains information about the BBS itself.

```
    Grotto de Blotto runs on an AT clone with 2.5 megs of RAM,
    a 66 meg and a 30 meg hard drive, a 60 meg tape drive for
    backups, and a 9600 baud external modem.  We have recently
    added a CD-ROM drive with the PC-SIG library, giving Grotto de
    Blotto about 300 megs of downloads.

    The system is verified access.  Although there is no fee for using
    Grotto de Blotto, users are expected to contribute their energy to the
    board in the form of messages, files, and so on.  People who sign on
    for the sole purpose of receiving files will rapidly discover their
    access privileges limited.
```

*Figure 2-10. General Information Bulletin*

Take a few minutes to read all the bulletins. They can give you background information about the BBS, the types of people who use it, and the services the BBS offers. It is a good idea to capture the bulletins to a disk file with your communications program. You can then review them later and print out any information that is particularly helpful. When you are done reading the bulletins, return to the main menu.

## Using Help

Almost all BBSes have help of one kind or another, ranging from simple prompt explanations like the ones shown in Figure 2-11 to a complete BBS manual that you can download from the BBS's file section.

```
┤ MAIN MENU HELP FILE ├

COMMAND                          WHAT IT DOES
------------------------         -------------------------------------------
[B]............Bulletins         Go to the Bulletins menu to read system news
[C]............Comments          Leave a private message for the Sysop
[F].........File System          Go to the Files menu for uploads and downloads
[G]............Goodbye           Log off board
[H]..........Help Level          Change amount of system help and prompts
[I]......Initial Welcome         Display the system policy message
[M].....Message System           Go to the Messages menu
[P].......Page the Sysop         Call the sysop (if she's in) for a chat
[Q]........Questionnaire          Add your comments to the user survey
[S]....System Statistics         Examine message, file, and user statistics
[U]............Utilities         Go to the Utilities menu
[V]........Verify a User         Search for a name in the userlog
[Y]........Your Settings         Change your password, city, or display options
[?].........Display Menu         Display the main menu
```

*Figure 2-11. Sample Help Screen for Main Menu*

To save yourself time looking for commands, capture and print the main menu screen and post it near your keyboard. Most BBSes have an Expert mode that suppresses the full main menu and only displays a line of options:

```
Select an option <B,C,F,G,H,I,M,P,Q,S,U,V,Y,?>
```

Since the 10 or 12 lines of main menu aren't redisplayed each time, using the BBS in Expert mode is much faster. This also means a cash savings if you are dialing long distance.

About half the BBSes now in operation offer only one or two lines of help for each command. However, many BBSes have *extended help* for the commands, as shown in Figure 2-12.

```
Bulletin.  This takes you to the Bulletins menu.

Once you have entered this command, the menu of system bulletins appears.
You can display a bulletin by entering the number or letter associated with
that bulletin.  You may read as many bulletins as many times as you like.
When you are ready to return to the Main menu, press [ENTER] at the prompt.
```

*Figure 2-12. Help on a Selected Command*

In addition to these two kinds of help, about 20% of all BBSes offer help on topics of general interest, as shown in Figure 2-13.

```
Help is available on the following topics:

     FILE - Files, sending, and receiving
     HELP - The Help system and how to use it
     MAIN - An overview of the commands on the main menu
  MESSAGE - Entering and reading messages
     UTIL - Using the system utilities

To get help on one of these topics, type the letter H followed by
the topic name shown in the left column of this table.
```

*Figure 2-13. Help on Topics*

Use your communications program to capture all of the help on the system for reviewing later.  An important point to remember is that BBSes are designed to be user-proof. It's almost impossible to enter a command that will cause any damage.  If you're not sure what to do next in a situation, feel free to experiment a little.  The worst you are likely to do is unexpectedly log yourself off of the BBS.

# LOGGING OFF

After capturing the bulletins and help files and looking around a bit, log off the BBS and review the information.  The most common command for logging off is *G*, although *X, T,* and *Q* are also used.  At the main menu prompt, simply enter the appropriate logoff command.  The BBS will ask you if you really want to log off now, in case you entered the logoff command by mistake.  Figure 2-14 shows a typical set of options when you log out.

```
Do you want to leave a comment for the sysop?

Y - Yes, leave a comment.
N - No, just log me out
C - Cancel, don't log me out yet

Command?
```

*Figure 2-14. Logout Options*

For right now, enter *N* to log out without leaving a comment. You'll have a chance to see how to enter messages in the next chapter. The BBS will log you out and hang up the modem, as shown in Figure 2-15.

```
It's now 9 Aug 1990 at 19:39:49.
On for 12 mins, 18 secs
17 min left for next call today
SAM, thanks and please call again!

2í √aπh
NO CARRIER
```

*Figure 2-15. Logout Screen*

*Never log off of a BBS by turning off the modem or exiting the communications program.* "Hanging up" on the BBS this way will at the very least tie up the BBS for a couple of minutes while it figures out that nobody is on the line anymore. In some cases, hanging up can cause the BBS to freeze until the sysop reboots the BBS.

# BECOMING AN EXPERT

When you first call a BBS, use your communications program's capturing features to save to a file all of the information that appears on the screen. After you log off, you can print the file and examine it at your leisure. Look for special requirements of the BBS. For example, you may have to leave your telephone number, answer a questionnaire, or send a photocopy of your driver's license before being granted access to the BBS.

Don't use pseudonyms until you are sure that it's accepted practice on a particular BBS. Enter your name and city the same way at all times. Put your passwords in a safe place, and don't use the same password for all the boards you call.

Read all the bulletins. These contain a considerable amount of information that will be helpful to you for using the BBS and its features. The same is true for all the online help you can find.

Feel free to experiment with the BBS's commands. You will certainly make a few mistakes here and there, but you will also learn a great deal about how the BBS works very quickly.

Never abuse a BBS in any way. If a sysop feels that you are intentionally trying to "crash" or damage the BBS, you may be barred from using the BBS entirely. In many states, you can be prosecuted for trying to crash a BBS.

As soon as you feel comfortable with the commands on a BBS, switch to Expert mode (usually by entering *X*) to save display time. You can always enter *?* or *H* to display help about the commands, or enter *X* again to display the full menu of options.

Use the appropriate command (*G, T, X,* or *Q*) to exit the BBS gracefully. Don't just "hang up."

Don't pay for membership in a BBS until you have explored the free BBSes in your area (but do contribute financially to any BBS you use regularly). The sysop is providing the BBS as a largely unpaid service and deserves a modicum of respect. If you don't like the way a sysop is running a BBS, call another BBS.

Don't dial an untested BBS number in the middle of the night or before 10:00 A.M. BBS numbers change frequently, and you may wake someone up.

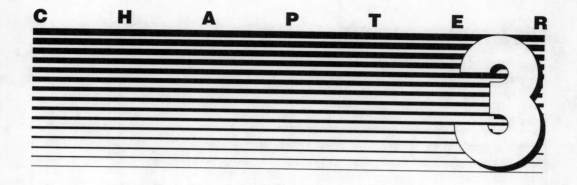

# READING AND ENTERING MESSAGES

This chapter will show how to read and enter messages and how to exchange messages with other BBS users. Before reading this chapter, be sure you know how to log on to a BBS, look around, and log off. These techniques are covered in Chapter 2.

Messages on a BBS give the quickest indication of what the BBS is like. Even if you're only using a BBS to upload and download files, you will still need to know how to read and enter messages to find out what's happening in relation to the BBS.

## THE MESSAGE SYSTEM

After logging on to a BBS, look for the command on the main menu that takes you to the message system. This is usually an *M*. When you enter this command, the message menu appears. Two sample message menus are shown in Figure 3-1.

```
┤ Message Reading Menu ├

<L>ist <N>ext <P>rior <R>eply <E>nter <S>-Scan Mail <#>Jump to Msg #

<M>ain Menu <G>oodbye <Enter>-Start Reading or Repeat Next/Prior


Command:


Msg Area #1 GENERAL
General Topics of Interest.
A)rea-Change L)ist R)ead E)nter I)ndex
S)tatistics G)oodbye M)ain-Menu
Msg: A L R E I S G M or ? for help:
```

*Figure 3-1. Sample Message Menus*

Some BBSes display the most recent message first, down to the oldest message last. The two primary advantages to this type of message system are that it is very easy to see the latest news and to keep track of several discussions at once. BBSes with this type of message system may not have a separate message menu at all.

The disadvantage to this sort of message system is that you have to sift through all the messages to follow a single conversation. If you're only interested in one conversation out of five or six, this can be difficult and tedious. Because of this, most BBSes keep related groups of messages in *topics* or *areas*. These are separate message systems on the BBS where people go to talk about specific subjects.

### Selecting a Topic

The following example shows how to select a topic and read the messages it contains. If you have already chosen a BBS that does not use topics, skip this section and go directly to "Reading Messages."

Enter the *A* command to change your message area. Figure 3-2 shows a sample of the message areas you are likely to see on a BBS.

```
===============================[ Topic Areas ]==================================
   A    GENERAL     Main message area, announcements
   B    CLASSIFIED  Items wanted or for sale/swap/trade
   C    JOBS        Need a job?  Know of a job?  Leave messages here.
   D    MUSIC       Any kind of music - fiddle & banjo stuff especially!
   E    OTHER BBS   Advertisements for other boards
   F    EQUALITY    New developments in women's rights
   1    IBM USERS   General room for IBM PC & Clone users
   2    IBM PROGS   IBM programs (general)
   3    IBM GAMES   IBM Games
   4    IBM UTILS   IBM Utilities
   5    MAC USERS   General room for Macintosh users
   6    MAC PROGS   Macintosh programs (general)
   7    MAC GAMES   Macintosh games
   8    MAC UTILS   Macintosh utils
   9    ECOLOGY     How can we help the world?
  10    HAM RADIO   Amateur radio

Currently selected topic is A, GENERAL

Topic?
```

*Figure 3-2. Sample List of Topics*

When you first log on to most BBSes, you default to the first topic in the list, usually MAIN or GENERAL. Make a note of any topics on the list that particularly interest you. At the prompt, enter the number or letter for the topic you want to examine. The BBS will switch to this topic and then return you to the message menu and await your next command.

**Note:** Many BBSes now have an interesting variation on topics known as *conferences.* Conferences can be either public or private, with invitation-only access. They differ from topics in that they usually combine both messages and files related to a particular subject in the same area, so you don't have to shift back and forth between the message menu and the file menu. Conferences also quite often have a *moderator,* a person who keeps the discussion alive and on the subject of the conference.

## Reading Messages

From the message menu, you can read or enter messages. Suppose you have logged on to a BBS and are looking at the general message area for the first time. In order to get an idea of the types of messages that appear on the BBS, read the first few messages.

At the message menu, enter the command for reading messages (this command is almost always *R*). You are then presented with several choices:

```
Starting from which message [1..356], <S>ince,
<L>ast, <F>rom, <T>o, <M>y, <->, <+>?
```

You can enter any one of the following options at this prompt:

[1..356]    A message number (in this case, from 1 to 356).

<S>ince     Read forward from the last message you read since the last time you were on the BBS (the BBS keeps track of the last message you read).

<L>ast      Read backward from the last (most recent) message.

<F>rom      Read the messages from you.

<T>o        Read the messages addressed to you or to "ALL" (any messages to "ALL" will be of potential interest to you).

<M>y        Read "my" messages (messages either from you or to you).

<->         *n-* read backward from message number *n*. For example, to read backward from message 300, enter *300-*. The higher the message number, the more recent the message.

<+>         *n+* read forward from message number *n*. To read forward from message, enter *300+*.

**Note:**  Not all BBSes will have all of these options for reading messages. Some BBSes will also use different keystrokes for the various functions. For example, the Read Forward command, designated here by a plus sign (+), is frequently designated with an *F* (for Forward). You should learn how to use the various message functions effectively. Then, when you log on to a new BBS, you just need to learn the different keystrokes used for the various commands.

Read through some of the messages to get acquainted with the process. For example, after entering *1+* to read forward from the first message, you see the Figure 3-3.

```
Message 1 on 12 Feb 90 10:59
From: JAY SATO
To: ALL
Subject: Hard Disk

    I have a Micro-Science hard disk, model HH612.  I need some
information about it so I can install and format it.  Any information you
have will be greatly appreciated.

Thanks
Jay

Read msg [1] [1..356], <ENTER>=Next, <R>eply, <B>ack Up,
<K>ill, <Q>uit, <*>Read Reply?
```

*Figure 3-3. First Message*

Take a moment to examine Figure 3-3.  The first four lines comprise the *message header*.  The first line tells what the message number is, and when it was entered on the BBS.  The second line is the name of the user who entered it.  The third line is to whom the message is addressed.  Addressing a message to "ALL" makes it clear that you are inviting everyone to read the message and that anyone may reply.  Messages can be addressed to everyone on the BBS or to specific users.  Some of the message selection functions will find messages addressed to "ALL," allowing users to see anything addressed to everyone.  The fourth line is the subject of the message.

After the message header comes the *text* or the *body* of the message.  The text can be any practical length, although most BBSes limit the number of characters in a single message to about 1900.  If you need to enter a longer message, split it into two or more messages.

Following the message text in Figure 3-3 is a list of options.  You can press [ENTER] to see the next message, reply to the message, back up to the previous message, kill (delete) the message, quit reading messages and return to the message menu, or read the replies to this message.  After pressing [ENTER], the next message appears.

```
Message 2 on 12 Feb 90 11:30
From: JANE FERGUSON
To: ALL
Subject: Need a CGA or EGA card, please

There has been a Reply to this message

Does anyone have a CGA or EGA card they'd be willing to sell cheaply?  I
had a bunch of spare computer parts lying around, so I'm putting together
a computer for my brother to learn on, but the display card I was going to
use turned out to be no good.

Give me a phone call at home or leave me a message on the board.

Yours Truly,

Jane

Read msg [2] [1..356], <ENTER>=Next, <R>eply, <B>ack Up,
<K>ill, <Q>uit, <*>Read Reply?
```

*Figure 3-4. Second Message*

Below the message header is a line that says that this message has a reply.  Enter an asterisk (*) to see the reply (shown in Figure 3-5).

```
Message 5 on 15 Feb 90 17:02
From: JIM BUCK
To: JANE FERGUSON
Subject: CGA card

There has been a Reply to this message

Jane:

I have an old CGA card that I'm not using.  I'll sell it to you
for $25.  I don't have specs on it, but I had it in my old PC
for a couple of years before I got my VGA card.

Whaddaya say?

Jim

Read msg [5] [1..356], <ENTER>=Next, <R>eply, <P>revious,
<K>ill, <Q>uit, <*>Read Reply?
```

*Figure 3-5. Reply to Second Message*

From the header, you can see that this is message number 5.  Entering an asterisk (*) skipped the messages in between the message from Jane Ferguson (message 2) and message 5. You can see that there is also a reply to this message, which is shown in Figure 3-6.

```
Message 12 on 16 Feb 90 20:47
From: JANE FERGUSON
To: JIM BUCK
Subject: Your CGA card


Jim:

Okay.  I'll stop by your place tomorrow on the way to folk dancing.  Thanks.

Jane

Read msg [12] [1..356], <ENTER>=Next, <R>eply, <P>revious,
<K>ill, <Q>uit, <*>Read Reply?
```

*Figure 3-6. Reply to Reply*

Suppose that you want to skip ahead in the messages a little. Entering *100* at the prompt displays message 100:

```
Message 100 on 3 May 90 16:22
From: SYSOP
To: ALL
Subject: Board policy

A lot of people have apparently been overlooking the changes in the board's
policy statement.  I'd like to have you all read the board policy and then
post any questions you have about it.  The board works better if everyone
is operating with the same assumptions.

Your Sysop,

M. D.


                                * * *


Grotto de Blotto is a BBS for swapping technical information and having adult
discussions on a wide variety of topics.  Use of this board is a privilege,
not a right.  Users are expected to act in a reasonably civil fashion.  Anyone
who cannot comply with these rules will be denied access.

More [Y]es, N)o, C)ontinuous
```

*Figure 3-8. First Half of Message 100*

Message 100 is from the sysop, Michael Dispater. When a message happens to be longer than a single screen, many BBSes ask you if you want to display the next screen of information. Your options are usually *Y* to show the next screen, *N* to stop displaying this message, and *C* (or *NS* for *nonstop* on some BBSes) to display the rest of the message without stopping. The remainder of message 100 appears in Figure 3-8.

```
The distribution of unlawfully copied or "hacked" software will not be tolerated
on this board under any circumstances.  Anyone who uploads such software will
have their access privileges revoked.

I cannot guarantee the accuracy of any information posted on this bulletin
board, nor can I guarantee the results of using software from this system on
any computer.  Please be careful.  If you have a problem, let me know, and I
will take whatever steps seem appropriate.

Cash contributions for the maintenance of this BBS are always welcome, but are
not necessary.  The best way to support this BBS is to use it.  Thank you.

                    Your Sysop, Michael Dispater

Read msg [100] [1..356], <ENTER>=Next, <R>eply, <P>revious,
<K>ill, <Q>uit, <*>Read Reply?
```

*Figure 3-8. Second Half of Message 100*

You could read through the entire message system one message at a time, but if there are many messages, it will take a long time.

## Scanning Messages

The *Scanning* command lets you skim the message headers to see what each message is about, to whom each message is addressed, and who posted each message. The Scan command works much like the read command. You simply tell the BBS which messages you want to scan, and the BBS displays the message headers for the selected messages. Figure 3-9 shows a sample scan of a few messages.

```
Starting from which message [1..356]? 349

Message 349    (03/29/90 19:46)   Fm : SYSOP
Subject: How I do backups...      To : GEORGE MONTGOMERY

Message 350 has been deleted

Message 351    (03/30/90 19:10)   Fm : DAN GEISS
Subject: I'MMMMM BAAAAAACCK       To : ALL

Message 352 is private

Message 353    (03/31/90 15:36)   Fm : MARV MOORE
Subject: New version of QMODEM    To : CHRIS HIGGINS

Message 354    (04/01/90 19:48)   Fm : JANE FERGUSON
Subject: New QMODEM???            To : CHRIS HIGGINS

Message 355    (04/02/90 05:28)   Fm : JIM BUCK
Subject: Hard Disk for sale       To : ALL

Message 356    (04/02/90 15:33)   Fm : CHRIS HIGGINS
Subject: Yes, a new QMODEM!!      To : JANE FERGUSON
End of Scan
```

*Figure 3-9. Sample Message Scan*

Private messages (discussed in the "Using Mail" section of this chapter) are not displayed when scanning unless you are allowed to see them. Similarly, messages that have been deleted do not appear on the list of messages.

With a large group of messages, you may find that it is most effective to read the first few messages to see where the conversation started and then the messages from the last week, and scan all the messages in between. Make a note of message numbers that look interesting so you can come back and read them later. This lets you see how a discussion has developed and who has been taking part in it.

You can pause the display at any time by pressing [CTRL-S]. This tells your computer to stop accepting data from the BBS. Pressing [CTRL-Q] resumes the display. These keystrokes can be used to pace the material to fit your reading speed when a BBS has a nonstop display feature.

## Searching for Messages

Suppose that you want to read all the messages that have to do with hard disks, or with something for sale, or that were written by Jane Ferguson. Most BBSes have a text search function that allows you to search for a specific word or phrase in the message header (and on some BBSes, in the message text as well). Here's how searching for messages works:

At the message menu, select the command for searching messages. This is usually *T* for Topic Search or *I* for Index. You'll see something like this prompt:

```
Topic of Msgs?
```

Enter the text you want the BBS to look for. For example, if you enter *sale,* the BBS will look for "sale" in the To, From, and Subject fields of all the messages you specify. Text searches do not usually differentiate between upper- and lowercase letters; entering *sale* will find "sale," "Sale," and "SALE." As another example, you could look for someone by the first three letters of their last name, such as *gut.* This would find you message headers to or from Gutman, Gutierrez, and Guthrie.

After you have entered the text to search for, you have to tell the BBS which messages in which you want to search for the text:

```
Search for text from message number (1-356)?
```

Specify the message to search from by entering its number. If you want to search through all the messages, enter *1.* The BBS proceeds to look for all message headers containing the specified text string. As it finds them, it will display the message numbers:

```
I found "sale" in the following messages:
10, 155, 207, 288
```

Make a note of the message numbers so you can read them with the read command. Some BBSes make it easier for you by displaying shortened versions of the message header fields as shown in Figure 3-10.

```
Scanning Messages...

Msg#    To              From                Subject
10      ALL             SYSOP                GARAGE SALE
155     ALL             GEORGE MONTGOMERY    FOR SALE: DISK DRIVE
207     GEORGE MONTGO   DAVE GEISS           FOR SALE: DISK DRIVE
288     ALL             JANE FERGUSON        COMPUTER FOR RESALE
```

*Figure 3-10. Alternate Display of Found Messages*

Many BBSes *mark* the messages you have found by searching. You can then read them quickly and easily by telling the BBS you want to read the marked messages at the read message prompt. Message marking differs from BBS to BBS. Check with the sysop or the BBS's help files for more information on how it is implemented.

## Other Useful Commands for Reading Messages

The Since or New Messages command will display all the messages in a topic that have been entered since the last time you logged on. This allows you to read the latest messages quickly and easily.

Some BBSes allow you to enter a number of commands at once. This is known as *stacking* commands. Each time the BBS needs you to enter a command, it performs the next command in the stack. For example, at the main menu, you might enter something like *M A 5 R S C* to perform the following commands consecutively:

- switch to the message menu (M)
- change the message area (A)
- specify area 5 (5)
- start reading the messages (R)
- specify that you want all the messages since you were on last time (S)
- read the messages continuously without stopping (C)

Unfortunately, some of the older BBSes do not have these features, but you can use your communications program's scripting capabilities to accomplish the same thing.

Remember that different BBSes will use varying keystrokes for commands and actions. However, the basic functions of selecting a topic, reading messages, scanning message headers, and searching for text are all about the same.

## ENTERING MESSAGES

Your own first message may be to express interest in something someone has offered for sale, to respond to a political opinion by another user, or even to tell a joke. Whatever it is, you'll find that entering messages is quick and easy.

Suppose that you decide to introduce yourself to the other BBS users. Having gotten to the message menu, you need to tell the BBS that you want to enter (or *post*) a message. Almost all BBSes use *E* to enter a message.

Once you enter *E*, the BBS displays something like the following:

```
To All, Sysop, or specific user?
```

The first thing you need to do is tell the system who you are sending the message to. Since you want an introduction to go to everyone, type *ALL*. The BBS will then prompt you for a subject:

```
Enter the subject of your message?
```

The BBS uses the subject when scanning or searching messages. At the subject prompt, enter a description of what your message is about: something like *Hello, everybody.* Many BBSes will allow you only about 40 characters for the subject, so be brief.

```
Is this message private (Y/N)?
```

If you make the message private, only the person to whom the message is addressed can read it. Since this message is to everyone, it should be public, so enter *N*. More about this feature is discussed later in the chapter.

You now enter the text of the message. In most cases, you'll see something like this display:

```
   Enter your text. Press [ENTER] twice to end. 72 chars/line, 80 lines max
   [-----------------------------------------------------------------------]
1:
```

The top line of the display shows that the message on this BBS can have 72 characters in each line of text and be up to 80 lines long. The number of lines and characters varies somewhat from BBS to BBS, but this is average. The line of dashes is 72 characters wide, and is displayed to act as a guide when you're typing. The line number (1:) appears on the left of the screen.

Start entering your message. As you type, the characters will appear on the screen just like using a word processor. You can press [ENTER] to end a line, or you can let the BBS format the message for you. Almost all BBSes automatically *wordwrap;* that is, the BBS figures out where to start a new line, so you don't have to press [ENTER] until you want to start a new paragraph. Figure 3-11 shows a sample message as first entered.

```
   Enter your text. Press [ENTER] twice to end. 72 chars/line, 80 lines max
   [-----------------------------------------------------------------------]
1: Hello!  My name is Sam Spade.  I'm new to using bulketin boards.  I
2: have an IBM and am using a 2400 baud modem.  I like QMODEM best.
3: Among my interests are banjo playing, ham radio, and homebrewing.  My
4: wife and I have three cats and six birds.
```

*Figure 3-11. First Draft of Message Text*

Notice the typo in the word "bulletin" in the first line. Fortunately, the BBS gives you several ways to correct mistakes and to add and delete text.

## Editing a Message

Pressing [ENTER] twice on blank lines tells the BBS that you want to edit or save the message you have been entering. You will then see a list of choices something like the following:

```
<A>bort, <C>ontinue, <D>elete, <E>dit, <I>nsert, <L>ist, <S>ave
```

Entering *E* for Edit (or *R* for Replace on some BBSes) lets you find a character or group of characters and replace it with another group of characters.

In this example, use the Edit command to get rid of the extraneous *k* in the word *bulletin*. However, if you simply told the BBS to replace *k* with nothing, it would remove *all* k's in the message and replace them with nothing. When using this command to correct a typo, you must enter enough characters to accurately identify the section of text you want to change. The Edit command prompt asks for the characters to change. You then enter the text you want to replace and a semicolon, followed by the character you want to insert. When you press [ENTER], the BBS will then find all occurrences of the old text and replace them with the new text. The Edit command prompt with the characters to find and replace looks like this:

```
Enter old text;new text or press [ENTER] for no change?
bulk;bull
```

Here are some things to remember when replacing text:

- The BBS assumes that any spaces, punctuation, and so on in either group of characters are to be looked for or replaced.

- The Edit command is *case-sensitive*. Looking for "THIS IS A TEST" will not find the line "this is a test" because the BBS is looking for capital letters.

- If your new text causes a line to exceed the maximum number of characters in a line, the excess characters are usually truncated.

When you are finished making changes to the text, press [ENTER] to return to the message commands.

## Adding Text

You can add more text to the message by entering *C* (for Continue). This positions the cursor at the start of the next blank line in the message, where you can type more text, as shown in Figure 3-12.

```
    Enter your text. Press [ENTER] twice to end. 72 chars/line, 80 lines max
    [-----------------------------------------------------------------]
1: Hello!  My name is Sam Spade.  I'm new to using bulletin boards.  I
2: have an IBM and am using a 2400 baud modem.  I like QMODEM best.
3: Among my interests are banjo playing, ham radio, and homebrewing.  My
4: wife and I have three cats and six birds.
5:
```

*Figure 3-12. Continuing a Message*

Pressing [ENTER] on blank lines takes you to the Message Editing Commands. A useful technique for inserting a blank line or two in the middle of the message is to type a space on the line and then press [ENTER]. The line is no longer "blank" because it contains a character, so the BBS will not go to the editing commands.

## Inserting and Deleting Lines

Use the Insert and Delete commands to insert and delete entire lines of text. To insert a line of text, enter *I*. When the BBS prompts you for a line number, enter the line number before the text to be inserted. For example, suppose that you want to add a line of text before line 3 in the message in Figure 3-12. When you enter *I*, the BBS asks you where to insert the line:

```
    Line number to insert new line before?
```

When you enter the line number, the BBS displays it and waits for you to enter text. The completed line of text right before pressing [ENTER] looks like:

```
    3: I write computer manuals for a living and do some freelancing.
```

When you press [ENTER], the BBS will insert this line of text at the position you specified and renumber the subsequent message lines. Enter *L* (for List) to see what the message looks like, as shown in Figure 3-13.

```
    Enter your text. Press [ENTER] twice to end. 72 chars/line, 80 lines max
    [-----------------------------------------------------------------]
1: Hello!  My name is Sam Spade.  I'm new to using bulletin boards.  I
2: have an IBM and am using a 2400 baud modem.  I like QMODEM best.
3: I write computer manuals for a living and do some freelancing.
4: Among my interests are banjo playing, ham radio, and homebrewing.  My
5: wife and I have three cats and six birds.
```

*Figure 3-13. Listed Message*

The inserted line appears before line 3. Note that the BBS does not reformat the message to smooth the margins.

You can delete lines of text the same way. Enter *D* to tell the BBS you want to delete a line. At the prompt, enter the line number. The BBS displays the line you specified and asks for confirmation. Enter *Y* to delete the line.

Some BBSes will let you delete a group of lines by letting you specify the beginning and ending line in the group. If you only want to delete a single line on a BBS like this, specify the same beginning and ending line.

## Cancelling a Message

To cancel (abort) a message in progress you enter *A* (for Abort) or *X* (for Exit message). The BBS will ask for confirmation. When you confirm by entering *Y*, the BBS will return you to the message menu. Figure 3-14 shows you an example of this.

```
Entry Command? a

Abandon the message in progress (Press [ENTER] for no)? y

Message abandoned.
```

*Figure 3-14. Cancelling a Message*

## Saving a Message

The Save command writes your message to the BBS's hard disk and records it as part of the message file. To save a message, enter *S* at the prompt. The BBS will respond with a message like:

```
Saving message to hard disk...
```

The BBS will return you to the message menu for your next command. The completed message as it appears in the message system is shown in Figure 3-15.

```
Message 357 on 1 Apr 90 18:26
From: SAM SPADE
To: ALL
Subject: Hello, everybody!

Hello!  My name is Sam Spade.  I'm new to using bulletin boards.  I
have an IBM and am using a 2400 baud modem.  I like QMODEM best.
I write computer manuals for a living and do some freelancing.
Among my interests are banjo playing, ham radio, and homebrewing.  My
wife and I have three cats and six birds.

Read msg [357] [1..357], <ENTER>=Next, <R>eply, <B>ack Up,
<K>ill, <Q>uit, <*>Read Reply?
```

*Figure 3-15. Completed Message*

Although composing messages as you type is acceptable for short messages, it's bad form to take up lots of online time to compose and type a long message. It is much better to write the message out beforehand using a word processor and then upload the message in ASCII format. You can upload several pages of text in about a minute and won't tie up the BBS for a long time. Chapter 4, "Sending and Receiving Files," describes the procedure for doing this.

## Using Electronic Mail

Suppose that you want to leave your phone number for the sysop, but you don't want to have everyone on the BBS to have it. In this case, you need to send the sysop *electronic mail* (also known as *email* for short, or just *mail*).

To send mail, you enter the addressee's user name at the message recipient prompt. Email is a message addressed to a specific person, rather than to everyone on the BBS. When addressees log on to the BBS, they are alerted that messages have been addressed to them. These messages can be made Public, so everyone will be able to read them, or Private, for reading only by the addressee.

However, just because a message is Private does not always mean that only the recipient will see it. The sysop can always read mail on the BBS, regardless of to whom it's addressed. Other people may also have *remote sysop* status; that is, they can dial in to the BBS and have all the privileges of the sysop just as if they were sitting in front of the BBS computer. If you really don't want someone other than the recipient to see something, you should just leave your phone number in email and talk to the recipient directly.

Some BBSes offer additional options for sending email. For example, you may be able to enter a password for the message so that only you and the recipient will be able to read the message. Of course, the recipient must know the password.

Another feature is the ability to send "carbon copies" to other people on the BBS. Check the help system on the BBS you are using for more information.

## Replying to a Message

Replying to a message is like email, as you are sending a message to a specific addressee. Unlike email, however, it links the reply and the message. This allows you to easily read a series of messages and replies in sequence.

Suppose you have read message 355 from Jim Buck advertising a hard disk for sale, shown in Figure 3-16.

```
Message 355 on 2 Apr 90 05:28
From: JIM BUCK
To: ALL
Subject: Hard Disk for sale

I have a 30 meg RLL drive for sale.  It works okay, but it is used.
I'm after $150 for it, and I'll help you install it for that price.

If you're interested, leave me email.

Read msg [355] [1..357], <ENTER>=Next, <R>eply, <B>ack Up,
<K>ill, <Q>uit, <*>Read Reply?
```

*Figure 3-16. Advertisement for Hard Disk*

After reading Jim's message, enter *R* for Reply. This will automatically prepare a message header for you, with the "To," "From," and "Subject" fields filled in. All you need to do is enter the message text. Figure 3-17 shows a reply to the message in 3-16.

```
Message 358 on 3 Apr 90 17:15
From: SAM SPADE
To: JIM BUCK
Subject: Hard Disk for sale

Jim: I'm interested in your disk drive.  Can we meet sometime and
talk about it?

Read msg [358] [1..358], <ENTER>=Next, <R>eply, <B>ack Up,
<K>ill, <Q>uit, <*>Read Reply?
```

*Figure 3-17. Reply to Advertisement*

When you save a reply, the BBS makes a note to inform Jim Buck the next time he logs on that there is a message waiting for him. The BBS also adds some information to the message you just entered and to Jim's message to show that they're related.

The BBS adds a line to Jim's message just below the message header that says there is a reply. To the message you just entered, the BBS adds a line saying to see message 355, the subject of your reply.

Someone reading Jim's original message will now see that there is a reply. They can then use the Read Reply command to skip any intervening messages.

You can also reply to a reply. An example of this appears in Figure 3-18.

```
Message 358 on 3 Apr 90 17:15
From: SAM SPADE
To: JIM BUCK
Subject: Hard Disk for sale
REPLY TO #355   SEE ALSO #363

Jim: I'm interested in your disk drive.  Can we meet sometime and
talk about it?

Read msg [358] [1..365], <ENTER>=Next, <R>eply, <B>ack Up,
<K>ill, <Q>uit, <*>Read Reply?
```

*Figure 3-18. Reply with Second Reply*

The lines under the message header now show that this message is a reply to an earlier message (REPLY TO #355), and also that someone has replied to this message (SEE ALSO #363). To see the reply without seeing the intervening messages, press an asterisk (*). Message 363 appears, as shown in Figure 3-19.

```
Message 363 on 4 Apr 90 08:44
From: JIM BUCK
To: SAM SPADE
Subject: Hard Disk for sale
REPLY TO #358

Sam: Delighted to get together with you on the weekend.  Is there
any particular time you're available?

Read msg [363] [1..365], <ENTER>=Next, <R>eply, <B>ack Up,
<K>ill, <Q>uit, <*>Read Reply?
```

*Figure 3-32. Second Reply*

Many BBSes also use a plus sign (+) to read forward through the replies and a minus sign (-) to read backward through the replies.

## Killing a Message

*Killing* a message is the act of deleting it from the message system. Killing messages frees room on the BBS's hard disk, often a valuable commodity. It also makes it easier for you to read messages addressed to you, as most BBSes will alert you to any messages addressed to you whether you have read them or not.

The Kill message command is about the same on all BBSes. To kill a message, first read the message you want to kill and then enter *K* at the message menu. The BBS may ask you to confirm your choice. When you enter *Y*, the BBS deletes the message from the message system.

Sysops can kill any message on the BBS. As a regular user, you can only kill messages that are to you or from you. If you try to kill someone else's message, the BBS will display a message like `Message cannot be deleted`.

## Message Etiquette

The ease and convenience of sending email will probably inspire you to start communicating frequently with other BBS users. Following are a few points of message etiquette to help you be a better BBS user.

### Message Formatting

- *Use paragraphs.*
  If you are entering a long message, break up your thoughts into paragraphs. Insert blank lines and indent the first lines just as if you were typing a letter. No one likes to read several screens of solid type. You can also press [ENTER] to reduce the width of your message text which makes the text easier to read.

- *Don't "yell" at the readers.*
  Don't use capital letters and lots of exclamation points TO EMPHASIZE YOUR MESSAGE!!! It may make the readers feel like you are shouting at them. Understated emphasis using asterisks is *much* better. You can also use the greater than (>) and less than (<) characters to highlight >>your<< ideas.

- *Be courteous and concise.*
  Close your messages as if they were letters. Use a closing such as "Yours Truly," or just a simple "Thanks," followed by a blank line and your name. The recipient already knows who sent the message by looking at the message header, but signing your messages adds a personal touch that is often overlooked with email.

### Announcements

Check with BBS policy before posting announcements asking people to show up for a get-together or a fund-raising activity; some BBSes have strict rules governing the types of announcements that are allowed to be posted.

### Buying and Selling

Many goods (such as computer disks) and services (such as babysitting) are bought and sold through BBSes. Almost all BBSes have a "For Sale" area just for posting advertisements. Before you enter your own ad, check the BBS's policy on advertisements. Most BBSes have a very specific policy about the type and number of ads they will allow. If there are too many ads for commercial businesses versus personal, classified-ad sort of messages, the phone company may start charging the sysop business rates for their phone service. Furthermore, if you enter a lot of ads as soon as you start using the BBS, the other users will think that the only reason you're there is to sell things, and they'll resent it. If you have that much to sell, consider taking it to a swap meet.

### Flame Mail

A message that disagrees violently with someone else's point of view is known as a *flame* or *flame mail*. Messages in some topics on a BBS (usually politics and religion) can get rather heated at times and can rapidly embroil other BBS users. As you start to compose your message, remember that while disagreement with someone's ideas is healthy, personal attacks are not. Remember that your messages are being read by real people, not a computer.

If you receive flame mail, laugh at it or ignore it. If you can't do either, try and talk to the sender personally, not on the BBS. Don't say anything on the BBS you wouldn't be willing to say face to face. You have a responsibility to prevent a flame-mail war from happening on the BBS.

Keep in mind that, since there is no way of entering your body language, tone of voice, or facial expressions with the message text, a dissenting opinion may sound like you are actually attacking someone. Many people have gotten in the habit of entering a sideways smiley-face like **:)** or **:D** as a quick way of expressing amusement or good feelings.

### Discretion

It is indiscreet to post a message that reveals another user's address, phone number, or other personal information without their explicit permission to do so. This is doubly true on BBSes that allow pseudonyms. Don't blow someone's cover—they may want to remain anonymous. Also, be discreet when meeting other BBS users face to face.

### Anonymous Topics

Many BBSes have anonymous message areas that do not show who a message is from. Anonymous message areas can be fun, because you can enter opinions that are different from the sorts of things you usually enter and see how people respond. Many times there are no real rules on posting anonymous messages whatsoever, allowing users to enter anything they like.

### Thank You's

The sysop is generally providing the BBS to its users as a service. Be sure to send the sysop mail giving thanks when appropriate. Thank you's are an often overlooked and underused form of praise, and sysops in particular rarely get enough of them.

## BECOMING AN EXPERT

There are three standard message functions you need to be familiar with: *reading, scanning,* and *searching*. Reading displays the complete message header and all the message text. Scanning displays just the message header to let you see if you want to read the message text. Searching looks through the message headers (and in some cases, the messages themselves) for words and phrases you specify. This is a quick way to look for messages on a particular topic.

Whenever you sign on to a new BBS, read or scan the messages to get a sense of the BBS and its users. Capturing the messages to disk or printer lets you examine them offline later.

A lively message system is vital to the health of a BBS. Contribute your energy to the BBS by entering messages frequently. Try to keep your messages short and to the point. Make the subject informative. Addressing messages to specific recipients makes it more likely that they will see and respond to your messages.

Consider yourself a guest in somebody else's house and act accordingly; be courteous towards the other BBS users. Don't ever leave a message that you don't want someone else to read, even if it's private. Keep it clean. Remember that the use of a BBS is a privilege, not a right.

Correspond with the sysop via email if you have questions about using the BBS. Sysops are generally very sympathetic to beginners. Not only are sysops used to dealing with beginners, they usually remember being beginners themselves.

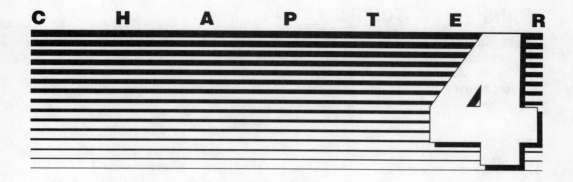

C H A P T E R

4

# SENDING AND RECEIVING FILES

Sending and receiving files and programs is known as *uploading* and *downloading*. Uploading is sending a file from your computer to a BBS. It is useful if you want to post a large message on several different BBSes and you'd rather not have to type it several times. Downloading is receiving a file from a BBS. This is useful when someone offers to put a program on a BBS for you to try out. Both uploading and downloading are very easy tasks to perform.

# TRANSFER PROTOCOLS

Before you try to send or receive files on your own, you need to understand the various ways you can transfer data. Most communications packages offer at least four or five ways to transfer data, and some offer as many as a dozen. This section will define the different transfer protocols and how to use them. In practice, you'll probably only use two or three protocols 90% of the time.

## ASCII

The ASCII protocol is the simplest and fastest way to send and receive text. You will use the ASCII protocol almost exclusively for uploading message text from an ASCII file on your computer.

However, ASCII protocol has several distinct disadvantages. First, each character is sent as a seven-bit ASCII character. This means that anything using extended ASCII characters will not be sent correctly. Although this is not frequently a problem with message files, it makes ASCII useless for sending and receiving programs, files that have been compressed with archiving programs (discussed later in this chapter), or other *binary files*. Binary files are programs, spreadsheets, and formatted files that contain extended ASCII characters.

Also, unlike the other protocols discussed in this section, ASCII protocol does no error checking of any kind. If there is any line noise, the information you receive can be corrupted without any indication that there was an error. Losing one or two characters may not be a problem when uploading a message, but it is critical when receiving a file containing data or a program.

Despite these disadvantages, ASCII is the only protocol that allows you to upload message text as if you were typing it. (You'll see how to do this a little later in the chapter.) The BBS interprets the characters it receives in ASCII protocol in the same way as it treats the characters you type.

**Note:** Files from most word processors contain special information that would be lost if you used ASCII protocol. To upload or download a word-processor file, you must either save it as an unformatted ASCII file or you must use a protocol that can handle binary files.

## XMODEM

When you logged on as a new user in Chapter 2, you entered X (for XMODEM) as the default transfer protocol. Regardless of what other transfer protocols your communications program and the BBS support, you can be sure that both will support XMODEM.

XMODEM is the most popular transfer protocol used in BBSes. Developed by Ward Christensen in 1978, XMODEM is a simple method of transferring files over phone lines. The transmitting computer sends each file as a series of 128-byte *blocks*. A block is simply a convenient way of dividing a file into manageable pieces. Each XMODEM block has a block sequence number and a *checksum*. A checksum is the total ASCII values of all the characters in a block. If any character is garbled in transmission, the checksum will be incorrect. The receiving computer will then send a signal to the sending computer to retransmit that block of data.

Unlike ASCII protocol, XMODEM (and all the other protocols discussed in this section) send and receive information eight bits at a time rather than seven bits. This means that you can use XMODEM for uploading and downloading programs and binary files.

One disadvantage to XMODEM is that it is slower than many of the protocols developed later. XMODEM is also not as "bulletproof" as some of the other protocols: the checksum can occasionally miss an error. Moreover, XMODEM and most of its variants rely heavily on exact timing. If the other computer is busy processing other requests, or you are working over long distances that add a time delay for the signal to get from one computer to the other, XMODEM may "time out" or generate false error conditions. One variant of XMODEM, known as Relaxed XMODEM, will help prevent the problem by increasing the amount of time between each acknowledgment to allow you to use XMODEM on busy multi-user systems.

XMODEM may also pad a file with up to 127 characters if the file does not exactly fit into 128-byte blocks. This padding will not hurt the file, but will take up extra space on your hard disk.

Despite these shortcomings, XMODEM is popular, dependable, and fairly reliable. It was the first protocol of its kind for BBSes, and almost all subsequent BBS protocols reflect some aspects of XMODEM in their design.

## XMODEM-CRC

XMODEM-CRC is XMODEM that uses a Cyclic Redundancy Check (CRC), a more complex and more accurate type of error correction than a checksum. XMODEM-CRC is preferable to regular XMODEM in situations where line noise is a problem. XMODEM-CRC and XMODEM take about the same time to transfer files.

## YMODEM

YMODEM is like XMODEM-CRC, but it uses 1024-byte blocks instead of 128-byte. Unlike XMODEM and XMODEM-CRC, YMODEM is a *batch* protocol: it allows you to send several files in a single transfer. The file name, size, and date are sent at the start of each new file. The computer receiving the files uses this information to save the files automatically.

You can use YMODEM and other batch protocols to download groups of files even when the computer is unattended because you don't need to enter the name of each new file you are downloading. This is particularly convenient if you are uploading and downloading business data files or other groups of files with similar names.

Because of the larger block size, YMODEM is much faster than XMODEM. Less time is lost to error checking and acknowledging each block. However, excessive line noise can actually make YMODEM *slower* than XMODEM because of the increased time to retransmit the larger blocks.

**Note:** Some BBSes and communications programs incorrectly call the XMODEM-1K transfer protocol YMODEM. XMODEM-1K is XMODEM format with 1024-byte blocks. Check to make sure that both the BBS and your communications program are referring to the same format before attempting to download a group of files.

## ZMODEM

ZMODEM, fairly new on the BBS scene, is similar to YMODEM as it can transfer a group of files without changing the file sizes and dates. One of ZMODEM's most impressive features is that it is able to transfer part of a file, lose the connection due to line noise or a system crash, and still finish the transfer without losing information. This feature makes ZMODEM highly desirable for transferring many large files over noisy lines or in situations where you may be cut off unexpectedly. ZMODEM uses a different technique than XMODEM and YMODEM for handling blocks of information. It can handle more relaxed timing than XMODEM, making it better for long-distance communications, and is also much faster than YMODEM.

Use ZMODEM whenever possible. Its biggest disadvantage is that many communications programs and BBSes do not yet support it. If your communications program does not already have ZMODEM, you may be able to find a standalone program for running ZMODEM as an external protocol.

## Kermit

The Kermit protocol, named for the frog, was developed at Columbia University in 1981. It is a machine-independent batch protocol that can be used to transfer files and data between mainframes and microcomputers.

Sadly, Kermit's strength is also its weakness. Because Kermit was designed to assume almost nothing about the computers and modems it is running on, a great deal of information is packed into each block of data. This makes Kermit effective, but very slow: even XMODEM is faster. Use Kermit only if you need a batch protocol and you don't have YMODEM or ZMODEM available, or if there are no other options for transferring files.

## Other Transfer Protocols

You may encounter other transfer protocols on BBSes or in different communications packages. Each of these will have various advantages, but they are likely to share the disadvantage of not being widely used. If a BBS knows a particular protocol and your communications program does not, you will not be able to communicate using that protocol.

# DOWNLOADING FILES

This section shows how to explore the BBS to see what kind of files are available for downloading.

## Types of Files

There are many different types of files that you may want to download from a BBS, including:

- *programs*—all types, including communications programs, games, word processors, spreadsheets, databases, and utilities
- *text files*—program manuals, general documentation, or stories written by other BBS users
- *picture files*—digitized pictures that are displayed on the screen of your computer

### Programs

Most BBSes have a wide variety of programs available for downloading. These programs include computer games, general-purpose and utility programs, and even full-scale computer applications such as spreadsheets, word processors, communications programs, and databases. Most of the programs available on BBSes are either *public domain* or *shareware*.

Public domain programs (also known as *freeware*) have been released for general, noncommercial distribution by the author(s).

Shareware is software that has been released for distribution and is licensed to be used for a trial period. If you like the software and intend to use it, you register your copy. The registration costs are usually very low because the author relies on hand-to-hand distribution from happy users, rather than duplicating her or his own disks. Registration frequently gives you additional value such as phone-in support, a printed manual, and free updates when the next version is released. Many shareware packages have an incentive for registering and then distributing the programs: the shareware company will pay you a kickback for each copy someone registers with your registration number.

Shareware and public domain software are usually as good as or better than similar commercial programs. Furthermore, you can try programs before you pay for them, much like taking a test drive in a new car. You are welcome to use public domain programs without paying for them at all. Most of the communications programs in Appendix A are shareware and are far better than anything available at twice the price.

### Text Files

Text files cover almost anything that is written. Some examples of text files you can find on a BBS are the following:

- program manuals for shareware and public domain software
- technical notes, such as a procedure for installing a half-height disk drive outside the chassis or circumventing an error in a program
- online newspapers and magazines such as *BoxOffice, NewsBytes, Infomat Magazine*, and *USA Today Decisionlines*
- stories, poetry, and fiction written by other BBS users

Text files can often be identified by the extensions DOC, MAN, ASC, or TXT.

### Pictures

In addition to programs and text files, there are thousands of digitized pictures available for downloading. With the proper viewing program, these can be viewed on any popular computer. Some BBSes are exclusively devoted to swapping picture files of all kinds. Picture files can frequently be identified by having one of the following extensions in their file name: MAC, GIF, PIC, PIX, GL, or MCP.

## Selecting a File to Download

Now that you have a little understanding of the various data transfer protocols, you're ready to try downloading a file. Downloading a file is very easy; the BBS and your communications program will tell you everything you need to know.

The following examples assume that you will be using an IBM-compatible computer with any one of several common shareware communications programs. However, the principles of uploading and downloading files presented here are the same, regardless of the type of computer you are using.

To select a file on the BBS to download, list all the files on the BBS available for downloading. To do this, go to the file menu from the BBS's main menu. Two sample file menus appear in Figure 4-1.

```
┌─ TRANSFER ──────── INFORMATION ──── UTILITIES ──── ELSEWHERE ─┐
│  [D]ownload file   [L]ist files   [H]elp (or ?)   [G]oodbye   │
│  [P]ersonal dwnld  [N]ew files    [X]pert on/off   [Q]uit     │
│  [U]pload file     [S]earch files                            │
└───────────────────────────────────────────────────────────────┘


 FILE MENU:
    [Q].........Quit to main menu      [I]....Information on a file
    [L].....List available files       [D].......Download a file(s)
    [S]....Stats on Up/Downloads       [F]...... File transfer info
    [G].........Goodbye (logoff)       [H]..............Help Level
    [?].............Command help       [M]..........MESSAGE SECTION
    [V].........View an ARC file       [R].........Read a text file
```

*Figure 4-1. Sample File Menus*

Almost all BBSes organize the files for downloading in topics or categories, much like messages. Unless you know there is a specific file on the system you want to download, you need to list the files by entering *L*. Figure 4-2 shows you a typical selection of the file topics.

```
 The available file areas are:

 [A] - General utilities        [B] - Bulletin Board Systems
 [C] - Games and fun stuff      [D] - Disk and drive utilities
 [E] - Communications           [F] - Music
 [G] - Programming languages    [H] - Word processors
 [I] - Printer programs         [K] - Macintosh
 [L] - C64 & C128               [M] - Amiga
 [N] - Atari                    [O] - Miscellaneous

 File area to list:
```

*Figure 4-2. File Areas*

From the list of file topics, select a specific category. For your first time downloading, try something fun. Select the Games category. Figure 4-3 shows a list of a typical games directory.

```
                          - GAMES AND FUN STUFF -

    NAME            BYTES   COMMENTS                         DATE UPLOADED
    =====================================================================
    F-16    ZIP     29824   F-16 combat game                   04-21-90
    BURGER  ZIP     23025   Make your own burger!              02-15-90
    PC-GOLF ZIP     37248   GOLF FOR YOUR PC                   03-23-90
    GEMINI  ARC     69632   2 player modem to modem games      03-23-90
    FTBALL  ARC     39936   A football game.  Not bad.         03-27-90
    NCRGOLF PAK    101504   A better golf game                 03-28-90
    AIRTRFK ZIP     45440   Air traffic controller game        04-29-90
    STARSH  ZIP     48256   Starship game. Real time.          05-29-90
    PCPOOL  ZIP     37376   Pool for your PC.                  01-29-90
    GOLF    ZIP     37760   a good golf game                   01-31-90
    STRIKER ZIP     68736   save the spies                     01-31-90
    HARDHATS PAK    32640   hardhat construction               01-31-90
    CHESS   EXE     10505   Good chess game for CGA card       02-24-90
    TENNIS  ZIP     23040   3D TENNIS GAME, ARCADE             03-16-90
    FIREWORK ZIP    26624   FIREWORKS DEMO ON YOUR SCREEN      04-23-90
    AIRPLANE ZIP    55296   LEARN TO MAKE PAPER AIRPLANES      04-23-90
    NEWTODAY ZIP   442496   Today: What happened today in history..03-19-90
```

*Figure 4-3. Directory of Game Files*

The first column in the directory lists the name of the file, followed by the extension. The next column is the size of the file in bytes. The third column is a brief description of the file. The last column is the date the file was uploaded on this particular BBS.

**Note:** A recent upload date is no guarantee that the file is the most current version.

Skimming the list, you can see that CHESS.EXE is only 10505 bytes. You can estimate how long it will take to download the file from this information by dividing the number of bytes in the file by the speed of your modem. For example, if you're using a 1200 bps modem, you can send or receive about 120 bytes per second, which is calculated like this:

$$8 \text{ data bits} + 1 \text{ start bit} + 1 \text{ stop bit} = 10 \text{ bits}$$

$$1200 \text{ bps}/10 \text{ bits per byte} = 120 \text{ bytes per second}$$

Allow an additional 10-15% for correcting transmission errors and time delays caused by the transfer protocol. A 10505-byte file like CHESS.EXE would take between 90 and 120 seconds to download with a 1200-baud modem or between 45 to 60 seconds to download if you are using a 2400-baud modem.  A file this size is good for practicing downloading.

## Starting the Download

From the files menu, enter D to download.  Depending on the BBS you are using, you may need to confirm the transfer protocol you want to use at this point.  The BBS will assume that you want to use XMODEM from the information you gave when you logged on, but you can change from XMODEM to another protocol if you wish.  Figure 4-4 shows a common protocol prompt.

```
Select a download protocol or press Enter for default:

Default protocol is: Xmodem

A) ASCII,  X) Xmodem, C) XmodemCRC, 1) Xmodem-1K, Z) Zmodem, B) Ymodem
Batch, Q)uit

Select:
```

*Figure 4-4.  Protocol Prompt*

For right now, press [ENTER] to stick with XMODEM.  (After you become more familiar with downloading, you can experiment with some of the other transfer protocols.)  The BBS will then tell you how many blocks are in the file and how long the transfer will take.  Figure 4-5 shows an example of this display.

```
There are 83 blocks, consisting of 10,505 bytes in this file.
Transfer time will be 3 minutes, 50 seconds.

Ready to Send CHESS.EXE using Xmodem. Press Control-X to cancel.
```

*Figure 4-5.  Download Time Display*

This message means the BBS is waiting to hear from your communications program that it is ready to receive.  As soon as you see this message, you need to tell your communications program to start receiving data.   You have about 40 seconds before the BBS will stop trying to send the file. On most IBM communications programs, you start downloading by pressing the [PgDn] key on your keyboard.  On Macintosh pro-

**4** Sending and Receiving Files

grams, you click on the appropriate "Receive a File" option. See the documentation for your communications program for specific details on starting a download.

Start the download. The communications program will display a menu of transfer protocols like those in Figure 4-6.

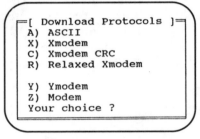

*Figure 4-6. Download Menus*

Because you have already told the BBS you will be downloading the file using the XMODEM protocol, select XMODEM from the list. Your communications program will now prompt you for the name with which to save the file you are downloading. A sample prompt is shown in Figure 4-7.

```
Enter name of file to upload or press <Esc> to abort:
>
```

*Figure 4-7. Filename Prompt*

Enter the name of the file exactly as it appeared on the BBS: *CHESS.EXE*. You can also specify an optional drive or path to save the file to if you wish.

**Note:** Because XMODEM doesn't pass the filename as part of the information tion sent to your computer, you could download the file CHESS.EXE into a file with a different name, such as CHESS2.EXE or even CHECKERS.EXE. If you are using YMODEM, ZMODEM, or another transfer protocol that tells your computer the name of the file, you may not have to enter a filename at all.

When you enter the filename, the communications program will display download information. This display will typically include the number of blocks received, the number of bytes received in the current block, the total bytes received, the average characters per second, and the efficiency of the transfer. The efficiency is the measure of how much of the actual file has been transferred. This does not count the bytes taken up with checksums, CRCs, or acknowledgments. Figure 4-8 shows a typical download information display.

```
===================[ Download a file ]===================
Press the PgDn key to stop downloading the file

Total blocks received    : 3      Bytes/block:   132
-- Long block errors      : 0      Total bytes:   396
-- Short block errors     : 0
-- SOH errors             : 0      Average CPS :   104
-- Complement errors      : 0      Efficiency  :   86.7%
-- Block number errors    : 0
-- Timeout errors         : 0
-- Resend block errors    : 0
-- Checksum errors        : 0
-- Last error message     :
```

*Figure 4-8. Download Information Display*

As the blocks are transferred from the BBS to your computer, you can check the progress by matching the number of blocks and the total bytes received against the total blocks and bytes in the BBS's display shown in Figure 4-8. When the file transfer is finished, the communications program will close the file and return you to the BBS. You will probably see a message from the BBS like Download successful.

## Cancelling a Download

If you need to cancel a download before you have completed it, you can press the [PgDn] or the [ESC] key. Depending on your communications program, you may also need to enter [CTRL-X] to tell the BBS to stop sending. The BBS will probably take a moment before responding with a prompt.

**Note:** *Don't cancel a download by hanging up!* At the very least, the BBS will take several minutes to realize that the connection has been terminated and reset the modem for the next caller. In many cases, however, hanging up in the middle of a download can "hang" the BBS, preventing further communication by anyone. The sysop then has to restart the BBS.

## Time Limits

Virtually all BBSes put limits on the amount of time you can spend per call or per day downloading software, but files or sets of files may take too long to download with your current access privileges. If you need to download a large file, leave a private message for the sysop explaining what you want and ask the sysop to set up a *personal,* or *private,* download. Many BBSes have a personal download option where the sysop designates certain files as personal files for you or a group of BBS users. You can then log on and download these files without the normal time limit on downloading.

If the BBS doesn't have this feature, you can arrange to send the sysop diskettes in a stamped mailer and simply have the files sent to you. Mailing diskettes to the sysop is also a good way to distribute software to a BBS. Check with the sysop to make sure the diskette is formatted correctly for the BBS's hardware. Use this option instead of uploading very large files to avoid tying up the BBS for a long time.

## Downloading Etiquette

You should plan your downloads for times when the BBS is not likely to be in high demand. If your communications program allows you to set up a *script,* a set of commands that it can perform automatically at a certain time, you may want to have the communications program log on to the BBS late at night and download the files automatically. In the morning, the downloaded files will be waiting for you, and the rest of the users will not have been inconvenienced. See your communications program's manual for information on how to do this.

Many BBSes require you to upload a certain amount of software for every piece you download or will give you credit for uploading files that extends time available for downloading files. Additional time may be granted on a one-for-one basis, or the BBS may have a ratio for uploads versus downloads. The general idea is that you are expected to contribute to the BBS as well as benefit from it.

In other words, file exchanges are expected to go both ways. It's very bad manners to do nothing but download files. Download only a few files at a time, then upload a file in return or contribute to the message system. BBS users who only take files will rapidly find their existing access privileges severely limited. Also remember that sysops constantly exchange information about problem users. If you develop a reputation as a file hog on one BBS, it may follow you.

# UPLOADING A FILE

Uploading a file is very much like downloading a file. You log on to a BBS, go to the appropriate file area, tell the BBS what protocol you are using, tell your communications program what file and protocol to use, and then go get coffee while the communications program does the work.

## Uploading Message Text

Rather than type in a large message, it's best to upload it in order to save time online with the BBS. Suppose that you want to post a message that announces an upcoming instrumental music presentation. The first thing you should do is create the message text using a word processor. As you prepare the text file, make sure that the lines of text are no more than 72 characters long to prevent the BBS from automatically wrapping the text to the next line. You may also want to put a space at the start of each blank line between paragraphs because pressing [ENTER] on a blank line usually returns you to the message editing menu. A sample of the message text ready to upload appears in Figure 4-9.

```
                    *    *    *    *    *
    This Saturday at 7:00pm, there will be a presentation of really
    first-rate piano and harp pieces at the Old Civic Auditorium.
    Several local musicians will be doing pieces by Debussy, Brahms,
    and Liszt.  Benefits from the show will go to the Old Civic
    Auditorium's building fund.

    For those of you who haven't heard Debussy in a live performance
    before, I strongly recommend you make plans to go to the show.
    I've been doing some sound work for the technical crew, and I've
    never heard anything so beautiful in my life!

    Tickets are $5 each at the ticket office.  Seating starts at 6:30
    and the show will last about 2 hours.
                    *    *    *    *    *
```

*Figure 4-9. Message Text Ready to Upload*

This message, though not too long to enter on one BBS, would be a nuisance to manually type in on several BBSes.

When you are satisfied with the way the message text looks, save it as plain ASCII text, without any special characters or formatting.

**Note:** Depending on your word processor, ASCII text may also be known as "nondocument mode" or "unformatted" text. Check your word processor's manual for more information.

To upload the text, log on to a BBS and go to the message menu. Enter *ALL* for the recipient and Music Presentation as the subject.

Rather than simply typing in the information at the standard message text prompt, upload the prepared file. Tell your communications program that you want to start an upload.

On most IBM communications programs, you start uploading by pressing the [PgUp] key on your keyboard. On Macintosh programs, you click on the "Send a Text File" option. See the documentation for your communications program for specific details on how to start an upload.

A list of protocol options will then be displayed. Select ASCII from the list of options.

Your communications program will now prompt you for the name of the file to be uploaded. This file should contain nothing but the message text laid out exactly as you want it to appear in the finished message. Figure 4-10 shows a sample filename prompt.

```
Enter name of file to upload or press <Esc> to abort:
>
```

*Figure 4-10. Filename Prompt*

After you enter the name of the file at the prompt, the communications program will open the file and start transferring the information in the file to the message text area. You will probably see the information displayed on the screen as it is transferred. When all the text in the file has been transferred, the communications program will pause for a few seconds and then return program control to you. Some communications programs may display the last few lines of the message you just uploaded.

Depending on the BBS, you will see either the Message Edit menu or the next available line for the message. You can save or edit the message with the BBS's standard message editing commands, customize the message by typing in additional text, or even upload a second block of text from a different file.

Uploading message text affords the advantages of using a word processor such as editing and spell-checking. One good way to experiment with uploading message text is to send a private message to yourself and see exactly what the finished message looks like.

## Uploading Programs

There are a few things you should consider before uploading a program to a BBS. One of the most important is to make sure that the file you are about to upload is relevant to the BBS. If the BBS specializes in programs written in C, they probably won't be interested in a music program for kids written in BASIC.

One interesting fact about uploading programs is that you can upload programs designed to run on one computer to a BBS run on a different type of computer. For example, a Commodore 64 program can be uploaded to a BBS run on an IBM. The BBS just acts as a storage facility; you are still unable to run the Commodore 64 program on the IBM used for the BBS. Because uploaded programs can only be run on the computer system which they were designed, you will frequently find file areas in the BBS categorized by the type of computer.

*Never upload copies of copyrighted programs!* This will probably get you kicked off the BBS permanently.

Almost all BBS sysops prefer that uploaded files be *compressed* with a compression program before uploading to save time and space.

## USING COMPRESSION PROGRAMS

The time that it takes to upload or download a file is directly related to how big the file is. If you could somehow shrink the file before sending it over a modem, the file would take that much less time to send. *Compression* programs (also known as archiving programs) do just that. They compress files and then restore them to their original size. Not only does this let you save time when modeming, you can store a group of related files in one big, compressed file known as an *archive*. To upload or download those files, you simply transfer the archive and then use the program to restore the original files.

Compression programs are available for every common computer system. Some of the most common IBM compression programs are PKZIP, PAK, ZOO, and ARC. Stuffit! is a popular compression program on the Macintosh. If a BBS has downloadable files compressed with a particular program, it will probably have the compression program available for downloading also.

Archives are usually identified by the file extension ARC, PAK, ZIP, or ZOO. Take a look at the files in Figure 4-11 for a moment. Many BBSes have a file menu option for viewing archives. Usually only one type of archive can be viewed. Figure 4-11 shows a sample listing for the archive file BURGER.ZIP.

```
Searching ZIP: BURGER.ZIP

Length   Method    Size    Ratio   Date      Time    Name
  25523  Reduced   18243   29%     10-01-87  15:25   BURGER.COM
  12840  Reduced    4110   68%     10-01-87  15:21   BURGER.PAS
   1337  Shrunk      672   50%     11-15-87  01:32   BURGER.DAT

  39700            23025   43%                             3
```

*Figure 4-11. View of Archive*

The first thing you probably noticed about the file BURGER.ZIP is that it actually contains three separate files. BURGER.COM is the actual program, BURGER.PAS is the source code for the program, which was written in Pascal, and BURGER.DAT is data for running BURGER.COM.

Now look at the columns in the table. The length column shows the original size of the file. The method column shows what the program did to the file to compress it. This can be any of a variety of options, such as "reduced," "shrunk," "squashed," "compressed," or "squeezed." You really don't need to worry about the compression method—the compression program uses the most effective method. The types of compression vary from program to program; see the program manual for more information about what it offers. The size column is the file size after compression, and the ratio column is the amount of space saved. The date and time columns are the original date and time of the file, the name of which appears in the name column.

The totals in Figure 4-11 show that the archive BURGER.ZIP saves 43% of the space taken up by the uncompressed original files. Programs can usually be compressed to about two-thirds of their original size. Documents and text files can shrink as much as 80%. The file BURGER.PAS in Figure 4-11 contains source code (text) and has shrunk 68%.

Some BBSes also have requirements about what format uploads should be in. For example, if a BBS uses ZIP formatting for large files, you won't make points by uploading a file in PAK format—the two formats can't be unpacked by the same compression program. Read the BBS's policy statement on uploading files for the BBS's rules. When in doubt, ask before uploading.

Collect several different compression programs for your computer. Different compression programs use different compression methods, some of which can't be unpacked by any other program. Compression programs are small and do not take up much room on your computer, so it won't be a problem to store them all.

# DEALING WITH TRANSFER ERRORS

There are a number of possible types of transfer errors that can occur when uploading and downloading. Most communications packages will check for these errors and report if they occur. The sample download information display in Figure 4-12 (also shown as Figure 4-8) lists a number of common errors, each of which is related to specific conditions when sending or receiving a block of data.

```
==============[ Download a file ]=============
Press the PgDn key to stop downloading the file

Total blocks received   : 3    Bytes/block:   132
-- Long block errors     : 0    Total bytes:   396
-- Short block errors    : 0
-- SOH errors            : 0    Average CPS :   104
-- Complement errors     : 0    Efficiency :   86.7%
-- Block number errors   : 0
-- Timeout errors        : 0
-- Resend block errors   : 0
-- Checksum errors       : 0
-- Last error message    :
```

*Figure 4-12. Download Information Display*

If you get one of these errors, you don't need to do anything. Transfer errors are almost always caused by line noise. Any slight burst of static on the line will change the value of some of the bits in the current block, and an error will result. The value of using an error-correcting transfer protocol is that the computer is smart enough to fix things without your help. If you get lots of errors when uploading or downloading a file, you may need to hang up and phone the BBS back on another line that may not have so much static. Otherwise, sit back and let the computer do the work.

Capture the file directories so you can examine them at your leisure and see which files you want to download. Many sysops make this process easier by keeping a catalog of the files on their BBS as a separate file you can download and print.

## PIRATE SOFTWARE

Occasionally, you will find "pirated" copies of programs mixed in with the legitimate software on a BBS. These may be "hacked" programs (copy-protected software that has had the software protection removed), copies of software that was not protected but is nevertheless not in the public domain, or a beta test copy of software that was uploaded for illegal distribution.

Whatever their source, pirated programs are illegal to own and illegal to use. Virtually all sysops actively discourage the uploading and distribution of pirated software. If you discover a program is actually an illegal copy of a legitimate program currently for sale, send email to the sysop so it can be removed from the BBS.

## COMPUTER VIRUSES AND TROJAN HORSES

When you upload and download files and programs from BBSes, you must be aware of the potential risks of encountering a *computer virus*. A computer virus is a program that attaches itself to another program, much like a real virus attaches itself to a cell. When the program is run, the virus "wakes up" and attaches copies of itself to other files and programs on the computer. This process generally continues until most of the programs on your computer are infected, at which time the virus may start erasing programs or data, corrupting files, or doing other unpleasant things to your computer and files.

Another type of program is known as a *trojan horse*. A trojan horse does not replicate itself; however, it is specifically designed to do nasty things to your computer. The most common type of trojan horse is a program that appears to be a game or an information file that, when run, formats your computer's hard disk, permanently erasing everything on it. Because trojan horses don't reproduce themselves, they tend to be extremely rare; as soon as they show their true nature, an alert goes out and all copies of the program get erased from the local BBSes.

### Taking Precautions

Despite the press coverage given to viruses, your chances of encountering a computer virus are actually rather small. You should not dismiss them as being nonexistent, however. Viruses do exist, and they can be expensive and painful to clean off a computer. There are several things you can do that will both minimize your chances of a virus attacking your computer and also make it easier to clean up after a virus attack.

The first step in being ready for a problem is to backup everything on your system regularly. Nobody really likes to do a backup. They're slow, they tie up the computer, and they're frequently a lot of work. Nevertheless, the time you invest in backing up the programs and files on your computer will be amply repaid if you ever have to format your hard disk and reload the information. If you don't have current backups of information, viruses and trojan horses can destroy months of your work.

As part of your backup policy, you should make sure that you have write-protected copies of the original system and application source diskettes. *Never* insert an original diskette into your computer unless it is write-protected. If your computer becomes infected, you'll need the originals to reinstall uninfected copies of the system software and applications.

The second step is to be careful where you download software. You are less likely to find viruses on BBSes that restrict uploads to registered, verified users because the sysop has a way to track BBS users down. Viruses are also more common on free BBSes than on those that require you to pay an access fee.

The third step is to never start your computer from any floppy disk other than the original, write-protected diskette that came with your computer. Many viruses can infect your system only if you start the computer from an infected floppy diskette. Similarly, if your computer normally starts from a hard disk, never start it from the floppy drive.

In general, you should always treat downloaded files, public domain software, and shareware with caution until you have checked them out. Run the programs on a computer without a hard disk or check them with anti-viral programs.

**Note for Macintosh users:** If you are using a Macintosh with an external SCSI drive, you can very easily disconnect the hard drive and then start the computer from a floppy disk. This will let you experiment with new software without risking an infection on the hard disk. Be sure to shut the computer off completely before plugging the hard disk back in. A virus may be able to live through the standard Macintosh "Restart" procedure.

## Detecting Viruses

One of the problems with detecting viruses is that by the time they actually start seriously affecting your computer's behavior, it may be too late to do much to prevent damage. There are, however, a number of early warning signs that may help you to catch a virus before it has had a chance to infect your entire system.

Because most viruses attach themselves to programs on your computer, the size of the programs will change. Check the size of your programs frequently, particularly the system files. If you see a sudden unexplained change in the size of a program, it's a good indication that you have a virus. For the same reason, you should also track how much space is available on your hard disk. Diminishing free space without the creation of new files is another indication of a virus.

Any unexplained change in the way your computer does things should be examined closely and the cause for it determined as soon as possible. Here is a list of symptoms that may indicate a viral infection on your computer:

- Unusual error messages related either to a specific device (such as a printer) or a specific program

- Unexplained hidden files or formerly hidden files that become visible

- Programs or files that disappear, move, or change their names for no reason

- A change in the volume labels on the hard disk or on floppy disks

- A sudden decrease in the free space on your hard disk

- A sudden decrease in the amount of available memory, for example, if you cannot load a program then bring up a memory-resident program or desk accessory

- An increase in the number of system failures when running standard programs

- An increase in the work the hard disk seems to be doing, particularly when a program should not be using the hard disk

- An increase in the amount of time programs take to load and run

There are a number of shareware and public-domain anti-viral programs for IBMs, clones, and Macintoshes. You can download these from BBSes or obtain them from computer user groups. These are good against the more common viruses, but they may not be proof against new viruses. It is also possible for some anti-viral programs to become infected themselves.

## Cleaning Up

If you have discovered a virus on your computer, here is what you need to do to clean it out and prevent reinfection.

First, try to determine when and how the virus entered your system. You may not discover how this happened until you are actually cleaning the system up. Also, determine how much of your system the virus has infected. Examine the contents of the batch files on your computer. Some viruses will write additional instructions in otherwise innocuous batch files that may pinpoint the source of the infection. If the hard disk is not infected, the process of cleaning up will be simpler.

Next, turn the computer off and restart from a clean, write-protected copy of the original boot diskette. Back up all the spreadsheets, documents, uninfected batch files, and other data files to diskettes formatted on an uninfected machine. Do not copy any of the programs, as they may be infected. Even more importantly, do not use any of the programs on the computer; you may infect the diskettes you are copying to. Set aside the diskettes containing the data you copied.

With all the data backed up, you're now ready to start the actual cleanup. If the hard disk appears to be infected, you should reformat it. Many of the anti-viral and virus detection programs will tell you which programs are infected.

If you're not sure whether the hard disk is infected, it is safest to assume that it is. Use your anti-viral programs to check any floppy diskettes that you used or formatted during the time your computer was infected. If you haven't determined the exact source of the infection, check any and all floppy diskettes used in the computer for the last 18 to 24 months. In many cases, the source of the infection was a diskette received at the time the computer was purchased, which guaranteed an infection from the start. Remove the viruses with the anti-viral programs or reformat the diskettes completely.

**Note:** When looking for the source of the infection, check every possibility. Don't assume that software from someone is safe because they seem like a nice person. Viruses have been on disks of software obtained and handed out by computer dealers, private users, and users' groups.

With the hard disk and floppy diskettes clean, you can recreate your directories or folders. Restore the system files and program files from the original, write-protected diskettes. Check your backup disks for signs of infection and, if they appear to be clean, restore the data files from the backup disks to your hard disk. Prevent a future reinfection by taking the precautions outlined earlier.

Take appropriate precautions when exchanging software. Cleaning up after a major viral infection is not fun. You will spend hours, sometimes days, checking and reformatting diskettes; unfortunately, there are no shortcuts. If you don't completely clean up your computer and diskettes, you will sooner or later have another infection. Worse, you may spread the infection to your friends and other BBS users. Uploading infected software can get you permanently kicked off of many BBSes, and has already gotten at least one BBS user sued by its sysop.

# BECOMING AN EXPERT

If you upload messages that are long or are to be duplicated on a number of different BBSes, use a word processor to create a plain, unformatted ASCII text file. Make sure the lines of message text are no more than 72 characters long so the BBS doesn't wrap the text to the next line. Use the ASCII protocol to upload the message text.

Check for a catalog of downloadable files on the BBS before downloading anything. This will help you plan your downloading and will also give you an idea of what files you can upload in return. Remember that many files are commonly available on BBSes everywhere. You can probably get the latest version of a communications program or a compression utility from most local BBSes, so you don't need to spend money on long distance when you can get the same programs from a BBS in your area.

Use ZMODEM or YMODEM for uploading and downloading whenever you can. Investigate other transfer protocols offered by the BBS and your communications program to see if there is something more effective that you can use.

If you discover you don't want to download a program, don't just hang up before you finish downloading. Use the appropriate set of commands to terminate the transfer. Hanging up in the middle of a download can crash the BBS.

Public domain software is free. Anyone can use it as long as they like. Shareware is not free; you are allowed to try it for a limited time before paying for it. If you download a shareware program that is useful to you personally, you have an obligation to pay for it. If the shareware is useful to your business organization, you are *required* to pay for it.

Keep track of your uploads versus your downloads. Try to upload at least one file for every six you download. Above all, don't get greedy. If the BBS has lots of files you want to add to your system, see if you can contact the sysop and arrange to get copies of them directly. As with the message system, you are expected to contribute to the life of the BBS.

Don't upload pirated software. Let the sysop know if you discover software on the BBS that is pirated.

Viruses are still not particularly common, but they do exist. Take care when exchanging software that your computer does not get infected with a computer virus. Do frequent backups and write-protect all of your original system and program diskettes. Note any changes in your computer's behavior. If your computer does become infected, clean out the infection completely, or you will risk a rapid reinfection. Alert others to the problems that you have encountered with a particular virus so that they can watch for it on their computers.

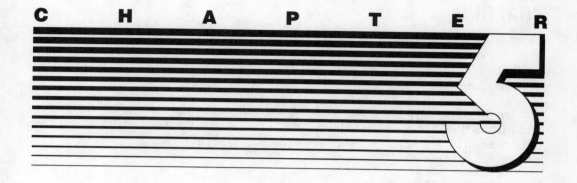

C H A P T E R 5

# CHATTING AND PLAYING GAMES

This chapter shows you how to have fun chatting with the sysop and other BBS users, how to play online games, and how to run programs. This introduces you to some of the more unusual features of BBSes.

# CHATTING

*Chatting* on a BBS is just what it sounds like: having a quiet conversation with some-one. The difference here is that you're typing rather than talking. Chatting allows you to talk to one or more persons over the phone lines, with the BBS providing the soft-ware and hardware connections.

The most common type of chatting is chatting with the sysop. However, many large, multi-line BBSes are designed to allow you to chat with several other BBS users at the same time. This section shows you how to do both types of chatting.

## Chatting with the Sysop

Most BBSes allow you to page the sysop by typing *C* for Chat or *O* for Operator Page. This command makes the BBS's computer start beeping, which lets the sysop know that someone wants to chat. If the sysop is around, she or he will break in and start typing. You can then type questions and comments directly to the sysop, just as if you were sharing a typewriter. A typical chat session with the sysop appears in Figure 5-1.

```
Hello.  This is Michael the sysop.  You rang?

Yes, thanks.  I'm new to this and wasn't sure how to get
back to the main menu.

Well...from where you are now, you can type X to exit the message
conference, then M to go back to the main menu.

Thanks.

You're welcome.  See you on the board...
```

*Figure 5-1. Chatting with the Sysop*

By watching the BBS computer, the sysop can see what you are doing on the BBS. If you are having trouble with something, the sysop may break in and chat with you even if you haven't paged. This might be a little surprising at first, as it will look and feel as if the BBS has suddenly taken over your computer and is typing for you.

The sysop will not be available at all times to answer pages from the BBS. The sysop may have even set up the BBS so that it does not beep between certain hours. In this case, you might see something like that in Figure 5-2.

```
I'm sorry, but I am unavailable to chat with you right now.
I am normally available between 8:00 and 10:00pm weekdays,
and at odd hours on the weekends.  You can leave me questions
in email, and I'll get back to you within a day or so.

Yours truly,

Michael
```

*Figure 5-2. "Sysop Unavailable" Message*

Don't keep paging the sysop if there's no response. Just leave a message to the sysop or a comment when you log off. Messages are better than comments because they are easier to respond to on most BBSes. Also, don't try to chat when the sysop is likely to be asleep. You aren't likely to get to chat, or worse, you'll wake them up.

Both you and the sysop can type at the same time in Chat, but typing at the same time has the same effect as two people talking at the same time: neither one knows what the other said. The easiest way to cue the person you are chatting with that you are turning the conversation back to them is to press [ENTER] twice at the end of what you have to say. Pressing [ENTER] twice will differentiate between pressing it once, which indicates a paragraph break.

## Chatting with Other BBS Users

Many multi-line BBSes have entire areas dedicated to chatting between BBS users. In fact, chatting between users is one of the primary reasons many BBSes have more than one line. Chatting with other BBS users is a lot of fun, and a good way to get to know them. Moreover, many BBSes have long-distance phone links that allow you to chat with people who are calling from other parts of the country and even other continents.

Many multi-user BBSes specialize in matchmaking or singles who want to meet other people. These BBSes tend to have the best-developed chatting options of any BBS. Chatting between BBS users can be done exclusively between two people (just like chatting with the sysop) or in a round-table discussion known as a *forum* or a *public conference*.

An essential feature of a multi-user BBS is a user list. This shows who is on the BBS at the moment and what they are doing. Figure 5-3 shows a sample user list from a typical matchmaking BBS.

| # | User ID | City | St | Sex/Age | Status |
|---|---------|------|----|---------|--------|
| 10: | Nancy 44 | Chicago | IL | F  31 | Chatting |
| 9: | Karen 72 | Chicago | IL | F  35 | Forum 1 |
| 8: | Michael 21 | Chicago | IL | M  23 | Chatting |
| 7: | Lynn 14 | Sydney | AU | F  30 | Forum 1 |
| 6: | John 43 | Chicago | IL | M  33 | Forum 1 |
| 5: | Sandra 6 | Seattle | WA | F  29 | Chat on |
| 4: | \<no caller\> | | | | |
| 3: | Mark 39 | Los Angeles | CA | M  33 | Page on |
| 2: | Robert 54 | Seattle | WA | M  38 | Page off |
| 1: | Dale 109 | Bellevue | WA | M  23 | Chat on |

*Figure 5-3. Sample Multi-User Log*

Most multi-user BBSes tend to use first names only and a user ID number for privacy. Pseudonyms are also common on multi-user BBSes. Many BBSes have special long-distance connections that allow you to log in from places all over the world at no charge to you for the long distance. Check the bulletins and help files on the BBS for information.

Figure 5-3 shows users logged in from places around the country and one user logged in from Sydney, Australia. The status display shows what each user is doing at the moment.

Two users, Nancy 44 and Michael 21, are in an exclusive chat. Karen 72, Lynn 14, and John 43 are in one of the open forum areas having a round-table discussion. Sandra 6 and Dale 109 have their chat option turned on. If someone enters the command for "chat with line 5" or "chat with line 1," Sandra or Dale will immediately be in an exclusive chat with someone. Mark 39 has the paging option turned on; if someone tries to chat with him, the BBS will send him a message telling him who is trying to chat with him. Mark can then respond immediately or finish what he is doing. Robert 54 has turned his page off. Other users will neither be able to bring him into an exclusive chat or have the BBS page him.

Figure 5-4 shows a portion of an exclusive chat between two BBS users.

```
You are now in exclusive chat mode.  Anything you type is immediately
echoed on the other person's screen.  To exit from chat and return to
the main menu, press CTRL-C.

          USER PROFILES
Michael 21            Nancy 44
Chicago, IL           Chicago, IL
23 years old          31 years old


Hi.  I've been wanting to ask you about something you
put in your profile.  It says that you like to dance.  What
kind of dancing?

Oh, well, I like folk dancing mostly.  I've been doing
squares and country dancing for about 2 yrs now.  Been trying
some swing dancing lately.  You?

Neat!  Yes, I do some country dancing.  I also play guitar
with a bluegrass group.

What's the name of the group?  Do you play at any of the
local dances?
```

*Figure 5-4. Exclusive Chat*

Take a look at the information at the top of the figure.  User names and profiles are displayed to show which two users are in chat.  Not all BBSes display user profiles, but some BBSes, particularly matchmaking BBSes, have users fill out a questionnaire as part of the logon procedure.  The information can then be *browsed* by any other BBS user who wants to find out a little more about you.

While you are chatting with one user, the BBS may show you who is logging on and logging off.  You can also get paged by other users.  Figure 5-5 shows examples of how this might look.

```
The group has played at a couple of the dances on Monday nights
[George 75 has logged on to line 4]
but only with other people in a large jam session.  You go to any
of those?

Only occasionally.  I work late on Monday nights, so it's tough to
get away.  I usually just head home and flake out in front of the tube.

What do you do for a living?

/Msg from Karen 72: Nancy, stop by Forum 1 before you leave.  We need
some technical advice on a hard disk question.

I run the computer maintenance department for a savings and loan.
```

*Figure 5-5. Messages and Pages while Chatting*

When George 75 logged on to the BBS, both users in the chat saw the announcement. However, the page from Karen 72 was addressed to user 44 (Nancy) and only shows up on Nancy's computer. Although Michael is chatting with Nancy, he would not see the page from Karen.

Leaving an exclusive chat is usually done by pressing [CTRL-C]. Figure 5-6 shows an example of this.

```
I just got a page from Karen 72.  She wants to ask me about
a hard disk.  I'm going to head over to Forum 1 for a few
moments.  Join me - Karen and I go dancing every so often.

Sounds good.  See you there!

[CTRL-C pressed!  Returning to main menu...]

Enter main menu option, or press ? to list>
```

*Figure 5-6. Ending an Exclusive Chat*

Round-table discussions are much like exclusive chats, except they can involve several people. Figure 5-7 shows the persons from the chat joining the conversation in Forum 1.

```
Now entering Forum 1.
Current members: Karen 72, Lynn 14, John 43, Nancy 44.
Enter /HELP for help, /QUIT to leave forum.

hi, everyone
Nancy 44: hi, everyone

Karen 72: That was quick!  Thanks.
Lynn 14: Hi Nance.
Karen, you had a question about disks?
John 43: hello
Nancy 44: Karen, you had a question about disks?

[Michael 21 has joined the forum]

Karen 72: Yes.  My hard disk has been getting really noisy over
Karen 72: the past few months.  It's gotten so loud I have
Karen 72: seriously considered wearing earplugs!  HELP!!!
Michael 21: Howdy folks.
```

*Figure 5-7. Joining a Forum*

In a forum, you type what you want to say on the screen. The BBS holds this until you press [ENTER], then it sends what you have typed to everyone with your user ID at the front of each line so that the other people in the forum know who is talking.

When Nancy 44 entered the forum, she typed "hi, everyone" and pressed [ENTER]. The BBS then sent this message to everyone else in the forum with her name and ID attached. The other forum members responded. While Nancy was typing her next comment, John sent his "hello." When Nancy pressed [ENTER] to send what she had just typed, the BBS displayed John's message and then displayed hers. The BBS had then announced that Michael 21 had joined the forum and the conversation continued.

You can see that chatting round-table style is a little different from an exclusive chat between two people. For one thing, the time delay between questions and their responses staggers the conversation. Frequently, you will find that you are answering a question posed a message or two before, while the other forum members are doing the same thing. The flow of the conversation may not be as clear as having a conversation in person, but you can communicate effectively nonetheless.

Forums allow you to *page* other BBS users even if they aren't currently in a forum. An example of this is the message from Karen 72 you saw in Figure 5-5. Paging another user this way has two advantages. First, you can communicate with someone you couldn't otherwise reach except by sending mail. For example, you can't break into an exclusive chat. In addition, pages are private; only the addressee sees them. You have already seen how you can page someone while they're doing something else. Figure 5-8 shows how you might send a private message to another user within a forum.

```
Nancy 44: Gee, Karen, my first thought is to check the screws
Nancy 44: and mounting brackets to see if they're tight.  Have
Nancy 44: you tried that yet?
/Msg from Karen 72: I saw Michael 3 weeks ago playing at a dance.  He's GOOD!

Lynn 14: I'm going to truffle off for now.  See ya.
John 43: see ya, keed  :-D

/SEND 72 Oh, really???  We could use another good band for dances! You
think...?
Karen 72: uh, no, I haven't.  I'll give it a shot.  Thanks.
[Lynn 14 has left the forum]

John 43: I had a bad disk bearing recently that made a lot of
John 43: noise.  I finally took the disk in for reconditioning
John 43: because I couldn't stand it anymore.

/Msg from Karen 72: Sure!  The band is really tight
```

*Figure 5-8. Paging within a Forum*

In this example, Nancy and Karen are sending private messages within the forum by typing */SEND* followed by the user number.  As in Figure 5-5, only they see the messages.

There are a few standard restrictions on paging other BBS users.  You are usually limited to about 80 characters of text in a single message.  Pages are meant primarily as a signalling device, not as yet another way of holding a conversation.  If the BBS user you are paging has set their session to "Ignore page" or "Page off," then you will get a message from the BBS saying that the user is unavailable for paging right now.  Similarly, you cannot send a page to someone in the middle of uploading or downloading a file, as the characters would be interpreted as line noise and trigger a transmission error.

You can usually perform a number of other commands while in a forum.  Commands are invariably preceded by a slash (/), usually at the start of a new line, followed by the command information.  Some of the common commands are:

| /B or /BROWSE | Browse a user's profile or questionnaire answers |
| /S, /SEND, /P, or /PAGE | Page another user with a private message |
| /?, /H, or /HELP | Display a list of the available commands in the forum |

/W or /WHO                      Display the user list (for example, Figure 5-3)

/Q or /QUIT                     Exit the forum and return to the main menu.

You should be aware of one additional command: the Ignore, or Squelch, command. You can enter something like */I (number) ON* or */IGNORE (number) ON* to suppress messages from the member whose number you use in the command (this command also appears as */X (number)* on some BBSes). Squelching a member in a forum completely prevents any of their messages, public or private, from appearing on your screen. For example, suppose Michael 21 has stepped away from his keyboard for a moment to answer the door, and one of his cats lies down on the keyboard (a surprisingly common occurrence when chatting). An example of this appears in Figure 5-9.

```
Michael 21: Uh, oh, the door.  Back in a moment.
John 43: There's a disk drive repair shop down in the south end
John 43: I recommend.
Nancy 44: I've tried them, I think.  They're good.
Michael 21:fedr09jjjmlk bbbbbbbbbbbbbbbbbbbbbbbbbbbbbbbbbbbbbbb
Michael 21:bbbbbbbbbbbbbbbbbbbbbbbbbbbbbbbbbbbbbbbbbbbbbbbbbbb
Michael 21:bbbbbbbbbbbbbbbbbbbbbbbbbbbbbbbbbbbbbbbbbbbbbbbbbbb
Karen 72:?????
Michael 21:bbbbbbbbbbbbbbbbbbbbbbbbbbbbbbbbbbbbbbbbbbbbbbbbbbb
/IGNORE 21 ON
[Ignore 21 now ON]
John 43: Sonomagun, what was THAT?
Nancy 44: I think his keyboard has fallen over or something. :D
```

*Figure 5-9. Squelching a Member*

The cat isn't pressing [ENTER] in this example to send the information. The BBS sends what you type when you press [ENTER] or when 240 characters have stacked up. The figure shows Nancy entering an Ignore command to prevent the spurious messages from appearing on her screen. To stop ignoring or "unsquelch" Michael 21, she would enter */I 21 OFF, /IGNORE 2 OFF,* or */X0 21,* depending on the BBS.

# DOORS

Since a BBS is a program running on another computer, it performs many tasks such as maintaining a system of messages and sending and receiving files. Many BBSes have incorporated the ability of one program to run another program to let you log on to the BBS and run applications such as word processors and spreadsheets, utility programs, and even games.

Running a program outside of the BBS is very much like opening a "door" in the BBS to another program. In fact, these entry points are commonly known as *doors*. Access to BBS doors and the ability to run external programs is a privilege that is frequently not given to new users. Running programs, particularly games, on the BBS can tie up the BBS for hours at a time.

How you open a door varies dramatically from BBS to BBS, but is generally related to selecting an option from the main menu or the file menu. This is not always the case, however, and you should check with the sysop of the BBS to find out the correct procedure for opening doors.

# GAMES

Although you can run many different kinds of programs through a door, almost all of the programs found on BBSes for running through doors are games. There are several classes of games commonly found on BBSes. The following sections describe each of these classes and give you an example of the type of games in that class.

## Simple Games

The first class of games on BBSes is simple games. These games are usually for simple entertainment. Examples of this class of games include number-guessing games, Nim, Hangman, and Battleship. The skill level necessary to master simple games is fairly low. ANSI graphics and sound features are used occasionally in simple games but are rarely elaborate.

If a simple game is set up for more than one person, the players must usually pass the keyboard of the computer back and forth. Only a few games in this class (notably Battleship) are designed for two people to play from two different locations. Figure 5-10 shows a typical Hangman game being played on a BBS. Some ANSI graphics characters are used for drawing the scaffold.

```
        HANGMAN!
I'm thinking of a word of 5 letters.

Your guess? A
Nope.
 _____
|           0
|
|
|
|
 _____
|_____|

Your guess? O
There is 1 O.
 = O = = =

Your guess? E
Nope.
 _____
|           0
|           |
|
|
 _____
|_____|

Your guess? I
There is 1 I.
 = O = I =

Your guess? C
There is 1 C.
 = O = I C

Your guess? T
There is 1 T.
 T O = I C

Your guess? P
There is 1 P.
 T O P I C

You beat the hangman and guessed the word!
The word was TOPIC.
```

*Figure 5-10.  Hangman Game*

## Gambling Games

Computer versions of poker, blackjack, slot machines, craps, and roulette wheels are very popular. Like simple games, gambling games require a relatively low skill level. ANSI graphics and sound appear frequently in gambling games and can be very fancy. Figure 5-11 shows an example of a game of five-card draw poker.

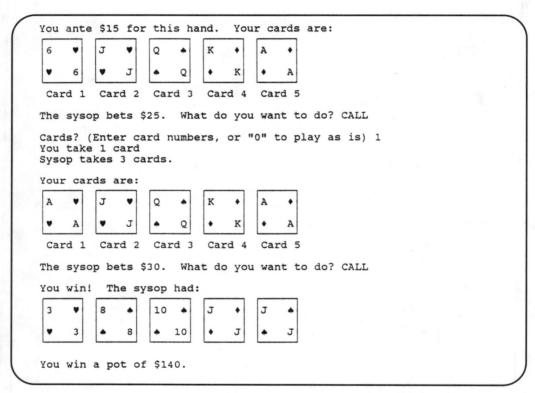

*Figure 5-11. Five-Card Draw Game*

Some BBSes require you to pay for access time, for which you receive a number of credits on account. An interesting variation on some BBS gambling games lets you use your credits to buy chips from the house and then gamble with the chips. If you win, you gain extra credits to use on the system. If you lose, you lose the credits. This makes the games much more exciting because you can actually win or lose something of value.

## Sports Games

The next class of games is sports and action games. Examples of sports games include electronic golf, baseball, football, and basketball. Sports games are usually single-player, although some versions will allow several players to share the keyboard on a computer. Only occasionally will you find a sports game that lets two BBS users from different locations play against each other simultaneously.

Sports games encourage you to compete against yourself more than against someone else. You are usually trying to beat your own best score. A sample of a golf game appears in Figure 5-12.

```
          Welcome to the Grotto de Blotto Country Club!

It's a perfect day for golf!

You're at hole 1.  The distance is 349 yards.  The par for this
hole is 4.  On your left are trees.

Choose a club (1-12), ? for help, or X to quit: ?

   #    CLUB    RANGE       #    CLUB    RANGE
   _    ____    _____       _    ____    _____
   1  Driver    310 yds     7  5-iron   170 yds
   2  3-wood    280 yds     8  6-iron   150 yds
   3  4-wood    260 yds     9  7-iron   130 yds
   4  2-iron    230 yds    10  8-iron   100 yds
   5  3-iron    210 yds    11  9-iron    80 yds
   6  4-iron    190 yds    12  Wedge     60 yds

"Range" is roughly how far the ball travels with a full swing.

Choose a club (1-12), ? for help, or X to quit: 1
Swing how hard (1-100)? 100

You sliced.  Your shot went 326 yards.
The ball is 46 yards from the cup, 30 yards offline in trees.

Choose a club (1-12), ? for help, or X to quit: 9

Swing how hard (1-100)? 35

Your shot went 42 yards.
The ball is on the green 9 feet from the cup.

Now using putter.  Putt how hard (1-30)?
You holed it!

Your score for hole 1 was 3.  A birdie!
Total par for the first hole is 4.
Your score so far is 3.
```

*Figure 5-12. Golf Game*

## Action Games

The class of games with the most members is probably action games. Action games are almost always for a single player, with either a limited amount of time or accelerating action to make the game harder. Road races, "escape the robots/mummies/snake/dragon," and dozens of miscellaneous "shoot 'em up" and "chase 'em" games are good examples of this class of games. Action games are the most likely to use full ANSI graphics and sound. Figure 5-13 shows a BBS user making the galaxy a little safer for carbon-based life forms.

```
    .   .   .   .   .   .   .   .      Stardate            3211.4
    .   .   .   .   *   .   .   .      Condition           Green
    .   .   .   .   .   .   .   .      Quadrant            6, 1
    *   .   .   .   *   .   .   .      Sector              8, 4
    .   *   .   .   .   .   *   *      Photon torpedoes    10
    .   .   .   .   .   .   .   .      Total energy        2695
    .   *   .   .   .   .   .   .      Shields             1000
    .   .   .  <E>  .   .   .   *      Invaders remaining  16
================================================================
    M)ove        L)ong range scan    P)hasers       Q)uit
    SH)ields      S)hort range scan   T)orpedoes     SAVE game
    C)omputer    G)alactic map        ?)Help         SC)ore
================================================================

Enter Command  > M
Enter a Course [1-8]  > 1.4
Enter Speed [0-8] > 1

ALERT! Alien invader in sector 3, 6!
================================================================
    .   .   *   .   *   .   .   .      Stardate            3212.4
    *   .   .   .   .   .   *   .      Condition           >RED<
    .   .   .   .   .  !@!  .   .      Quadrant            6, 2
    .   .   .  <E>  .   .   *   .      Sector              4, 4
    *   .   .   .   .   .   .   .      Photon torpedoes    10
    .   .   .   .   .   .   .   .      Total energy        2677
    .   .   .   .   .   .   .   .      Shields             1000
    .   .   .   .   .   .   *   .      Invaders remaining  16
================================================================
    M)ove        L)ong range scan    P)hasers       Q)uit
    SH)ields      S)hort range scan   T)orpedoes     SAVE game
    C)omputer    G)alactic map        ?)Help         SC)ore
================================================================

Enter Command  > P
Phasers locked on target.
Energy available =  1677 units
Numbers of units to fire > 1000

 1098 unit hit on invader at sector  3, 6

    **** INVADER DESTROYED ****
The universe is saved.  Take a bow.
```

*Figure 5-13. Sample Action Game*

## Adventure Games

Adventure games are descriptive "text" games that tell you what you see and then let you enter commands to make your character in the game do things. There are adventure games for almost all possible scenarios: descending into a set of caves, travelling around the world, searching for pirate gold in the Caribbean, journeying to Mars, becoming a wizard or a knight and defeating a monster, and traveling through time.

Like sports games, adventure games are designed for one player. Because adventure games are text-based, ANSI graphics and sound are almost never used. The skill level necessary to really enjoy an adventure game is medium. Problem-solving skills are extremely valuable in adventure games. You should also plan on drawing maps of where you've been, showing the name of the location and the direction to and from the previous room or area. Figure 5-14 shows the start of a typical adventure game.

```
Welcome to the Castle de Blotto Adventure.  Type HELP for help.

You are in a forest.  There are paths in all directions.
What do you want to do?  go north

You are in a forest.  There are paths in all directions.
What do you want to do?  go north

You are in a clearing.  There are paths north, south, and west.
What do you want to do?  go north

You are on a lawn that obviously used to be well-cared for, but
is now heavily overgrown.  Ahead of you is a large castle.
There are paths north and south.
What do you want to do?  go north

You are at a ruined wall.  You can go east, west, or up.
What do you want to do?  go up

You climb over the wall.  On the other side of the wall is a
rather swampy looking moat.  There is a drawbridge drawn up on
the wall of the castle.  As you are looking around, you see a
large sea serpent surface briefly on the far side of the moat.
You can go east or west.
What do you want to do?  go east

You are at the east side of the castle.  You see that the
castle wall has collapsed, leaving a hole big enough for you
to get through.  The rubble has filled in parts of the moat
and it looks like you can walk across it to get to the castle.
You can go north, east, or west.
What do you want to do?  go west
```

*Figure 5-14. Castle de Blotto Adventure Game*

## Political and Economic Games

Political and economic games are the most rich and complex of all the games on BBSes. There are games such as Hamrbi and King, in which you buy and sell land, plant grain, and rule an agrarian society. These are single-player text games that require a fair amount of thought and planning to win. Then there are much larger games such as Trade Wars, where you run a freighter from planet to planet buying and selling; Galactic Empire, where you set up your own planet and try to conquer other planets; and Galactiwars, a complex game that involves trading, conquest, and diplomacy. Most of the large political and economic games are specifically designed to have a number of players entering a set of moves each day, though not necessarily at the same time.

Games in this class require a significant amount of skill to win, although they are relatively easy to understand. They also can take a long time to play. In single player games, the time can be several hours per game; for a multiple player game with one turn a day, the game can take an hour a day for several months.

The complexity and depth of political and economic games, combined with the unpredictability of the other players, makes these games the most exciting and addictive of all the games you are likely to find on a BBS. Figure 5-15 shows a very small portion of a typical interstellar trading game.

```
Command?  move
Select space warp to move you to sectors 2, 3, 4, 5, 6, 7: 2

You are now in sector 2.
Command? move
Select space warp to move you to sectors 15, 12, 1: 15

You are now in sector 15.
Command? move
Select space warp to move you to sectors 27, 8, 20, 93: 27

You are now in sector 27.
Planet in sector: Snelgreb
Command? land

On Ship   Isotopes   Metals   Equipment   Software   Medicine
================================================================
$8000        0         0         15          10         10

We want 10 units of equipment.  How many are you selling? 10
We offer 20000.  What is your counter-offer? 22000.
Sold!
We want 25 units of software.  How many are you selling? 10
We offer 35600.  What is your counter-offer? 40000.
We offer 35800.  What is your counter-offer? 38000.
Our final offer is 35800.  What is your counter-offer? 36000.
Sold!
We have 40 units of isotopes.  How many are you buying? 20
We offer 52000.  What is your counter-offer? 48000.
We offer 50500.  What is your counter-offer? 50000.
Sold!

You are now in sector 27.
Planet in sector: Snelgreb
Command? move
Select space warp to move you to sectors 15, 93, 110: 110

You are now in sector 110
Squad of fighters in sector
Select space warp to move you to sectors 108, 114, 103, 100
Attack, Retreat, Bribe?  retreat
Your retreat was successful.
```

*Figure 5-15. Sample Interstellar Trading Game*

# Other Games

In addition to the other classes of games listed, there are miscellaneous games and diversions that don't fit well into any category. These include things like counselling programs with which you can discuss your personal problems, games to test your extrasensory perception, trivia games, and chess.

# BECOMING AN EXPERT

When you are chatting, remember that you're talking to a person, not a machine. All the basic rules of telephone etiquette apply: don't hog the conversation, don't interrupt, and don't say anything that you wouldn't be willing to say to the person's face. Chatting is casual conversation. It is not deathless prose or great literature. Relax and have fun. Many BBSes designed to help people get to know each other through chatting have the most sophisticated chatting features. Look for matchmaking, singles, or adult BBSes.

Opening doors may require more access privileges than you currently have. Check with the sysop to find out what's available on the BBS and what the rules are for using doors.

Although there are many programs that you can run on a BBS, almost all of the programs are games and entertainments. These range from simple number- and word-guessing games like Nim or Hangman to vast multi-player games that require the computer to keep track of the moves and actions.

You may have to enter your logon password again when you close a door. This additional security feature prevents someone else from running the game and then being able to learn your password upon returning to the BBS.

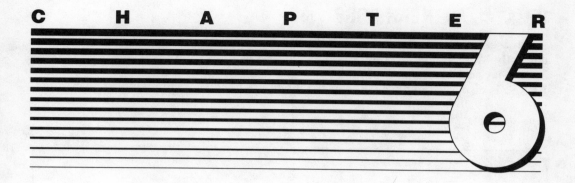

C H A P T E R

6

# LINEAR BBSES

This chapter describes how to use six of the most popular linear BBSes: RBBS-PC, Fido, OPUS, PCBoard, WILDCAT!, and TBBS. It presents a brief history of each BBS and sample screens that allow you to take a look at specific features of these common BBSes.

## WHAT IS A LINEAR BBS?

A *linear BBS* is organized hierarchically, like an organization chart. Almost all BBSes currently in operation are linear. The examples in the earlier chapters for Grotto de Blotto have all been modeled after linear BBSes. (Another family of BBSes, *room* BBSes, is discussed in the next chapter.) Figure 6-1 shows a sample linear BBS structure.

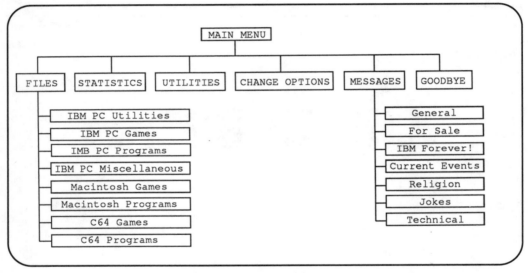

*Figure 6-1. Linear BBS Structure*

The distinguishing factor of a linear BBS is that the main menu is the starting point for almost all activities on the BBS. The main menu lists the classes of options available, including the message system, the file system, and chatting. After selecting one action, you generally have to move back up to the main menu and then down another leg to perform another action. For example, if you were entering messages in the message area and wanted to download a file, you first would have to leave the message area, return to the main menu, and then select the file area.

Most of the functions are separate on linear BBSes. For example, the message section, file area, and the utilities section are each in their own distinct and separate areas. After selecting a function from the main menu, a submenu such as a file or menu shows the options available under that section.

Because linear BBSes use menus and submenus, *commands at each level may use the same keys to mean different things.* For example, entering *M* at most main menus will take you to the message section. When you are already at the message or file menu, entering *M* usually returns you to the main menu.

Because the general BBS functions are divided into separate menus, you only have to remember a few single-key commands for each menu rather than having many different two-character commands. Furthermore, because command letters tend to indicate the type of command (such as G for Goodbye), a well-designed linear BBS is easy to use and understand.

## HOW TO USE THIS CHAPTER

When you first log on to a BBS, the name of the type of BBS usually appears on the logon screen. If the BBS is a type you are not familiar with, turn to the section which describes that type of BBS to see what commands and features you are likely to encounter. Each section will display enough information about a BBS to let you understand how that particular BBS program works. If you cannot identify the type of a particular BBS, look through each section of this chapter or refer to a list of BBS phone numbers that may identify the type of BBS software used.

Although this chapter looks closely at a number of the most popular types of linear BBSes, it is not possible to list all of the features each type of BBS provides in this limited space. For more details, you may refer to the BBS manuals, usually available as a downloadable file on the BBS. If you don't see one, leave a message for the sysop.

In addition, almost all BBSes have been customized in some way by their sysops to better serve their BBS users. Not only do many BBS programs encourage the sysops to experiment with menu structure and features, there are hundreds of programs that can also be used to customize a BBS. Some sysops further augment their BBSes with unusual hardware options, such as access to CD-ROM libraries, mainframe computer networks, and even shortwave satellite uplinks. Check with your sysop to find out what changes have been made to the BBS.

## RBBS-PC

RBBS-PC, "The Remote Bulletin Board System for the IBM PC," is a very popular BBS. It was written by Tom Mack, with major contributions by Jon Martin and Ken Goosens. The software was first released in July of 1983.

One of the reasons for RBBS-PC's popularity is that it was the first general-purpose BBS program for the IBM PC. Mack's stated goal in creating RBBS-PC is to encourage the free exchange of information. As a result, RBBS-PC is designed to help users swap messages and files on any subject.

Mack has released the BASIC source code for RBBS-PC to the public domain, which lets sysops and programmers customize RBBS-PC to fit their special applications and computers.

## Logging On

Logging on to an RBBS-PC BBS for the first time looks like the procedure shown in Figure 6-2.

```
What is your First name? Sam
What is your REAL! Last name? Spade

Checking Users...
Name not found
Are you 'SAM SPADE' ([Y],N)? y
What is your CITY, ST.? Seattle, WA
```

*Figure 6-2. Initial Logon Screen for RBBS-PC*

After entering your city and state, RBBS-PC may display a message from the sysop about system policy. Be sure to capture the system policy and study it. Taking a few moments to familiarize yourself with a BBS's policy at the start will save time and prevent misunderstandings later on.

Next, you have a chance to change the information you entered a moment ago, hang up, or register as a new user. Figure 6-3 shows you what happens when you choose to register.

```
SAM SPADE from SEATTLE, WA
C)hange name/address, D)isconnect, [R]egister? r
Enter PASSWORD you'll use to logon again? ........
Re-Enter PASSWORD for Verification (Dots Echo)? ........
Please REMEMBER your password
```

*Figure 6-3. Registering as a New RBBS-PC User*

## Setting Options

Once you have registered your name and password, you need to set display and file transfer options. Figure 6-4 shows a typical RBBS-PC procedure for setting options.

```
CAN YOUR TERMINAL DISPLAY LOWER CASE ([Y]/N)? y
UPPER CASE and lower

* Ctrl-K(^K) / ^X aborts. ^S suspends ^Q resumes *
G)raphics:  Three options tailor the visual output to your PC system:

                N)one, A)scii graphics, C)olor graphics

N)one means that you want only typeable text, like this sentence.

A)scii: Ascii graphics uses all 255 characters in the IBM character set.
Most IBM PC compatible systems can properly receive ASCII graphics.
Your system supports the IBM PC character set if you see characters
such as the heart♥ and straight line ──.

C)olor: C)olor graphics uses all 255 IBM characters and the ANSI screen
commands to provide color and sound effects and music.  For this to
work properly your communications package must support ANSI.  Your
system supports ANSI screen commands if this blinks in green.

Preferences can be changed with the Utilities command G)raphics.
GRAPHICS for text files and menus
Change from N to N)one, A)scii-IBM, C)olor-IBM, H)elp ([ENTER] quits)? a
Text GRAPHICS: Ascii
Do you want COLORIZED prompts ([Y],N)? n
Highlighting Off
```

*Figure 6-4. Setting Display Options for RBBS-PC*

One standard feature in RBBS-PC is the message that tells you to press [CTRL-K] or [CTRL-X] to abort, or [CTRL-S] to stop. By pressing [CTRL-K] or [CTRL-X], you can stop the display of a long bulletin or a list of files. RBBS-PC then returns you to the menu prompt. You can use these key combinations at almost any time in the BBS to stop whatever is happening and return to the menu. Several other BBSes also have this feature, although slightly different commands may be used.

After setting the display options, you need to tell RBBS-PC what file transfer protocol you want to use. The standard procedure for selecting a default protocol is shown in Figure 6-5.

```
File transfer protocol: The method you want to use to transfer files to
RBBS-PC ("upload") or to obtain files from RBBS-PC ("download").

1. You may want not to have a default transfer protocol if you use a
variety of protocols. Select the N)one option and RBBS-PC will ask for
your preferred protocol before each file transfer.

2. The protocol you want RBBS-PC to use must also be used by your
communications package.  Protocols available in RBBS-PC include Ascii
(no error checking), Xmodem, Xmodem/CRC, Ymodem, Kermit, Windowed
Xmodem.  Xmodem is the most widely supported, Ymodem is faster.

3. You can override the default by specifying the protocol on the same
command line as D)ownload or U)pload.  E.g. "D;SD.COM;C" downloads file
SD.COM in Xmodem/CRC no matter what the default protocol is.
Default Protocol

C)rc Xmodem
X)modem
Y)modem (1K Xmodem)
A)scii (TEXT FILES ONLY!!!)
B)atch Ymodem (DSZ)
K)ermit
Z)modem (Batch)
M)egalink  (Batch)
S)ealink (Batch)
J)MODEM (DATA COMPRESSION)
N)one - Cancel

Select Protocol? y
PROTOCOL: Ymodem (1K Xmodem)
```

*Figure 6-5. Setting RBBS-PC File Transfer Protocol*

RBBS-PC displays information about selecting a file transfer protocol to make it easier for users unfamiliar with the BBS.  At the bottom of Figure 6-5, you can see the list of available file transfer protocols.  In this example, the protocol selected for the download is YMODEM.

One special feature of RBBS-PC is *turbokeys:* the ability to type a character and have the BBS perform the command without having to press [ENTER].  Turbokeys are very handy and can speed up your movement around the system once you become familiar with a BBS.

Once you have completed the logon procedure, you will usually see a message that tells you the BBS is logging you in as a user, followed by general information about the version of RBBS-PC software the BBS is running on and standard system information such as baud rates, phone numbers, and the name of the sysop.  Figure 6-6 shows an example of the system information.

```
Logging SAM SPADE
RBBS-PC CPCxx.xx NODE 1   OPERATING AT  3/12/2400 BAUD,N,8,1
24 hours a day

Sysop: Michael Dispater          236 Megs Online

This system is for mature IBM users wishing to exchange public
domain software and shareware.

At least 15 NEW file(s) since last on
```

*Figure 6-6. RBBS-PC System Information*

The *node* tells which phone line of the BBS you have logged in on. On a BBS with a single phone line, this will always be *1*. If you are logged in on the second line of a two-line BBS, the node will be *2*.

If you have previously logged in on this BBS, you will see something like the user profile shown in Figure 6-7. The user profile lists your calling history as well as your default user options.

```
Times on: 2  Last was: 03-29-90 15:01
Files Downloaded: 0  Uploaded: 0

Your PROFILE (Use Utilities to Reset)
Novice
Text GRAPHICS: None
Highlighting Off
PROTOCOL: Xmodem
UPPER CASE and lower
Line Feeds On
Nulls Off
Prompt Bell Off
SKIP   old BULLETINS in logon
CHECK new files in logon
TurboKey Off
Autodownload Off
```

*Figure 6-7. RBBS-PC User Options*

After the user profile, the BBS usually displays the bulletin menu. Figure 6-8 shows a typical bulletin menu.

```
* Ctrl-K(^K) / ^X aborts. ^S suspends ^Q resumes *

******************** Bulletin Menu  ********************
*  1 - ACCESS LEVELS (more time, upload/download, etc)   *
*  2 - Hardware and software used on this BBS            *
*  3 - How to get your own copy of the RBBS-PC software  *
*  4 - The story behind the Grotto de Blotto             *
*  5 - Other BBSes in Seattle and the Puget Sound        *
*  6 - not in use                                        *
*  7 - Archiving utilities explained                     *
*  8 - not in use                                        *
*  9 - not in use                                        *
* 10 - not in use                                        *
**********************************************************
Read what bulletin(s), L)ist, N)ew ([ENTER] = none)? 1
```

*Figure 6-8. RBBS-PC Bulletin Menu*

To read a specific bulletin, enter the number of the bulletin. For example, to read the
bulletin on access levels, you would enter *1*. To list the bulletins (to display the menu
of bulletins if you are using expert mode), enter *L*. To see just the new bulletins, enter
*N*. To skip the bulletins entirely, press [ENTER].

After pressing [ENTER], RBBS-PC checks for messages addressed to you in the main
message area.

RBBS-PC then tells you how much time you have left on the BBS for this call and displays the main menu. The standard RBBS-PC main menu looks very much like the
one in Figure 6-9.

```
Checking messages in MAIN..
Sorry, Sam, no mail today...

RBBS-PC CPCxx.xx Node 1

Caller #  33561  # active msgs: 704  Next msg # 2438

 19 min left

RBBS-PC  M A I N   M E N U
— MAIL ——————— SYSTEM ————————— UTILITIES ——— ELSEWHERE —
 [E]nter Messages [A]nswer Questions [H]elp (or ?)  [*]oors
 [K]ill a Message [B]ulletins        [*]oin Conferences [F]iles
 [P]ersonal Mail  [C]omment          [*]iew Conferences [G]oodbye
 [R]ead Messages  [I]nitial Welcome  [X]pert on/off  [Q]uit
 [S]can Messages  [O]perator Page    [U]tilities
 [T]opic of Msgs  [W]ho else is on    * = unavailable  [@]Library

MAIN command <?,@,A,B,C,E,F,H,I,K,O,P,Q,R,S,T,U,W,X>!
```

*Figure 6-9. RBBS-PC Main Menu*

Some sysops will make their menus fancier using ANSI graphics to create borders or pictures, but you should be able to quickly spot the similarities between this menu and the one in Figure 6-10.

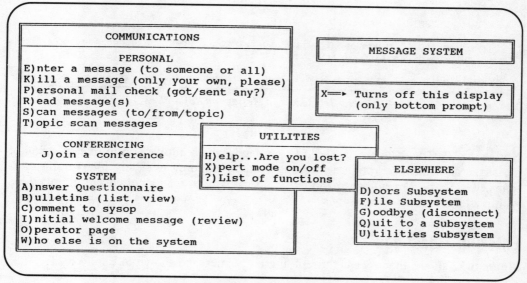

```
        COMMUNICATIONS                      ┌─────────────────────────────┐
  ┌─────────────────────────────┐          │       MESSAGE SYSTEM        │
  │         PERSONAL            │          ├─────────────────────────────┤
  │ E)nter a message (to someone or all)   │                             │
  │ K)ill a message (only your own, please)│ X═► Turns off this display  │
  │ P)ersonal mail check (got/sent any?)   │      (only bottom prompt)   │
  │ R)ead message(s)            │          └─────────────────────────────┘
  │ S)can messages (to/from/topic)
  │ T)opic scan messages
  │                    ┌───────────────────────────┐
  │      CONFERENCING  │        UTILITIES          │
  │    J)oin a conference        │
  │                    │ H)elp...Are you lost?     │
  │         SYSTEM     │ X)pert mode on/off        ┌─────────────────────┐
  │ A)nswer Questionnaire │ ?)List of functions    │      ELSEWHERE      │
  │ B)ulletins (list, view)      │                 ├─────────────────────┤
  │ C)omment to sysop  │                 │ D)oors Subsystem
  │ I)nitial welcome message (review)       │ F)ile Subsystem
  │ O)perator page     │                 │ G)oodbye (disconnect)
  │ W)ho else is on the system    │        │ Q)uit to a Subsystem
  └─────────────────────────────┘          │ U)tilities Subsystem
```

*Figure 6-10. RBBS-PC Main Menu with Graphics*

## Reading Messages

A distinguishing feature of RBBS-PC is that the message commands are part of the main menu, rather than being put into a separate menu. This shows the importance that the message system has in RBBS-PC BBSes. To read a message, enter *R*. Figure 6-11 shows a sample message being read.

```
MAIN command <?,A,B,D,E,F,H,I,J,K,O,P,Q,R,S,T,U,V,W,X,Z>? r
Message base MAIN
Msg # 1-164 (H)elp,S)ince,L)ast, T)o,F)rom,M)ine, text, [Q]uit)? 113

Msg #:  113
 From:   JANE FERGUSON           Sent: 03-22-90 06:08
   To:   SAM SPADE               Rcvd: -NO-
   Re:   TECHNICAL INFORMATION

I saw your hello blurb and I wanted to ask you a question about keeping
cockatiels.  It's kind of involved.  Could I phone you maybe or stop by?

More [Y]es,N)o,C)ontinuous,A)bort,R)eply,T)hread,=)reread,+,-,K)ill? r
```

*Figure 6-11. Reading a Message on RBBS-PC*

Notice that RBBS-PC offers a *Thread* command, which allows you to trace a string of messages and replies through a message system, skipping over any intervening messages. Using the Thread command is the fastest way to read a conversation imbedded within a larger group of messages.

## Entering Messages

Figure 6-12 shows the process for replying to the message shown in Figure 6-11.

```
Quote JANE FERGUSON'S message (Y/[N])? n
Make message p[U]blic, p(R)ivate, (P)assword protected, (H)elp? r
Sending personal mail to JANE FERGUSON

Type message 50 lines max (Press [ENTER] to quit)

    [----------------------------------------------------------------------]
 1: Be glad to have you stop by sometime.  I am always delighted to show
 2: off the birds.  What day is good for you?
 3:

A)bort,C)ont,D)el,E)dit,I)nsert,L)ist,M)argin,R)ev subj,S)ave

Edit Sub-function <A,C,D,E,I,L,M,R,S,?>? s
Adding new msg # 121.
Receiver will be notified of new mail
```

*Figure 6-12. Replying to a Message on RBBS-PC*

When you reply to a message, RBBS-PC lets you quote the original message. By putting the last few lines of the message to which you're replying, the recipient can see to what you're referring. This feature is very helpful for keeping the thread of a conversation going between users that don't sign on more than once or twice a week.

Notice in Figure 6-12 that you can password-protect messages. Password protection gives you an extra level of security for confidential messages.

RBBS-PC has all the standard message editing functions. It also allows you to set the margins on your message and revise the subject in the message header.

## Getting Help

RBBS-PC has good online help. To get help, enter *H* or a question mark (*?*). Figure 6-13 shows the help screen for the main menu.

```
=================[ MAIN MENU HELP ]============================
A)nswer Questionnaire — answer questionnaires on various topics
B)ulletin listing — see system bulletins and news
C)omment for SYSOP — leave a private message to the sysop
D)oors - run games and other programs
E)nter message — leave mail for a specific user or everyone
F)iles menu — files are downloaded/uploaded here
G)oodbye — log off the BBS
H)elp — help for any command, section, or general topic
I)nitial welcome message — repeats the logon message
J)oin a conference — change to a new message area
K)ill a message — erase a message
O)perator page — page the sysop for a chat
Q)uit — log off, or go to files or utilities sections
P)ersonal mail — list messages addressed to you
R)ead message(s) — select and read messages
S)can messages — display the message headers
T)opic scan — search messages for names or subjects
U)tilities — change your user profile here
W)ho — who else is on now?  (RBBS-PC can support up to 36 callers)
X)pert mode — turn the menus off (expert mode) and on (novice mode)
```

*Figure 6-13. Main Menu Help Screen on RBBS-PC*

Many RBBS-PCs also will let you get extended help on commands or specific topics. Figure 6-14 shows a typical extended help display.

```
Extended help is available on the following:

COMMANDS:   Enter the first letter of the command, such as U for U)pload

TOPICS:     Enter one of the following for help on a specific topic
   FILE - help with commands on the file menu
   HELP - more about the help system and how to use it
   MAIN - help with commands on the main menu
   UTIL - help with the utility menu
   ARC  - help on compressed and archived files

The default help is for the current section you are in.

ENTER QH (quit help) to exit help.
HELP with (LETTER or TOPIC, [ENTER]=MAIN, [QH]=quit HELP)?
```

*Figure 6-14. Extended Help Display on RBBS-PC*

## Downloading Files

Downloading files on an RBBS-PC is a straightforward operation. Figure 6-15 shows a typical file menu.

```
           RBBS-PC   F I L E   S Y S T E M
  --- TRANSFER ---- INFORMATION ---- UTILITIES ---- ELSEWHERE
  [D]ownload file  [L]ist files   [H]elp (or ?)  [G]oodbye
  [P]ersonal dwnld [N]ew files    [X]pert on/off [Q]uit
  [U]pload file    [S]earch files
                   [*]iew ARCs    [*] = unavailable

  FILE command <?,D,G,H,L,N,P,Q,S,U,V,X>?
```

*Figure 6-15. RBBS-PC File Menu*

Enter *L* to list all the files available for downloading or *N* to list the files added to the BBS since the last time you called. After choosing a file to download, start the download by entering *D*. Figure 6-16 shows a typical procedure for downloading a file.

```
FILE command <?,D,G,H,L,N,P,Q,S,U,V,X>? d
Download what file(s)? skater.zip
Searching for SKATER.ZIP
File Size    : 21 blocks  21248 bytes
Transfer Time: 1 min, 42 sec (approx)
Ymodem (1K Xmodem) SEND of skater.zip ready.  <Ctrl X> aborts
```

*Figure 6-16. RBBS-PC Download Procedure*

From here, start downloading the file on your computer using your communications program's download procedure.

## Uploading Files

Uploading files on an RBBS-PC is even simpler than downloading files. RBBS-PC asks for the name of the file or files you want to upload and then uses the default transfer protocol you have specified. When you get done uploading, you can add a brief comment about the file. This comment is displayed when the file is listed by other BBS users. Figure 6-17 shows a typical upload procedure.

```
FILE command <?,D,G,H,L,N,Q,S,U,V,X>? u
Name file(s) to upload? german.zip
Searching for file...

Upload disk has 33052672 bytes free
YMODEM receive of GERMAN.ZIP ready!

Upload successful
Describe GERMAN.ZIP (/ if for SYSOP only)
 |--+--1+0--+--2+0--+--3+0--+--4+0
? A pair of German language tutorials
```

*Figure 6-17. RBBS-PC Upload Procedure*

## Utilities

*Utilities* are general-purpose programs that help you do things such as set display options, change your password, and check on various system statistics. Figure 6-18 is a typical RBBS-PC utilities menu.

```
              RBBS-PC  U T I L I T I E S
   - DISPLAY ---------- INFO ---------- SYSTEM ---------- ELSEWHERE -
   [E]cho pref        [H]elp (or ?)   [B]aud Rate Change  [Q]uit
   [G]raphics         [R]ead Profile  [C]lock Time-Date
   [L]ines/Page       [S]tatistics    [F]ile Protocol
   [M]essage margin   [U]ser log      [P]assword Change
    * = unavailable                   [T]oggles

 UTIL command <?,B,C,E,F,G,H,L,M,P,Q,R,S,T,U,X>?
```

*Figure 6-18. RBBS-PC Utilities Menu*

Entering *T* will display a list of things that you can *toggle* on or off, like a light switch. Options you can usually toggle include checking the old bulletins and displaying new files when you log on, full menus versus command lines (also called novice versus expert mode), and turbokeys. Check the RBBS-PC you are using for more information on the available toggles.

## Other Interesting Features

RBBS-PCs have a variety of interesting features such as doors and multi-user capabilities. This section lists several of the features you may encounter on RBBS-PCs in your area.

### Doors

Many RBBS-PCs have extensive doors to games and other programs. There may be just a few games or perhaps an entire library of options.

### Multiple Users

RBBS-PC supports multiple users, and an increasing number of RBBS-PCs have two or three incoming phone lines. One common variation is to have most of the lines servicing the primary area for the BBS, and then have one line—known as a *foreign exchange line*—for calls from another area. The BBS then serves as a hub of activity for callers from a broad area.

### Library

A relatively new feature on RBBS-PCs is the Library command, @. You use this command to access additional file areas on the RBBS-PC. Most commonly, you will use the @ command to access an RBBS-PC's *CD-ROM drive*, a data-storage unit that uses a compact disk to store several hundred megabytes of data and files.

CD-ROM is not in use by most sysops yet, but some sysops have installed CD-ROM drives with the PC SIG (Special Interest Group) software collections. The PC-SIG contains thousands and thousands of programs, files, and archived software packages for people with MS-DOS computers.

### Stacking Commands

RBBS-PC allows you to stack commands by separating them with semicolons. For example, if you wanted to read a list of messages, you could enter *r;12;57;63;101;219;300* at the main menu prompt. RBBS-PC would perform the first command in the stack (r), then when the resulting prompt to Read which message? appeared, RBBS-PC would perform the second command in the stack (12), and so on. When all the commands in a stack have been performed, RBBS-PC returns control to you.

### Netmail

RBBS-PC supports *netmail* (networked mail) and *echomail,* which you can use to send messages and files from one BBS to any other BBS anywhere in the world. Netmail and echomail are discussed in Chapter 8, "Extending Your Reach."

## Logging Off

You can log off of an RBBS-PC in two ways. The first is to enter *G* for Goodbye. You can also log off of the BBS by entering *Q* for Quit at the File or Utility menu. RBBS-PC will then ask you if you want to quit the conference or session; or if you want to quit to the file, utility, main, or library menu. If you select the commands for a different section, RBBS-PC will shift you to that menu without having to go through any intervening menus. Quitting a conference removes you from that conference, and RBBS will not check for mail in that conference until you rejoin it. If you quit the session, RBBS-PC logs you off and hangs up the modem. Figure 6-19 shows an example of logging off the BBS this way.

```
QUIT C)onference, S)ession or to section F)ile, [M]ain, U)til or @)Library! s
End session (Y,[N])! y

Now: 03-29-1990 at 14:06:32
On for 4 mins, 23 secs
 56 min left for next call today
SAM, Thanks and please call again!
f£^g/Å+)∫x
NO CARRIER
```

*Figure 6-19. Logging Off on RBBS-PC*

## Comments

The availability of the source code and the simplicity of the command structure has made RBBS-PC a very popular BBS. If you are interested in learning how to set up your own BBS using RBBS-PC, you are encouraged to read *The Complete Electronic Bulletin Board Starter Kit* by Charles Bowen and David Peyton. This book tells you how to set up and customize an RBBS-PC and comes with a copy of the RBBS-PC software on two diskettes. See the bibliography for more information on how to find this book.

# FIDO

Fido is an easily recognized, simple BBS to use. Written by Tom Jennings, Fido was designed as a message system, with file capability later added. The examples shown in this section are from version 12, the most popular version of Fido, only recently made available as shareware.

Fido's simplicity can make experienced users feel that it is not as feature-rich as other linear BBSes. On the other hand, Fido is very straightforward in its functions. There are only a few commands to remember at each level. If you already understand the basics of BBSing, you will have no trouble using Fido.

## Logging On

One of the things that makes a Fido BBS recognizable is the picture of Fido and his bowl. Many Fido BBSes include this as part of the logon screen. Figure 6-20 shows a typical logon screen for a Fido BBS.

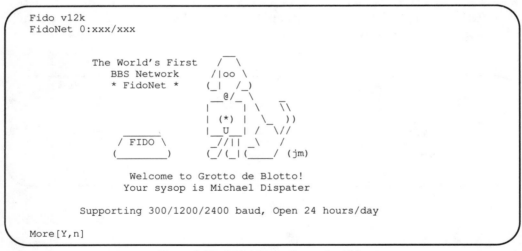

*Figure 6-20. Initial Logon Screen for Fido*

Although the dog-with-diskette picture in Figure 6-20 is popular, not all Fido BBSes use it, preferring instead to insert their own logon picture or bulletin. After the initial logon screen, the BBS asks for your first and last name.

```
Your FIRST name: Sam
Your  LAST name: Spade
Sam Spade? [Y,n]: y
Wait ...
Where are you calling from? Seattle, WA
Seattle WA? [Y,n]: y
Choose a password: gumshoe
Gumshoe? [Y,n]: y
   You will now be asked to REPEAT your password just to make sure you
have it right.  Dots will be echoed.

   Please remember your password.  You'll need it to log onto the BBS the next
time you call.

Password: .......
```

*Figure 6-21. Registering as a New Fido User*

Fido only looks for basic logon information when you are registering.  You can use the Change command at the main menu to change your user options.  After you enter the requested information, you will probably see a bulletin about the BBS and its policies, followed by the main Fido menu.

```
           New users: Read this now!
=================================================

This BBS is maintained for exchanging messages, technical
information, and public domain software and shareware.

If you are a new user, you are only allowed 10 minutes on
the BBS today.  I will change your status to allow you more
access time within the next few days.
=================================================

MAIN Section:
M)sg-Section F)ile-Section B)ulletins
S)tatistics C)hange P)age-Operator
L)ist-Callers A)ns-Questionnaire V)ersion
G)oodbye
Command (?=help) :
```

*Figure 6-22. Bulletin and Main Fido Menu*

Even if the sysop is not displaying the picture of the dog with the diskette, a Fido BBS is recognizable by the sparse, utilitarian look of the menus.  Like most BBSes, Fido is divided into a main menu section, a message section, and a file section.  General-purpose commands, such as Change and Page-Operator, are listed at the main menu.

## Setting Options

After logging on, use the Change command in the main menu to review your display options. When you enter *C* at the main menu prompt, the BBS displays the options you can change. Figure 6-23 shows you how to change the display to show text continuously without being prompted for each screenful.

```
Command (?=help): C

---- Personal Info ----
Name            : Sam Spade
Address         : Seattle WA
Password        : Gumshoe
Help Level      : All

---- Your System ----
Number of Columns: 80
Number of Lines : 24
"More[Y,n]"     : ON
Tab Expansion   : ON
Filler Nulls    : 0

N)ame A)ddress P)assword H)elp-Level W)idth
L)ength M)ore T)abs F)iller-Nulls
Command [Q=quit] (?=help): m
Pause every 24 lines is now Off

---- Personal Info ----
Name            : Sam Spade
Address         : Seattle WA
Password        : Gumshoe
Help Level      : All

---- Your System ----
Number of Columns: 80
Number of Lines : 24
"More[Y,n]"     : OFF
Tab Expansion   : ON
Filler Nulls    : 0

N)ame A)ddress P)assword H)elp-Level W)idth
L)ength M)ore T)abs F)iller-Nulls
Command [Q=quit] (?=help):
```

*Figure 6-23. Change Options in Fido*

## Getting Help

With version 12 of Fido, you can specify a command at the menu you are using and Fido will display help for that command. Online help is new to Fido with version 12.

If you want to find out more about the options you can change, enter a question mark (*?*) at the prompt. Fido will then display general help about the commands you can use. You can get more specific help by entering the command followed by a question mark, in this case, *C?*. Figure 6-24 shows an example of Fido's online help.

```
        C H A N G E   S E T T I N G S

    This is where you change your name, password, and so on, as well as your
    general display options.  Fido will use the settings you enter the next
    time you log on.

    For more specific help on a command, enter the command followed
    by a question mark.  For example, enter N? for more help on the
    N)ame command.
```

*Figure 6-24.  Context-sensitive Help in Fido*

## Reading Messages

Enter *M* at the main menu to go to the message menu.  The BBS will put you in the default message area.  Figure 6-25 shows an example of this.

```
MAIN Section:
M)sg-Section F)ile-Section B)ulletins
S)tatistics C)hange P)age-Operator
L)ist-Callers A)ns-Questionnaire V)ersion
G)oodbye
Command (?=help): m
Wait ...

Message Area   1: Public Messages
Total messages:    63
Highest message:   66
Highest read:       0

N)ext P)revious E)nter K)ill T)o-You
A)rea-Change R)eply C)ontinuous L)ist
S)earch U)pdate-Msg G)oodbye M)ain-Menu
Command or Message Number 1-66 (?=help) [0 N]:
```

*Figure 6-25.  Fido Message Menu*

The first time you enter an area during a session, the BBS will display the number of messages in the area, the highest message number in the area, and the highest message number you've read.  In the example in Figure 6-25, there are 63 messages, of which the highest is message number 66, and you have read none of them (because you're a new user).  This feature is very handy for checking for new messages in an area.  If the highest message number and the highest message number you've read are the same, there are no new messages in the section.

You can read specific messages by entering the message number at the prompt.  You can also enter *N* and *P* to see the next and previous messages.  Unlike many other BBSes, however, there is no Read command.

```
Message Area   1: Public Messages
N)ext P)revious E)nter K)ill T)o-You
A)rea-Change R)eply C)ontinuous L)ist
S)earch U)pdate-Msg G)oodbye M)ain-Menu
Command or Message Number 1-66 (?=help) [0 N]:
#1   21 Apr 90  15:34:27 [34]
From: Sysop
To:   All
Subj: Purpose of message area

[NOTE: Message modified on 23 Apr 90  08:42:21]
This message area is for general information, announcements, howdy-do's,
and so on.  If you want to talk about technical issues, go to the Technoids
area.  Classified ads go in the For Sale/Wanted area.  If it's fun or just
idle chatter, it goes in here.

Your Esteemed Sysop,

Michael

Message Area   1: Public Messages
N)ext P)revious E)nter K)ill T)o-You
A)rea-Change R)eply C)ontinuous L)ist
S)earch U)pdate-Msg G)oodbye M)ain-Menu
Command or Message Number 1-66 (?=help) [1 N]:
```

*Figure 6-26. Reading a Message on Fido*

In Figure 6-26, the number in the brackets in the command prompt is the number of the last message you read (0 in this case, because you have read no messages in this section at all).  The *N* says that, if you press [ENTER], you will automatically see the message with the next highest message number.  In other words, to scroll through the messages in an area one at a time, you simply have to press [ENTER] for each new message.  Each time you read a message, Fido updates the number in the brackets at the command prompt to show the number of the message you just read.

When you enter *N* or *P*, the BBS displays the next or previous message and also changes the direction in which Fido reads the next time you press [ENTER].  For example, if you enter *P* to read the previous message, Fido will display the previous message and change the letter in the brackets from *N* to *P.*

Fido has several other commands that will help you read messages. Entering a less than sign (<) selects the message with the lowest number and sets Fido to read forward. For example, if the lowest message were 5, the command prompt would look like [5 N]. Similarly, entering a greater than sign (>) selects the message with the highest number and sets Fido to read backward. If the highest message were 243, the prompt would show as [243 P]. The plus (+) and minus (-) commands let you thread through a conversation in the messages. You can reply to a message and delete the original at the same time by using the RK (for Read, then Kill Message) command.

One feature of Fido that is not common to most BBSes is the ability to change a message you have already saved. You can do this by entering a *U* at the message menu, and Fido will let you use the standard message editing commands. When you finish changing the message and save it in its new form, Fido adds a line at the top that says when the message was changed (an example of this appears in Figure 6-26).

One additional feature of Fido's message system worth noting is that the number in brackets next to the message date indicates how many times the message has been read by BBS users.

## Entering Messages

To enter a message in Fido, simply enter *E* at the message menu. At the prompts, enter the recipient and whether or not the message is private. Entering a message on a Fido BBS is demonstrated in Figure 6-27.

```
Message Area    1: Public Messages
N)ext P)revious E)nter K)ill T)o-You
A)rea-Change R)eply C)ontinuous L)ist
S)earch U)pdate-Msg G)oodbye M)ain-Menu
Command or Message Number 1-66 (?=help) [66 N]: e
This will be message #67
From: Sam Spade
To: Michael Dispater
Subject: Hi, and thanks
Private? [y,N]: y
(System operator can read (PRIVATE) messages)
Maximum message length, lines: 138
Enter your message, blank line to end
Words will wrap automatically

 1: Just wanted to say "Hi."  A couple of friends recommended I log on
 2: and take a quick look around.  It's a very nice BBS and I'll be back
 3: in the next couple of days.  I'd appreciate access to the file areas
 4: as I have a couple of new shareware releases to upload.
 5:
 6: Yours Truly,
 7:
 8: Sam
 9:
S)ave C)ontinue-adding A)bort L)ist E)dit-Line
D)el-Line I)ns-Line H)eader (?=help): s
Saving your message
```

*Figure 6-27. Entering a Message on Fido*

The message editing commands are self-explanatory. One message editing command that is a little unusual is the Header command, which lets you change the subject in the message header.

## Downloading Files

Enter *F* at the file menu to list the files in an area. Enter *L* to locate either a specific file or set of files. The BBS searches through all the file areas to which you have access for files with names that match the ones you entered. Figure 6-28 shows an example of looking for the Fido manual on a typical Fido BBS.

```
File Area   1: Fido v12 Tools
F)iles D)ownload U)pload A)rea-Change T)ype
S)tatistics L)ocate G)oodbye M)ain-Menu
Command (?=help): l
Filename(s) to search for: guide.arc
    1) Files for Fido
GUIDE.ARC    25 Aug 88    61706 Fido v12 Callers' Guide
*   2) IBM-PC & compatibles utility programs
    3) Games and fun for IBM-PCs and compatibles
    4) Communications programs for IBM-PC and compatibles
    5) Word processing programs & text file utilities
    6) Newly uploaded files + *** FILE CATALOG ***
Found 1 matching files

File Area   1: Fido v12 Tools
F)iles D)ownload U)pload A)rea-Change
S)tatistics L)ocate G)oodbye M)ain-Menu
Command (?=help):
```

*Figure 6-28.  Locating a File on Fido*

The asterisk by the second category indicates that this file area contains files from FidoNet.  These are files that are transferred from one BBS to another.  FidoNet is an option of Fido and other participating BBSes that lets you route messages and files through a network of BBSes throughout the U.S. and the world.  FidoNet is discussed in Chapter 8, "Extending Your Reach."

Downloading a file on a Fido BBS is about the same as downloading on most other linear BBSes.  When you have located the file you wish to download, enter the name of the file or files and specify the transfer protocol.  Unlike earlier versions of Fido, version 12 supports ZMODEM.  The file being downloaded in Figure 6-29 is the user's guide to version 12 of Fido.

```
Command (?=help): d

A)scii, Z)modem, X)modem, XC)modem-CRC, K)ermit, T)elink
Transfer Type: A Z X XC K T (?=help): xc
XMODEM/CRC transfer
File(s): guide.arc
Ready to send "guide.arc"
61,706 Bytes total, 07:09 transfer time
Start now, or five Control-X's to abort

Sent 1 files, 61,706 bytes in 5:51 (including
start time), or 175 bytes/sec
File Area   1: Fido v12 Tools
F)iles D)ownload U)pload A)rea-Change
S)tatistics L)ocate G)oodbye M)ain-Menu
Command (?=help):
```

*Figure 6-29.  Downloading a File on Fido*

At the end of the download, Fido displays statistics about the download process and returns you to the file menu.

## Uploading Files

Switch to the appropriate file area and tell the BBS you want to upload a file. You then specify the file transfer protocol and the name of the file to be transferred. The example in Figure 6-30 shows an ASCII text file being uploaded into a file area.

```
File Area   3: Games and fun for IBM-PCs and compatibles
F)iles D)ownload U)pload A)rea-Change
S)tatistics L)ocate G)oodbye M)ain-Menu
Command (?=help): u
A)scii, Z)modem, X)modem, XC)modem-CRC, K)ermit, T)elink
Transfer Type: A Z X XC K T (?=help): a
ASCII Text transfer
Filename: license.fun

Ready to receive "License.fun"
Start now, or five Control-X's to abort
Want your text echoed back to you? [Y,n]: n
Control-C, Control-Z, Control-X, or Control-K to stop


File contains 1,862 characters

Received 1 files OK
Wait ...
Please describe LICENSE.FUN : Fun version of standard software license.
```

*Figure 6-30. Uploading an ASCII File on Fido*

When the ASCII file is finished uploading, you will need to enter [CTRL-C], [CTRL-Z], [CTRL-X], or [CTRL-K] to tell the BBS you've finished uploading the file. Fido then displays statistics about the file and asks for a one-line description of the file. The BBS then returns to the file menu.

## Other Interesting Features

Fido, along with some other BBSes, lets you enter [CTRL-C] or [CTRL-K] to stop the command or the display of text and return to the menu prompt. This will come in handy if you started displaying a several-page message that you are not interested in. Entering [CTRL-C] or [CTRL-K] stops the output without having to wait for the More? prompt or for the message to end.

If you aren't sure what to do at a menu prompt, take advantage of Fido's help. Enter a command letter followed by a question mark. You should also download and read Scot Kamin's *Caller's Guide,* an easy-to-read user's manual for Fido version 12. Ask your sysop for more information on downloading it from the Fido BBS you are using.

## Logging Off

To log off a Fido BBS, you enter *G* at any of the three menus, as demonstrated in Figure 6-31.

```
MAIN Section:
M)sg-Section F)ile-Section B)ulletins
S)tatistics C)hange P)age-Operator
L)ist-Callers A)ns-Questionnaire V)ersion
G)oodbye
Command (?=help): g
Logging Sam Spade off at 23 Apr 90  08:46:48
d∏∫=R, Á[
NO CARRIER
```

*Figure 6-31. Logging Off a Fido BBS*

## Comments

Fido's utilitarian design and stark appearance may not be enough for BBS users who are used to a wide variety of menu options and screens surrounded by borders of graphics characters. Fido is nonetheless a good, extremely stable BBS that is easy to learn and use.

## OPUS

According to the system operator's manual, OPUS is "Militantly Public Domain." The explanation of this is that OPUS is copyrighted and has a limited license solely to ensure that it remains available for no money. The license for using OPUS states that you may freely use and distribute OPUS as long as it is used in a lawful and friendly manner, there is no money charged for OPUS, and the BBS is not part of a government or government-controlled office (which must pay a license fee). If money is collected for using OPUS, a $50 donation must be paid to the *Shanti Project,* an AIDS support group in San Francisco, for each copy of OPUS that goes online.

OPUS is a very attractive, easy-to-use BBS that focuses heavily on sending and receiving messages. It also has extensive file transfer protocols. OPUS's above-average documentation includes a user's manual and a sysop's manual.

## Logging On

Logging on to an OPUS BBS for the first time is much like logging on to most other linear BBSes. Figure 6-32 is a typical logon procedure for an OPUS BBS.

```
* Network Address 1:xxx/xxx Using BinkleyTerm Version 2.00

Welcome to Grotto de Blotto OPUS xxx/1!
Please press your Escape key to enter the BBS, or wait a few moments.
Thank you.  Now loading BBS.  Please wait...

OPUS-CBCS v1.03a

300/1200/2400/9600
USR HST Modem

What is your FIRST name: Sam
What is your LAST name: Spade
Sam Spade [Y,n]? y

Please type your CITY and STATE: Seattle, WA

Now, you need to select your secret password.
A password must be a single word (NO SPACES). It can be as long
as 15 characters and can include letters, numbers, or punctuation.
There is NO difference between uppercase and lowercase letters.

Type the password you plan to use on this system: .......
Let's see if I recorded what you think you typed!

Please type your new password one more time: .......
```

*Figure 6-32. Initial Logon Screen for OPUS*

When you log on to an OPUS BBS, you will see any logon information for the BBS and then will be asked for your name. If the BBS has no record of your name, you will be asked for your city and state, followed by a password.

**Note:**   OPUS BBSes are commonly part of a BBS FidoNet, a network discussed in Chapter 8, "Extending Your Reach."

After entering your city, state, and password, you generally specify some display options, as seen in Figure 6-33.

```
Does your system support ANSI screen controls [y,N,?=help]? n

Use the OPed full-screen editor [Y,n,?=help]? y

OPUS boards are pretty easy to get around in.  If you want help,
try using the "?" key.  Most of the prompts have help screens.

                    [=------=]
     [=---------=+ BULLETINS +=---------=]
                    [=------=]

    (A)   News on Viruses
    (B)   Files and Downloading
    (C)   User Guide To Opus
    (D)   Introduction to Echomail
    (E)   Upcoming Events
    (F)   Donations
    (Q)   Quit - Return to the Main Menu

   [=--------------------------=]

       Enter A,B,C,D,E,F, or Q:
```

*Figure 6-33.  Display Options and Bulletin Menu on OPUS*

The first question asks you if you want the BBS to add graphics characters to the menus and screens.  Entering a question mark (*?*) displays three blocks on screen using graphics characters.  If you don't see three blocks on your screen, enter *N*.  If you see three blocks, enter *Y* if you want enhanced screens.  As always, adding graphics to the screens makes them prettier, but it also takes longer to draw them than if you are just displaying text.

The second question asks if you want to use the OPUS full-screen editor.  For now, enter *N*.  The editor is discussed a little later in this section under "Entering Messages."

After answering the questions on the options you want, you may see the bulletin list. You enter the letter of the bulletin you want to see or enter *Q* to quit to the main menu, shown in Figure 6-34.

```
MAIN MENU: Type `?' for help
M)essage section    F)ile section      G)oodbye (logoff)   S)tatistics
A)ns Questions      B)ulletin          Y)ell at sysop      C)hange setup
V)ersion
Select:
```

*Figure 6-34.  Main Menu in OPUS*

## Setting Options

Like Fido, OPUS has a *C* command on the main menu to change your setup options. Figure 6-35 shows the Change Setup options.

```
MAIN:
M)essage section    F)ile section     G)oodbye          S)tatistics
B)ulletin           Y)ell for sysop   C)hange setup     O)pening Menus
V)ersion            ?)HELP
Select: c


The CHANGE SETUP Section

City.......................Seattle, Wa

Help........NOVICE      Nulls.......0
scrn.Width..80         scrn.Length 24      Tabs........YES
More?.......YES        Video mode..TTY     Scrn. clear YES      IBM Chars...YES


CONFIG:
P)assword           H)elp level       N)ulls
W)idth of screen    L)ine length      T)abs
M)ore               V)ideo            S)creen clear
F)ull screen editor I)bm characters   Q)uit
?)HELP
Select:
```

*Figure 6-35. Changing Options in OPUS*

OPUS displays a list of available options and commands to enter to change a specific option. To change an option, enter the letter of the option. "Yes/No" options, such as the `More?` prompt and `Tabs` (instead of spaces) are changed as soon as you enter the command letter. Options that require numeric input, such as the screen width and nulls options, will prompt you for a number. Options that require you to choose an answer from a list, such as the help and video mode options, will display a list of possible entries and a letter to enter for each one.

## Reading Messages

You can get to the message menu from the main menu or the file menu. OPUS uses standard message areas and commands. Figure 6-36 is an example of reading a few messages on OPUS.

```
The MESSAGE Section
There are 45 messages in this area. The highest is #47
You haven't read any of these.

A)rea change      N)ext msg        P)rior msg       =)read non-stop
+)read reply      -)read original  L)ist brief      S)can text
Q)uit to Main     F)ile section    G)oodbye         ?)HELP
Y)ell for sysop
Select: =

From:    Jane Ferguson
To:      George Montgomery               Msg #1, 14-Mar-90 04:16pm
Subject: Re: Resume Programs

I don't put job references on my resumes either.  I prefer to give them out
if I am asked for them.  It gives me more control over the interview process.




From:    Rick Summers
To:      Sysop                           Msg #2, 14-Mar-90 05:16pm
Subject: Get a degree.

Yeah, I think that a degree is pretty necessary, too.  Certainly a h.s.
diploma is an absolute minimum if you ever want to make more than $4 an hour
I think that a bachelor's degree in something is also important, although
a friend of mine tells me that he has made an excellent career as a programmer
and technical writer without one.
```

*Figure 6-36. Reading Messages on OPUS*

If you want to read all the messages nonstop from where you are, enter an equals sign (=). OPUS will display all the messages in an area until there are no messages left or until you enter [CTRL-K]. If you press [ENTER] at the prompt, OPUS displays the next or previous message, depending on whether you were reading forward or backward through the messages.

## Entering Messages

OPUS has two types of message editors. The first is known as *LORE* (for line-oriented editor). With LORE, you enter the changes you want to make to one line of a message. Entering a message on an OPUS BBS is about the same as any other BBS if you are using LORE.

The second editor is *OPed*, the OPUS editor. OPed is a *full-screen* message editor. This means that you can move the cursor around on the screen to make changes, very much like a standard word processor.

The OPUS editor uses a basic set of commands to move the cursor and edit the message. There are usually two different commands to perform each action. The first set of commands uses standard keyboard keys. The second set uses control key combinations similar to commands found in programs such as WordStar and SideKick. Depending on your personal preferences, you can use either set of commands to perform an action. Figure 6-37 shows a table of the commands used in the OPUS editor.

```
Action                      Key(s) to press

Backspace                   BACKSPACE or CTRL-G
Move one line down          DOWN ARROW or CTRL-X
Move one line up            UP ARROW or CTRL-E
Move forward one screen     PGDN or CTRL-C
Move back one screen        PGUP or CTRL-R
Move one column left        LEFT ARROW or CTRL-S
Move one column right       RIGHT ARROW or CTRL-D
Move to start of line       HOME or CTRL-QS
Move to end of line         END or CTRL-QD
Delete to end of line       CTRL-QY
Toggle insert mode          CTRL-V
Save message                CTRL-Z or CTRL-KD
Cancel message              press ESCAPE twice or CTRL-KQ
Get online help             CTRL-K?
```

*Figure 6-36. OPUS Editor Commands*

The OPUS editor works like a simple word processor. You can move around in the text with the commands shown in Figure 6-37 as you could in any common word-processing program. If you have specified the OPUS editor rather than LORE in your options, OPUS will use the editor whenever you enter or reply to a message. When you enter *E* to start a message, the cursor is always at the start of the first line (shown in Figure 6-38 by an underscore) and the addressee and the subject appear in the lower part of the screen. The majority of the screen will be blank, with a cursor at the top, indicating where the text will start to appear.

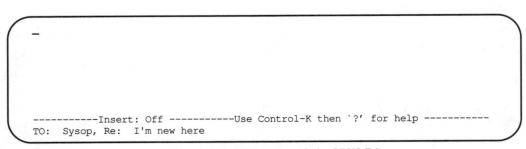

```
    _



    ----------Insert: Off ----------Use Control-K then `?' for help -----------
    TO:  Sysop, Re:  I'm new here
```

*Figre 6-38. Starting a Message with the OPUS Editor*

Start typing your message. The text will automatically wrap to the next line, so you don't need to press [ENTER] at the end of a line. To change something in a previous line, just move the cursor to the position and change it. Insert text by entering [CTRL-V] to turn on the Insert mode. If you need help at any time, enter [CTRL-K?]. Figure 6-39 shows the message started in Figure 6-38 just before saving.

```
This is the first time I have tried the OPUS editor, and I am very impressed.
I'm new to this BBS so I'm still learning some of the features.
Please leave me mail about some of the other features unique to OPUS.

Yours Truly,

Sam Spade

_


-----------Insert: Off -----------Use Control-K then `?' for help -----------
TO: Sysop, Re: I'm new here
```

*Figure 6-39. Message Created with the OPUS Editor*

The OPUS editor lets you quote information from the message you are replying to, allowing the person to which your message is addressed to see what you are responding to. This feature is very helpful when responding to a long message, or to a specific part of a message.

The OPUS editor displays the original message four lines at a time in the lower portion of the editor screen. You can copy those four lines of text into your reply. To start reading the original message, enter [CTRL-KR]. Figure 6-40 shows the sysop replying to the message in Figure 6-39.

```
  > This is the first time I have tried the OPUS editor, and I am very
impressed.
  > I'm new to this BBS so I'm still learning some of the features.
  > Please leave me mail about some of the other features unique to OPUS.
  >

Sam: I'd recommend you download the OPUS user manual for the most
complete answer to your question.  I think there are a lot of nice
features in OPUS, and it would be easier and faster for you to read
the overview in the manual than for me to tell you about all of them.

Sorry, I don't mean to sound unhelpful.  I'll be glad to answer
questions about specific features any time you like.

Yours, Michael

--------------------Insert: Off ------------------ QUOTE ------------------
  > This is the first time I have tried the OPUS editor, and I am very
impressed.
  > I'm new to this BBS so I'm still learning some of the features.
  > Please leave me mail about some of the other features unique to OPUS.
  >
TO: Sam Spade, RE: Welcome!
```

*Figure 6-40. Replying to a Message with the OPUS Editor*

The lines in the lower window are from the original message. To include these four lines in the body of your message, enter [CTRL-KC]. OPUS then copies those four lines into your message at the current cursor position. Quoted lines are preceded with a greater than (>) symbol. To read the next four lines in the original message, enter [CTRL-C].

**Note:** You cannot back up and read the previous four lines of a message. If you overshoot the lines of text you want, you must enter [CTRL-KR] to quit reading the original, then enter [CTRL-KR] to start reading the original message again. This positions you at the start of the original message. You can then read forward until you find the lines you want to copy.

## Getting Help

You can get help at any prompt by entering a question mark (?). OPUS will display a menu of the commands for which help is available. Figure 6-41 shows the help options for the main menu.

```
MAIN:
M)essage section    F)ile section      G)oodbye          S)tatistics
B)ulletin           Y)ell for sysop    C)hange setup     O)pening Menus
V)ersion            ?)HELP
Select: ?

HELP: MAIN MENU
M)essage section    F)ile section      G)oodbye          S)tatistics
O)pening Menus      B)ulletin          Y)ell at Sysop    C)hange setup
U)ser list/search   L)ocal BBS list    V)ersion

Which command do you need help with?
> u


  USER LIST/SEARCH
  Displays any or all users based on matching a string of characters
  you enter.  Entering no search string lists all users.

  For example, entering the search string "dav" would list:
    David Retsnif
    Dave Peacock
    Ron Davies
```

*Figure 6-41. Online Help on OPUS*

## Downloading Files

File operations in OPUS are done from the file menu.  Enter *F* to locate the file or files you want to download.  Once you have located a file to download, enter *D* to start the download process.  Figure 6-42 shows a typical download on an OPUS BBS.

```
The FILES Section.
File area #  1 ... General files

A)rea change     S)tatistics      Q)uit to Main     M)essage Section
F)ile titles     G)oodbye         Y)ell for sysop   ?)Help
L)ocate
Select: d


Select a method.
 Z)modem
 X)modem
 Y)modem
 M)odem7
 S)ealink
 K)ermit
  Q)QUIT      (cancel the transfer)


Select: y
What do you want to receive? userdoc1.arc

File:   userdoc1.arc
Size:   224640 bytes (1756 xmodem blocks)
Time:   zmodem=15:36 xmodem/telink=20:48 sealink=18:43

Mode:   Ymodem

Begin receiving now or send several CONTROL-X's to cancel.


Transfer complete
```

*Figure 6-42. Downloading a File on OPUS*

You can change file areas with the *A* command. If you know the number of the area you want to change to, you can follow the *A* with the area number. For example, to change to area 4, you could enter *A4* or *A;4*.

If you want to see an ASCII text file, you can enter *T* and specify the filename. OPUS will type the file on the screen. You can read the file, and also use your communications program's screen capture utility to copy the information to a disk file on your computer.

OPUS also lets you view the contents of archived files with the extensions of .ARC (Archive) and .LBR (Library). Enter *C* and tell OPUS which file you want to view.

## Uploading Files

Uploading a file on OPUS is very easy. Select the area to upload the file to, then tell OPUS what transfer protocol you want to use and the name of the file you are uploading. After the transfer is complete, you must also enter a short description of the file. Figure 6-43 illustrates the upload procedure.

```
The FILES section
File area #1   General files
A)rea change   F)ile titles   T)ype (show)   G)oodbye       U)pload
D)ownload
S)tatistics    M)ain menu      C)ontents
Select: u

Select a method.
 Z)modem
 X)modem
 Y)modem
 M)odem7
 S)ealink
  Q)QUIT      (cancel the transfer)

Select: y
What file will you be sending? GERMAN.ZIP

Ready to receive GERMAN.ZIP using Ymodem
Begin sending now or send CONTROL-X twice to cancel.

Transfer complete

Thanks for the upload, Sam Spade.

Please describe GERMAN.ZIP: Shareware for brushing up your German.
```

*Figure 6-43. Uploading a File on OPUS*

## Other Interesting Features

Some OPUS BBSes use a "callback" system for instant user registration for local users. An example of this appears in Figure 6-44.

```
          N E W   U S E R    R E G I S T R A T I O N

Enter the number to your MODEM line.  After you log off this BBS, do not exit
from the communication program you are using.  This BBS will then call you at the
number you are about to enter.  You may see 'RING' appear on your screen or a
light on the modem showing that you have an incoming call.

When you know the phone is ringing, enter 'ATA' followed by a <CR> or let
the modem answer if it is able to by itself.  The modems will take a moment or
two to establish a good connection.  You may see CONNECT... and/or garbage char-
acters on your screen as the modems agree on how to communicate.

You will have three chances to enter your logon password.  If you enter the correct
password, the BBS will immediately upgrade you to the level of "registered user."
If not, the system will call you back one more time and try again.

Do you wish to register (Y/N) y

Enter the number to your MODEM line   ###/###-#### :
```

*Figure 6-44. Automatic Registration on OPUS*

The BBS will call you back at the number you give and prompt you for your password. The BBS then logs the phone number in its user information files. The sysop can use this number to phone you directly in the future if necessary.

## Logging Off

Logging off an OPUS BBS is done by entering *G*, as shown in Figure 6-45.

```
MAIN:
M)essage section    F)ile section      G)oodbye           S)tatistics
B)ulletin           Y)ell for sysop    C)hange setup      O)pening Menus
V)ersion            ?)HELP
Select: g?

Disconnect [Y,n,?=help]? y


Leave a note to the sysop [y,N,?=help]? n
Thanks for calling, Sam.
Your total downloads to date are 0 kilobytes.
Your total uploads to date are 0 kilobytes.
g»#~2@(~t
NO CARRIER
```

*Figure 6-45. Logging Off an OPUS BBS*

## Comments

Although it is one of the newer BBSes, OPUS is gaining rapidly in popularity. The software is free for noncommercial uses and the documentation is of high quality. The commands are easy to use and understand, the online help is good, and the documentation for the sysop is above average.

## PCBOARD

PCBoard is manufactured by Clark Development Corporation and was first released in 1983. PCBoard has many options at the main menu, extensive online help, and menus and displays that can be customized. PCBoard is not shareware; you must purchase the software from the manufacturer.

## Logging On

When you log on to a PCBoard for the first time, you will see something like the procedure shown in Figure 6-46.

```
What is your first name? Sam
What is your last name? Spade

SAM SPADE not found in USER's file.
(R) to re-enter your name or (C) to continue logon as a new user? c
```

*Figure 6-46. Initial Logon Screen for PCBoard*

After you enter your name, the BBS checks to see if you are in the user log. If it can't find your name, it lets you retype it or log on as a new user. Figure 6-47 shows you what happens when you continue the new user registration process.

```
                        N O T I C E
  This BBS requires that you use your REAL name so you can be verified.
  The verification process will NOT be started until after you leave a
  COMMENT FOR THE SYSOP (C command) or a MESSAGE for SYSOP (E command).
  Be sure to save any comments or messages using the S for Save command.


  Would you like to register with Grotto de Blotto? (Enter=YES)?
                              (------)
  Password (One word please!)? ........
                              (------)
  Re-enter password to verify? ........

                                  (------------)
  City and State calling from? Seattle, WA

                                  (-------)
  Business or data phone # is? 800-626-8257

                                  (-------)
  Home or voice phone # is?    555-4588

                                  (---------------)
    Computer brand & model???? Real IBM PC


    (A) Ascii (Non-Binary)
    (X) Xmodem (Checksum)
    (C) Xmodem-CRC (CRC)
    (Y) 1K-Xmodem (PCBoard Ymodem)
    (F) 1K-Xmodem-G (PCBoard Ymodem-G)
    (B) 1K-Ymodem (DSZ/Forsberg)
    (Z) Zmodem (DSZ/Forsberg)
    (K) Kermit (PCKermit/Columbia U)
    (N) None

  Default Protocol Desired (Enter)=no change? y

  Please wait - Adding name to Quick Index File ...

  Registration Information Saved . Many thanks!
```

*Figure 6-47. Registering as a New PCBoard User*

As you can see, the logon procedure for new users tends to be a bit more extensive on PCBoard BBSes than on some other BBSes. Notice in Figure 6-47 that the BBS shows you exactly how many characters you can enter in each field. PCBoard also supports more transfer protocols than most BBSes. This may be very useful if you plan to do a lot of uploading and downloading.

Following the logon procedure, you will probably see the information shown in Figure 6-48. Like many other linear BBSes, you can check the message areas as part of the logon procedure to quickly see if you have any mail waiting. After this, most PCBoard BBSes will display your user options.

```
Scan Message Base Since 'Last Read' (Enter)=yes?

(Ctrl-K) or (Ctrl-X) Aborts, (Ctrl-S) Suspends.

Scanning Main .....
  Msgs For You: None
 Msgs From You: None
New Msgs Avail: 32

              (M123456789012345678901234567890123456789)
MBase Areas: XXX      XXXXXX XX
MBase Scans: XXX      XXXXXX XX
Caller Num.: 62150
Conferences: 1
Lst Date On: 03-31-90
Expire Date: 03-31-91
# Times On : 1
Page Length: 23
Expert Mode: Off
Security Lv: 15
# Downloads: 0
# Uploads  : 0
Bytes Avail: 380000
L/Msg. Read: 0
High Msg. #: 117
Active Msgs: 79
Tr/Protocol: 1K-Xmodem (PCBoard Ymodem)
```

*Figure 6-48. User Options on PCBoard*

The display in Figure 6-48 appears each time you log on. You can also look at this information by entering *V* for View Settings at the main menu. The display shows the options you have selected, together with a number of statistics about your user account and the BBS. "MBase Areas" has an X under each message area you are registered in. "MBase Scans" shows the message areas to scan for personal mail. The rest of the information is fairly standard: what number of caller you are, the conferences you are entered in, when you were last on the BBS, when your BBS account will expire, how many times you've been on the BBS, your page length, and other general information on your status with the BBS.

After the user options, PCBoard displays the main menu (shown in Figure 6-49).

```
===[ Grotto de Blotto Main Menu ]===
A)bandon Conference   H)elp Functions       O)perator Page      T)rans. Protocol
B)ulletin Listings    I)nitial Welcome      OPEN a DOOR         TS)Txt Srch Msgs
CHAT between NODEs     J)oin a Conference    P)age Length Set    U)pload a File
C)omment to SYSOP      K)ill a message       Q)uick Msg Scan     V)iew Settings
D)ownload a File       L)ocate Files(name)   R)ead Messages      W)rite User Info
E)nter a Message       M)ode (Graphics)      REPLY to Msg(s)     X)pert On/Off
F)ile Directories      N)ew Files(date)      RM)Re-Read Mem #    Y)our Per. Mail
G)oodbye (Hang up)     NEWS file display     S)cript Question    Z)ippy DIR Scan

 [CHAT] = Talk to users on another phone line! [OPEN] a DOOR application

(42 min. left) Main Board Command?
```

*Figure 6-49. PCBoard Main Menu*

As you can see, the main PCBoard menu is packed with commands. The reason for this is that the message and file commands are at the main menu, rather than in separate menus of their own. Although this may be a little confusing at first, it allows you to get to the command you want without having to go through an intermediate menu.

PCBoard BBSes also use commands with more than one letter. This eliminates the problem of picking command letters for different commands with the same first letter, such as Read and Reply. For example, to open a door, you type *OPEN*. To reply to a message, you type *REPLY*. To chat with other users on a multi-line PCBoard BBS, you would type *CHAT*.

## Setting Options

Setting options on a PCBoard BBS is a little different from other linear BBSes. Instead of choosing a display option from a list on a display options menu, you choose the command for the specific display option from the main menu. Although this is not difficult, it can make changing several options a little more time-consuming.

Some of the commands that you can use to set options are:

*M*   to select the graphics display mode

*P*   to set the *page length* (the number of lines displayed on the screen at a time)

*T*   to change the default file transfer protocol

*W*   to write your user information

Figure 6-50 shows an example of changing the page length to zero, which will eliminate the `More?` prompts and display information continuously.

```
(26 min. left) Main Board Command? p

Page Length is currently set to 23.
Enter new length (0)=continuous, (Enter)=no change? 0
Page length now set to 0
```

*Figure 6-50. Setting the Page Length on a PCBoard*

You can change your user information (name, address, and the message bases you want to automatically scan for mail) with the *W* command. Figure 6-51 shows the user information you can change with this command.

```
(29 min. left) Main Board Command? w

  NOTE:  Press (Enter) for `no change' to any item!
                        (------)
Password (One word please!)?

                        (SEATTLE, WA            )
City and State calling from?

                        (800-626-8257 )
Business or data phone # is?

                        (    555-1617)
   Home or voice phone # is?

                        (REAL IBM PC               )
  Computer brand & model????

             system map: (-----1-----2-----3-----)
                        (M123456789012345678901234567890123456789)
                        (XXX      XXXXXX XX                      )
     Message Bases to Scan?

User Record Updated with Any Changes.
```

*Figure 6-51. Changing User Information on a PCBoard BBS*

## Reading Messages

To read a message, enter *R* at the main menu. Then enter the appropriate message read command at the prompt. Entering *S* (as in the example in Figure 6-52) reads the next message after the one you last read.

```
(H)elp, (1-411), Message Read Command? s

Date: 03-19-90 (16:26)              Number: 250
  To: SYSOP                          Refer#: NONE
From: JANE FERGUSON                   Read: 03-18-90 (07:09)
Subj: COMMENT                        Status: PUBLIC MESSAGE

Michael: Hello.  I hope you are well.  Many thanks for telling me about
the Syzygy Cafe.  The food was very, very good.  My aunt and uncle are
coming to town shortly, and I'll take them there.  Know of any good Thai
places?  Ever since the Thai House closed down, I haven't been able to
find a good Thai meal anywhere.

(H)elp, End of Message Command?
```

*Figure 6-52. Reading a Message on a PCBoard BBS*

PCBoard has an impressive array of message reading commands. Not only do you have the standard options of reading the next and previous messages and entering a specific message number, there are also commands that let you look for new messages (*S*), display messages in nonstop mode (*NS*), and look for messages left for you (*Y*) or by you (*F*). You can also read "memorized" messages—messages you marked for later examination with the text search command.

## Entering Messages

To enter a message on a PCBoard BBS, you enter *E* at the main menu or at the read message prompt. You first enter standard message header information, shown in Figure 6-53.

```
(103 min. left) Main Board Command? e
                         (------------)
           To (Enter)=`ALL'? Sysop
     Subject (Enter)=abort? Hello
  Message Security (H)=help? N
```

*Figure 6-53. Entering a Message Header on a PCBoard BBS*

On a PCBoard BBS, you can make messages public by entering *N* for No security or private by entering *R* for Recipient only. You can also assign a password to the message to prevent any other reader from killing it by entering *S* for Sender. *G* for Group assigns a password to the message—only those people with the password can read the message. This last option is very good for posting semi-private messages that affect only one group of people.

Once you have entered your message header and security, you can enter the text. Figure 6-54 shows a message being entered on a typical PCBoard BBS.

```
    Enter your text. (Enter) alone to end. (72 chars/line, 99 lines maximum)
    (-----------------------------------------------------------------------)
 1: Sysop:
 2:
 3: Hi.  I'm interested in finding out more about PCBoards in general and
 4: Grotto de Blotto in particular.  Have you got information about the BBS
 5: that I can download to get a better idea of what PCBoard is like?
 6:
 7: Yours,
 8:
 9: Sam Spade
(A)bort, (C)ontinue, (D)elete, (E)dit, (H)elp, (I)nsert, (L)ist, (S)ave
Text Entry Command? s

Saving Message # 6998 ...............
```

*Figure 6-54. Entering a Message on a PCBoard BBS*

## Getting Help

PCBoard BBSes have very good online help. You can enter *H* or a question mark (*?*) at any prompt and get extensive help on any command. Figure 6-55 shows typical help available for the Read command.

```
 (R)ead Messages - Function Help
 ─────────────────

 Subcommands:   (#) (E) (C) (F) (Y) (S) (NS) (+) (-) (RM) (TS) (NEXT) (PREV)

                (#) a message number between 1 and 9999999
                (E) allows entering a message
                (C) allows entering a comment
                (F) selects only messages left by you
                (Y) selects only messages left for you
                (S) selects messages above the last one you have read
                (NS) displays text in non-stop mode
                (RM) re-read previously "memorized" message number
                (RM+) re-read "memorized" message number plus forward read
                (RM-) re-read "memorized" message number plus backwards read
                (+) or (-) added to the end of a (#) forces either a
                    forward or reverse read respectively.
                (+) alone reads messages forward from present position
                (-) alone reads messages backwards from present position
                (TS) search message headers for specific text
                (NEXT) reads next higher message number available
                (PREV) reads next lower message number available
                (Enter) alone ends message read function

                Message numbers and the other commands above can be
                stacked if desired.  (i.e. 'R F Y S', etc.)

 Description:   Allows reading messages left on the system.  All public
                messages will be displayed, along with private messages
                left either by you or for you.  If a message has more
                display lines than what your (P)age Length is set for,
                a "(H)elp, More?" prompt will appear asking for your
                input.  Multiple message numbers to read can be entered
                on the same command line if desired.  Additionally,
                combinations of the above commands can be entered on the
                same command line if desired.
```

*Figure 6-55. Sample Online Help on a PCBoard BBS*

## Downloading Files

With most other linear BBSes, when you enter a file command, the BBS displays the file menu. From this menu, you can then list the files in each file area, download or upload a file, and so on. On PCBoard, you will probably need to use the *F* (for File Directories) command to locate a file first before downloading it. Figure 6-56 shows a list of file directories on a PCBoard BBS.

```
 ╔════════ FILE DIRECTORY (MAIN BOARD AREA) ════════╗

        1 General Programs
        2 Communications Programs
        3 Business and Education
        4 Word Processing and Editors
        5 Data Base Stuff
        6 Utilities
        7 Home/Personal/Entertainment
        8 Games (text, non-graphics)
        9 Games (graphics or color)
       10 Games (EGA)
       11 Text Files
       12 Ham Radio Programs
       13 BBS Programs and Utilities

 (H)elp, (1-13), File List Command? 1
```

*Figure 6-56. Selecting a File Directory on a PCBoard BBS*

After selecting the file directory to list, PCBoard shows you the files in the directory. Figure 6-57 contains the file list for the general programs directory selected in Figure 6-56.

```
 ***** DIRECTORY #1 *** GENERAL PROGRAMS ****************************

 | filename |  | size |  | date |  |         description for this file      |

 PCBUSR11.TXT   27592   11-19-89   NEW revised edition PC Board Users manual!!!
 SYSLOG11.ZIP   23731   01-17-90   Computer use recording program
 FLUSHOT1.6      8064   02-14-90   The latest release of Flu Shot!! Version 1.6
 206LST02.90    28532   02-11-90   Western Washington BBSes February 1990
 CHKUP.ARC      80896   05-24-90   Checkup program for viruses- protect HD!!
 WHERE26.ZIP    16067   05-20-90   Excellent file searching utility
 FSP_151.ZIP    54931   04-28-90   Latest version of FluShot (antivirus) program

 (H)elp, (1-13), File List Command?
```

*Figure 6-57. File List of General Programs Directory on a PCBoard BBS*

PCBoard BBSes let you save a little time here. Rather than making you return to the main menu to enter *D* to start a download, you can enter *D* at the menu prompt here. As a matter of fact, you can tell PCBoard you want to download, upload, or view an archived file at any More? prompt when you are listing a file directory.

When you enter *D* to start the download, the BBS asks you for the filename you want to download, then prompts you for the transfer protocol. PCBoard BBSes support a wide variety of transfer protocols, as you can see in Figure 6-58.

```
Filename to Download (Enter)=none ? flushot1.6
Checking file transfer request.  Please wait ...

   (A) Ascii (Non-Binary)
   (C) Xmodem-CRC (CRC)
   (F) 1K-Xmodem-G (Full flow)
   (G) Ymodem-G (DOOR 1 only)
   (K) Kermit (DOOR 1 only)
   (O) 1K-Xmodem (Old Ymodem)
   (W) WXmodem (DOOR 1 only)
   (X) Xmodem (Checksum)
   (Y) Ymodem Batch (DOOR 1 only)
   (Z) Zmodem (DOOR 1 only)
=> (N) None

Protocol Type for Transfer, (Enter) or (N)=abort? x
Download Time:   .6 minutes (approximate)
Download Size:   8064 bytes (63 blocks)
Total Will Be:   35656 bytes
Protocol Type:   Xmodem (Checksum)
File Selected:   FLUSHOT1.6
(Ctrl-X) Aborts Transfer

Transfer Successfully Completed!!!!!!!!   (200 cps avg.)
```

*Figure 6-58. Downloading a File on a PCBoard BBS*

When the file transfer is completed, the BBS tells you the average speed of the file transfer.

## Uploading Files

To upload a file on a PCBoard BBS, enter *U* at the main menu or at a `More?` prompt or command prompt in the file directory. Unlike most other BBSes, PCBoard asks you the name of the file before you upload it. Other than this difference in order, the uploading procedure is standard. Figure 6-59 shows a typical upload using XMODEM.

```
Filename to Upload (Enter)=none? license.fun
Checking file transfer request.  Please wait ...
Before beginning, enter a description of (LICENSE.FUN).
  (----------------------)
? Fun version of a software license.

   (A) Ascii (Non-Binary)
   (C) Xmodem-CRC (CRC)
   (F) 1K-Xmodem-G (Full flow)
   (G) Ymodem-G (DOOR 1 only)
   (K) Kermit (DOOR 1 only)
   (O) 1K-Xmodem (Old Ymodem)
   (W) WXmodem (DOOR 1 only)
   (X) Xmodem (Checksum)
   (Y) Ymodem Batch (DOOR 1 only)
   (Z) Zmodem (DOOR 1 only)
=> (N) None

Protocol Type for Transfer, (Enter) or (N)=abort? x
Upload Drive :  8513536 Bytes Free Disk Space
Upload Status:  Screened Before Posting
Protocol Type:  Xmodem (Checksum)
File Selected:  LICENSE.FUN
(Ctrl-X) Aborts Transfer

Transfer Successfully Completed!!!!!!!!  (176 cps avg.)

Thanks for the file Sam!
```

*Figure 6-59. Uploading a File on a PCBoard BBS*

## Other Interesting Features

Many PCBoard BBSes have an extensive selection of doors. The most common door on PCBoard BBSes is ProDoor. ProDoor extends PCBoard's file capabilities and gives you other transfer protocols (such as ZMODEM) not normally supported by PCBoard. You can also perform a number of file compression and decompression activities here. Perhaps most convenient is the ability to compress unread messages into a single file for downloading and reading offline later. This can save you a considerable amount of time connected to the BBS.

Conferences on a PCBoard BBS may also have file areas. Once you have joined a conference with the *J* command, you can upload and download files to the conference's file area.

The PCBoard software has extensive chatting commands. If you are logged on to a PCBoard with multiple nodes, you will be able to chat privately or in open forums.

You can use *Z*, the Zippy Dir Scan command, to look for text in the file directories. You can specify up to 20 characters of text to search through the file directories for.

Finally, like many other BBSes, PCBoard lets you stack commands. Be sure to separate your commands with a space.

## Logging Off

To log off of a PCBoard BBS, enter *G*. Figure 6-60 demonstrates logging off of a typical PCBoard BBS.

```
(27 min. left) Main Board Command? g
Thanks for calling, Sam.  You were connected for 18 minutes.
J●j?-█%╦
NO CARRIER
```

*Figure 6-60. Logging Off a PCBoard BBS*

## Comments

Most PCBoard BBSes focus heavily on message conferences. These conferences are frequently networked with other BBSes. See Chapter 8, "Extending Your Reach," for more information on how this is done.

PCBoard is extremely flexible. You can enter commands at the main menu and in other locations on the system so you don't have to return to the main menu. The wide range of commands and the extensive online help both contribute to making PCBoard a very popular BBS.

## WILDCAT!

WILDCAT! was written by Jim Harrer and Rick Heming, partners in Mustang Software, Inc., and was first released in 1986. Unlike many other BBSes, WILDCAT! was actually designed more for businesses than for hobbyists. Because businesses need reliable information, WILDCAT! has extensive security options the sysop may use to ensure that sensitive messages and files are routed in a timely and secure fashion. This slant has also stimulated a strong interest among hobbyists in the general BBS community, where WILDCAT! has a rapidly growing popularity.

WILDCAT! is available both as shareware and as a registered product. The registered version has more features and a very good sysop's manual.

## Logging On

The logon procedure for WILDCAT!, shown in Figure 6-61, is fairly standard.

```
What is your First Name?  Sam
What is your Last Name?  Spade
Looking up Sam Spade... Please wait.

Your Name "Sam Spade" was not Found in the User Data Base

Is Your Name Spelled Correctly? y

Where are you Calling From [City, ST] ? Seattle, WA
Seattle, WA, Correct [y/n] ? y

Please Select a Password ?    gumshoe
Re-enter Password to verify : *******

What is your Computer Type ? IBM
IBM, Correct [y/n] ? y

For later verification please enter your Birth Date:
MM/DD/YY
03/21/56
03/21/56, Correct [y/n] ?
MM/DD/YY
03/21/56
03/21/56, Correct [y/n] ? y

Please Enter your VOICE phone number:
XXX-XXX-XXXX
800-626-8257
800-626-8257, Correct [y/n] ? y
```

*Figure 6-61. Initial Logon Screen for WILDCAT!*

After entering the standard logon information, set your default options for displaying information and file transfer protocols, as shown in Figure 6-62.

```
You may customize the number of lines per screen display.

Please enter your display size.  [ENTER] = 23 lines.
------------------------------------
We suggest that you choose [S]elect to indicate you will make a choice
prior to each download.  This will allow you to use additional external
protocols such as ZMODEM for file transfers, or to quickly see and
change choices as new protocols are added.
------------------------------------

Please select a default Protocol:

S) Select for each download (all available protocols will be allowed)

X) Xmodem    C) Xmodem/CRC    Y) Ymodem  O) Xmodem-1K   A) ASCII

Select [S X C Y O A]:

WILDCAT!'s Hot Key Feature:
  WILDCAT! has the ability to execute single key stroke commands without
  waiting for a carriage return.  If you use this feature, you'll be able to
  process commands with one keystroke instead of two (i.e. No C/R required).
Do you wish to use HOT KEYS? [y/n] n

Color menus are available on this BBS.  Here are some color samples:
BLUE, GREEN, RED, WHITE.

Be certain you can see these colors BEFORE turning Color On!

Do you want color menus?  [y/n] n

Press [ENTER] to continue...
```

*Figure 6-62.  Entering Options on WILDCAT!*

WILDCAT! has a "hot key" feature that allows a single-letter command to be executed without pressing [ENTER]—much like RBBS-PC's turbokeys.  If you have a color monitor and your communications program can interpret ANSI graphics codes, the names of the colors will be displayed in color on your screen.  If you don't have this capability, you will see ANSI codes before and after the names of the colors.

Once you enter the user information, you see the bulletins (if any).  Figure 6-63 shows the bulletin menu.

```
You are the 14,961st caller.

        Congratulations Sam.  You have managed to reach:
                        Grotto de Blotto
              Your smiling sysop: Michael Dispater

The Following Bulletin(s) have been updated since your last call:
1, 2, 3, 4, 5

        ╡        Grotto de Blotto Bulletin Menu        ╞
        1 - Rules, rights, and responsibilities.
        2 - Current BBS list for the Greater Puget Sound
        3 - Some notes about files and downloading
        4 - Announcement - BBS Get-together in September!
        5 - Getting increased privileges on this BBS


You have been on for 4 minutes, with 16 remaining for this call.
Enter Bulletin # to Read, [L]ist Bulletin Menu, or [ENTER] to continue: 4

        ╡ Meet the people you've been talking to! ╞

        October 14 will be the next Grotto de Blotto get-together.
        Come meet all of the folks you've been nattering with on the
        BBS for months now!  The fun starts at 7:00 pm at the Seattle
        location of Mel's Amazing Pizza, and continues as long as the
        pizzas or the appetites hold out.

        RSVP on the BBS in the "Notes to the Sysop" area.
```

*Figure 6-63. Bulletin Menu on WILDCAT!*

After the logon information and bulletin menu, you will see the main menu.  A typical WILDCAT! main menu appears in Figure 6-64.

```
Sam, your quote for today is:

It is always the best policy to tell the truth, unless
of course, you are an exceptionally good liar.
                    —Jerome K. Jerome—

Checking your MAIL BOX...       Sorry, your mail box is empty.

    *    Message Section contains 225 active messages, numbered: 1 - 225.
    *    Highest Message you've read is number 0.

Press [ENTER] to continue...

MAIN MENU:
[M]............Message Menu        [F]..............Files Menu
[C]....Comments to the SYSOP       [B]............Bulletin Menu
[P]..........Page the SYSOP        [I]...Initial Welcome Screen
[Q]..........Questionnaire         [V]...........Verify a User
[Y]...........Your Settings        [S].......System Statistics
[U]............Userlog List        [L]...........Live Programs
[N]..............Newsletter        [G].......Goodbye & Log-Off
[H]..............Help Level        [?]............Command Help
[W]...........Who is Online        [T].....Talk to other nodes

You have been on for 5 minutes, with 35 remaining for this call.

MAIN MENU [M F C B P I Q V Y S U L N G H ? W T]:
```

*Figure 6-64. Main Menu on WILDCAT!*

The quote of the day, shown right before the main menu, is a popular feature of WILD-CAT! BBSes. This quote is selected at random from a large file of quotes maintained by the sysop.

## Setting Options

Enter *Y* (for Your Settings) to set your general user and display options. Figure 6-65 shows changing the page length setting from the standard 23 lines of display to 0, which will let information display continuously without stopping to ask More?

```
  Present setting for : Sam Spade

  A. Password        : *              Security level : 10
  B. Computer type   : IBM            No. of calls   : 2
  C. Phone number    : 800-626-8257   High message   : 0
  D. Birth date      : 03/21/56       User since     : 02/02/90
  E. Screen length   : 23             Last call      : 02/02/90  00:01am
  F. Color menus     : YES            Last new files : 02/02/90  00:01am
  G. Erase prompt    : YES            Downloads      : 0 Files, OK
  H. Calling from    : Seattle, WA    Uploads        : 0 Files, OK
  I. Hot keys        : NO
  J. Folders open    : A,B,C,D,E,G,I,J,K,Z
  K. Default protocol : ALL
  L. Chat status     : Available

  Setting to change [A..L], [ENTER] to Quit: E
  Number of Lines Per Page ? 0
```

*Figure 6-65. Changing Settings on WILDCAT!*

WILDCAT! has three different levels of user menus and online help.  Entering *H* lets you set the menus at one of three help levels, as shown in Figure 6-66.

```
  Current help level is set at: NOVICE

  [N]ovice  : Complete menus, full help.
  [R]egular : Option line only, little help.
  [E]xpert  : No help.

  Change to which help level [N R E], [ENTER] to Quit: r

  You have been on for 2 minutes, with 13 remaining for this call.

  MAIN MENU [M F C B P I Q S N G H ?]: h
  Current help level is set at: REGULAR

  [N]
    : Complete menus, full help.
  [R]egular : Option line only, little help.
  [E]xpert  : No help.

  Change to which help level [N R E], [ENTER] to Quit: E

  You have been on for 2 minutes, with 13 remaining for this call.

  MAIN MENU:
```

*Figure 6-66. Setting the Help Level on WILDCAT!*

Novice level gives complete menus and full help.  All the menus and displays shown in the figures are set at the Novice level.  Regular level does not display the menu, but does display single commands at the prompt.  Expert level gives the prompt only, with no commands whatsoever.  You can set the help level from the main, message, or file menus.

## Reading Messages

Entering *M* at the main menu displays WILDCAT!'s message menu, shown in Figure 6-67. From the message menu, you can read and enter messages, switch to the file menu, or log off.

```
MESSAGE MENU:

[Q]....Quit to the Main Menu      [U]..Update Folders for Mail
[R]............Read Messages      [S]............Scan Messages
[E].........Enter a Message       [D]........Delete a Message
[T].............Text Search       [C]......Check Personal Mail
[G].......Goodbye & Log-Off       [H].............Help Level
[?]............Command Help       [F]...........FILE SECTION

You have been on for 5 minutes, with 35 remaining for this call.
Folders Open: B,C,F,G,O
MESSAGE MENU [Q U R S E D T C G H ? F]: r
Starting from [1..56] [S]ince, [T]o, [F]rom, [M], [H]elp
[ENTER] to Quit:
==============================================================================

Message 1                              DATE/TIME: 04/14/90 13:27
From    : JANE FERGUSON                RECEIVED : YES
To      : ALL                          PRIVATE  : NO
Subject: First message! Yay!           THREAD   : NO
Folder : A, "General messages"

 I see that I'm the first message on the BBS!

 Actually, it doesn't count... I'm only entering the first message
 after the hard disk was reconfigured, but it is still message number one.

Msg # 1  [1..56] [R]eply, [F]orward, [K]ill, [P]ublic, [N]onStop,
[M]ove, [E]dit, [H]elp, [Q]uit,
[ENTER] to for Next Message:
```

*Figure 6-67. Reading a Message on WILDCAT!*

Most of the features on the message menu are pretty standard. You can read a specific message by entering the message number, reply to the message, read forward, kill the message, read the messages nonstop (without pausing after each message), get help, or return to the message menu. Pressing *P* makes a private message public or a public message private.

WILDCAT! keeps messages in *folders*. Folders are like message areas except that you can have more than one folder open at a time. Many BBSes using message areas will only allow you to read and enter messages in the current message area. The Move command lets you move a message from one folder to another. Opening and closing folders is done with the *U* (Update Folders for Mail) command, as shown in Figure 6-68.

```
MESSAGE MENU [Q U R S E D T C G H ? F]: u

  [A] - C Language Questions          [B] - General Discussion
  [C] - Bulletin Board Systems Issues [D] - C Language Programming
  [E] - For Sale (Computer Items)     [F] - Folkdancing
  [G] - Live Music and Performing Arts [H] - Operating Systems
  [O] - WILDCAT! Questions            [R] - Reviews of Software

Folders currently open: B,C,F,G,O

[O]pen message folders, [C]lose message folders, [ENTER] to Quit: o
Open which Folder(s)? e

  [A] - C Language Questions          [B] - General Discussion
  [C] - Bulletin Board Systems Issues [D] - C Language Programming
  [E] - For Sale (Computer Items)     [F] - Folkdancing
  [G] - Live Music and Performing Arts [H] - Operating Systems
  [O] - WILDCAT! Questions            [R] - Reviews of Software

Folders currently open: B,C,E,F,G,O
```

*Figure 6-78. Opening a Folder on WILDCAT!*

You normally read messages in message number order. If you want to read the messages in folder order, you can enter an exclamation mark (*!*) after the message number. For example, to read all the new messages after 250 in folder order, you would enter *251!* at the prompt. You would then see all the messages in Folder A with message numbers greater than or equal to 251, followed by the messages in Folder B, and so on. You can read messages in reverse by adding a minus sign (-) after a message number.

**Note:** An easy way to read all the new mail since you last logged on in folder order is to enter *S* (for Since) followed by an exclamation point (*!*) at the prompt.

Any new mail addressed to you since the last time you logged on is automatically marked for reading when you log on. You can read this quickly and easily by entering *M* to read all marked mail. You can also mark mail by entering *C* (Check for personal mail). This command marks all mail addressed to you, regardless of when it was entered.

You usually must have a folder open to read the messages in the folder. However, you can read marked mail even though a folder is currently closed.

## Entering Messages

Entering a message on WILDCAT! is much like entering messages on any other linear BBS. Figure 6-69 shows a message being entered on a WILDCAT! BBS.

```
MESSAGE MENU [Q U R S E D T C G H ? F]: u
Enter a message.
This will be message # 57
To [C/R = ALL] : Sysop
Would you like a note dropped in your box confirming
when MICHAEL DISPATER receives this letter [y/N] ? y
Send Carbon Copy # 1 to ([ENTER] if None):
Subject: Bargain on 9600-baud modems
Private [y/N]?

     Enter your text. (Enter) twice to end. (73 chars per line, 150 lines max)
     (----+----1----+----2----+----3----+----4----+----5----+----6----+----7--)

  1: Michael:
  2:
  3: I heard about a bargain on 9600 baud modems the other day that you might
  4: be interested in.
  5:
  6: The Electronics Swap Shop picked up a batch of 9600-baud modems from a
  7: computer firm that went out of business.  These are used, but they have
  8: a 30-day guarantee, so it should be possible to pick up a real bargain.
  9: I already bought one myself, and it works fine.
 10:
[A]bort, [C]ont, [D]el, [E]dit, [L]ist, [I]ns, [H]elp, [+]Subj, [S]ave: s
Save to which Folder?  "?" for list: ?
```

*Figure 6-69. Entering a Message on WILDCAT!*

There are a few relatively unusual features offered by WILDCAT!.  With the Carbon Copy option, you can send copies of a message to up to nine other people on the BBS. The Return Receipt Requested feature tells WILDCAT! to send you a message with the date and time the message was received.

The message entry commands are fairly typical, but what happens when you save the message is not.  WILDCAT! lets you save the message to any folder to which you have access.  Entering a question mark (*?*) at the `Save to which Folder?` prompt will give you a list of the message folders, like the list of folders shown  previously in Figure 6-68.  After you specify the folder to which to save the message, WILDCAT! will save the message and return you to the message menu.

## Getting Help

WILDCAT! has very good online help.  To get help on a command, enter a question mark (*?*).  Figure 6-70 shows part of the online help for the message menu.

```
- More - [C]ontinue, [S]top, [N]onStop: C
appears at the end of text entry and has its own associated help
prompts.

FILE MENU - Presents the File menu directly, where activity
such as uploading and downloading take place.

GOODBYE - Disconnects and terminates the connection.

QUIT TO THE MAIN MENU - Return to the main menu area.

READ MESSAGES - Reading messages involves selection of the
messages to be read from a sub-menu.  The choices within the READ
command are fully explained in a help file within that area.

SCAN MESSAGES - Scanning messages differs from reading in
that the text of the messages is not displayed, only the header
information. It is used in cases where a quick review of the messages is
needed.

TEXT SEARCH - Text search looks for messages which contain a
user specified text string in the message header. The header
information includes the TO:, FROM: and SUBJECT: fields.
```

*Figure 6-70. Online Help on WILDCAT!*

As you can see from Figure 6-70, WILDCAT!'s online help is fairly extensive.  Help is available for all three menus, as well as for several command prompts including the message entry command prompt.

## Downloading Files

Downloading a file on WILDCAT! is done from the file menu.  You can reach the file menu by entering *F* at the main menu or the message menu.  The file menu appears in Figure 6-71.

```
FILE MENU:

[Q]........Quit to Main Menu        [I]....Information on a file
[L].....List available Files        [D].......Download a File(s)
[U]........Upload a File(s)         [N]......New Files since [N]
[T].............Text Search         [S]....Stats on Up/Downloads
[F]......File Transfer Info.        [G]........Goodbye & Log Off
[H]............Help Level           [?]............Command Help
[M].........MESSAGE SECTION         [V].........View a ZIP file
[R].......Read a TEXT file

You have been on for 12 minutes, with 48 remaining for this call.

FILE MENU [Q I L D U N T S F G H ? M V R]:
```

*Figure 6-71. File Menu on WILDCAT!*

Files are kept in areas.  To list the files in an area, enter *L*.  After you select the file areas to examine, WILDCAT! lists the files in the selected areas.  If you don't know what the areas are, enter a question mark (*?*) to list the file areas themselves.  Once you identify the file you want to download, enter *D* at the file menu.  Figure 6-72 shows a sample download.

```
FILE MENU [Q I L D U N T S F G H ? M V R]: d

Please select a transfer protocol:

Z) Zmodem      K) Kermit        M) MegaLink     J) Jmodem      W) WXmodem
S) SeaLink     2) BiModem
Y) Ymodem      O) Xmodem-1K    C) Xmodem/CRC  X) Xmodem      A) ASCii
G) Ymodem/G    F) Xmodem-1K/G Q) Quit

Select: c

Enter the File Name to Download? newfiles.zip


Protocol Selected  : Xmodem\CRC
Number of blocks   : 34
Number of bytes    : 4,290
Est. transfer time :  0 minute(s), 22 seconds.

Ready to Send NEWFILES.ZIP. Press Control-X to abort.

File successfully transmitted.  Averaged 137 CPS
```

*Figure 6-72. Downloading a File on WILDCAT!*

The first two lines of protocols are external, and the second two lines are internal.  You can use the internal Ymodem and Ymodem/G batch protocols to download up to 50 files or upload up to 250 files in a single session.

## Uploading Files

Uploading files on WILDCAT! is similar to uploading files on other BBSes.  However, WILDCAT! offers a few extra features that are very attractive.  As Figure 6-73 shows, WILDCAT! lets you enter two lines of descriptive text rather than the standard one line on other BBSes.  More importantly, WILDCAT! lets you enter a message *immediately* after uploading a file without, having to return to the message menu.  The BBS even uses the file name as the subject of the message.

```
FILE MENU [Q I L D U N T S F G H ? M V R]: u

Choose your upload protocol:

Z) Zmodem     K) Kermit      M) MegaLink    J) Jmodem      W) WXmodem
S) SeaLink    2) BiModem
Y) Ymodem     O) Xmodem-1K   C) Xmodem/CRC  X) Xmodem      A) ASCii
G) Ymodem/G   F) Xmodem-1K/G Q) Quit

Select: C

   Please enter the filename > license.fun

Save File to Which Area ("?" for choices) ? m

Do you wish to password protect this file [y/n] ? n

Enter description for LICENSE.FUN:

You may enter up to 2 lines 40 characters long:

          1----+----10----+----20----+----30----+----40
Line 1: Fun version of a software license.  This
          1----+----10----+----20----+----30----+----40
Line 2: is for a real software product.

Ready to receive LICENSE.FUN via Xmodem\CRC...
Press Control-X to abort.
C
Upload Successful, end of file verified!
Granting upload compensation of 3 minutes.

Would you like to leave a more detailed message about this file? y
Enter a message.
This will be message # 58
To [C/R = ALL] :
Would you like a note dropped in your box confirming
when MICHAEL DISPATER receives this letter [y/N] ? y
Send Carbon Copy # 1 to ([ENTER] if None):
Subject: Re: Upload of LICENSE.FUN
Private [y/N]?

    Enter your text. (Enter) twice to end. (73 chars per line, 150 lines max)
    (----+----1----+----2----+----3----+----4----+----5----+----6----+----7--)

  1: Uploaded LICENSE.FUN.  It's an example of what software licenses could
  2: be with a little imagination.  As far as I know, it's for a real
  3: product.  It appeared at a software company I used to work at about three
  4: years ago, and I've hung on to it ever since.
  5:
[A]bort, [C]ont, [D]el, [E]dit, [L]ist, [I]ns, [H]elp, [+]Subj, [S]ave: s
Save to which Folder?  "?" for list: ? A
```

*Figure 6-73.  Uploading a File on WILDCAT!*

## Other Interesting Features

One of the nicest of WILDCAT!'s many features is the ability to stop the current display at any time by pressing the space bar. For example, if you are displaying online help or a list of files, you can return to the menu by pressing the space bar. WILDCAT! immediately stops the display and asks you to press [ENTER] to continue. Other BBSes usually use a [CTRL-K] or [CTRL-C] combination.

Another good WILDCAT! feature is *smart menus*. If a menu is displaying and you press a key for a command, the BBS immediately stops displaying the menu and performs the action requested. This feature is only available on version 2.0 and above.

## Logging Off

Logging off of WILDCAT! can be done at any of the menus by entering *G*. Figure 6-74 shows the standard logoff procedure.

```
MESSAGE MENU: [Q F R E D C G H ] > g

Are you sure you wish to log off [y/n]? y

Total time logged was 22 minutes, with 18 minutes remaining for 03/09/90.
Thank you for calling, Sam.

`ïY7b <WGû
NO CARRIER
```

*Figure 6-74. Logging Off on WILDCAT!*

## Comments

WILDCAT!'s security and flexibility make it well suited for a wide variety of specific and general BBS applications. It combines clean, simple menus with a good selection of commands and options, letting both beginning and experienced users use it effectively. WILDCAT! has good online help. It is easy to configure and customize and has extensive, easy-to-read documentation for the sysop.

## THE BREAD BOARD SYSTEM (TBBS)

The Bread Board System (TBBS) was designed and created by Philip Becker. It was originally released in 1981 for the TRS-80 Model I and III computers. In 1984, the software was switched to run on IBM computers. TBBS is designed specifically as a multi-line BBS; the current version, 2.1, can handle up to 32 users simultaneously on a single IBM AT and maintain the same performance as many single-user BBSes.

## Logging On

Because TBBS software is so easy to customize, each TBBS you log on to is likely to look different. However, although the TBBS you log onto may look different, it will still exhibit the basic characteristics shown in this section. Figure 6-75 has a typical logon procedure.

```
Welcome to Grotto de Blotto
Michael Dispater - System Operator

First Name? Sam
Last Name? Spade
Calling from (City,State)? Seattle, WA

TBBS Welcomes SAM SPADE
Calling From SEATTLE, WA
Is this correct? y
# Chars per line on screen(10-132)? 79


<A>IBM PC          <B>VT-52      <C>COMMODORE 64 <D>VT-100
<E>COMMODORE128 <F>Televid 925  <G>AMIGA         <H>H19/H89/Z19  <I>VIDTEX
<J>TRS-80 1/3    <K>ATARI        <L>ADM-3

Enter letter of your terminal, <CR> if not listed: a

Terminal Profile Set to:
No ANSI codes Allowed
IBM Graphics Allowed

Upper/Lower Case
Line Feeds Needed
0 Nulls after each <CR>
Do you wish to modify this?
```

*Figure 6-75. Sample Logon Procedure on TBBS*

If you aren't in the user log, TBBS asks you for display information. TBBS does most of the work for you by asking you what kind of computer or terminal you are using, and then using defaults for that type of computer. The terminal profile displayed at the bottom of Figure 6-75 shows the typical defaults for an IBM PC.

TBBS next asks if you want to pause at the bottom of each page and then prompts you for your password, as shown in Figure 6-76.

```
Do you wish to have a pause after each display page (Y/N)? N

Please Enter a 1-8 character Password to be used for future logons.   This
password may have any printable characters you wish.   Lower case is considered
different from upper case and imbedded blanks are legal.   REMEMBER THIS
PASSWORD.   You will need it to log on again.

Your password? gumshoe
You are authorized    30 mins this call
```

*Figure 6-76.  Completing the Logon Procedure on TBBS*

After you have finished entering the logon information, the bulletin menu is likely to appear.  Figure 6-77 shows a typical bulletin menu and one of the bulletins.

```
**** Grotto de Blotto Bulletins ****

<N>ew Callers Bulletin
<A>bout Grotto de Blotto
<G>raphic ANSI Displays
<C>ommodore Special Instructions
<U>ser Log Information Stats
<L>ist Members & Expiration Dates
<F>ind Members & Expiration Dates
<->Go to previous menu
<=>Go to main menu

Command: n

Type P to Pause, S to Stop listing

                  Welcome to Grotto de Blotto
                  =============================

Grotto de Blotto is running TBBS software with a total of 6 telephone lines
I have expanded over the years from a single line system to the current config-
uration.  I will keep adding phone lines as necessary to handle the call load.

Grotto de Blotto has an extensive message base and receives over a thousand new
messages a day.  You can also apply for FidoNet(tm) access, which will allow you
to send and receive messages around the world.

Grotto de Blotto handles special interest forums for a number of local groups,
including the Puget Sound chapter of the Society for Technical Communications,
the Radio Amateurs of Seattle, and the Greenwood Singers.  If you would like to
start a forum for your group, please leave me email and we'll talk about it.

Contributions to defray the costs of running this system are always welcome.

- Michael Dispater, Sysop
```

*Figure 6-77.  Bulletin Menu and Bulletin on TBBS*

A couple of TBBS's typical features can be seen in Figure 6-78. For one thing, menu options have the command enclosed in angle brackets, such as <N>. Another feature is the ability to return to the previous menu by pressing a key—in this example, the minus key (-). Since TBBS frequently has several levels of menus, it is easy to move back one menu instead of having to go all the way back to the main menu. Finally, when you are displaying information such as a bulletin, new messages, or a list of files, you can enter *P* to pause the display (press [ENTER] to resume the display) or *S* to stop the display entirely and return to the current menu.

Entering an equals sign (=) at the bulletin menu takes you to the main menu. Figure 6-78 shows a typical main menu on TBBS.

```
Grotto de Blotto Main Menu
************* ———
<G>oodbye-Log Off

2 Connected on Line 2
Restricted Access File Section on this line

<B>ulletins
<C>onferencing between Users
<D>oors
<E>mail
<F>iles
<I>nformation on Grotto de Blotto
<M>essage Areas
<P>olicy Statement
<R>ead Current News Bulletin
<S>ystem Utilities
<T>alk with the Sysop
<U>pload a Confidential File to Sysop
<V>oting and Surveys
<W>ho has called recently

<Z>Contributions !
<H>elp Files

Command:
```

*Figure 6-78. Sample Main Menu on TBBS*

Often, a multi-user BBS will reserve a line exclusively for certain tasks such as file transfers. The message 2 Connected on Line 2 shows which node (phone line) you have connected to, and the message following it shows what you can and can't do through that particular line.

Once again, you can see that the commands are enclosed in angle brackets. You should also remember that each TBBS is likely to have different commands and options at each menu, although general categories of functions, such as messages, files, and utilities, will all be available.

## Setting Options

To change your user options, you need to enter the command for "Utilities," "System Options," or "Reconfigure your System," depending on how the TBBS is set up. When you do so, you will see a list of available system options something like the one shown in Figure 6-79.

```
GROTTO DE BLOTTO System Options

<1>Terminal Settings
<2>Password
<3>Terminate and Re-login
<4>Time on System
<5>Prompt Level
<6>Who Else is on the System
<7>Userlog (Database Search)
<8>Chat with Sysop
<9>Statistics
<B>ack to Main Menu

Command: 1
                    Change User Profile:

A - Set ANSI codes On/Off       G - Set IBM Graphics On/Off
W - Set Terminal Width          T - Set New Terminal Type
L - Set Line Feeds On/Off       C - Set Lower Case On/Off
N - Set # of Nulls              M - Set Message Entry Prompt
U - Set File Upload Protocol    D - Set File Download Protocol
P - Set Page Pause (-more-)     S - Show Current Settings

Type Selection or ? for help, <CR> to exit: A

Can your terminal display ANSI codes? N
```

*Figure 6-79. Changing Options on TBBS*

As you can see, TBBS lets you use numbers as well as letters for commands.

## Reading Messages

TBBS allows the sysop to extensively customize the way the message areas are organized. For example, if a TBBS has a lot of message areas, the sysop can have broad categories of messages such as "IBM" and "Writing." These major categories are then subdivided into subcategories such as "Hardware," "Software," and "For Sale" under "IBM." Each subcategory is a message area. Figure 6-80 shows an example of a TBBS with subdivided message areas.

```
GROTTO DE BLOTTO Message System
Master Menu

<1>General
<2>Fun Stuff
<3>Computers
<4>Gaming

<F>iles Subsystems
<P>revious Menu
<B>ack to Main Menu

Command: 1

    GROTTO DE BLOTTO Message Base
General Subjects Menu
>/< Next/Prev Msg Section

<1>General Comments
<2>Visitor's Book
<3>Other BBS
<4>For Sale/Wanted
<5>Suggestion Box
<6>Tell It To Michael
<7>What's Next?

<P>revious Menu
<B>ack to Main Menu

Command:
```

*Figure 6-80. Selecting a Message Area on TBBS*

From here, you can select a message area. Figure 6-81 shows several new messages being read from the "What's Next?" area.

```
GROTTO DE BLOTTO Message Base
What's Next - What's in store for BBSes next?
+/- Next/Prev Msg Area

<S>can Messages
<R>ead Messages
<E>nter a Message
<P>revious Menu
<B>ack to Main Menu


Command: r

Pause after each msg(Y/N)? n

Msg#:  434 *WHAT'S NEXT?*
03/05/90 20:31:29
From: MITCH OSSIAN
  To: ALL
Subj: WHAT'S HAPPENING IS:
I think that BBSes will continue to get larger and faster as costs continue
to go down on hardware.


Msg#:  473 *WHAT'S NEXT?*
03/06/90 14:49:26
From: THAD JUENGER
  To: ALL
Subj: ON THE HORIZON
The history of BBSing suggest that we'll have BBSes that are capable of doing
a lot more things, but not a lot faster.


Msg#:  477 *WHAT'S NEXT?*
03/07/90 22:23:31
From: JANE FERGUSON
  To: THAD JUENGER  (Rcvd)
Subj: REPLY TO MSG# 473 (ON THE HORIZON)
Thad: I disagree with part of what you said.  The early BBSes didn't do a lot
compared to BBSes today because the hardware wasn't able to support it.
Having an AT or a 386 (as some BBSes do) with a fast hard drive allows the
computer to do the same task a great deal faster.
```

*Figure 6-81. Reading Messages on TBBS*

The message commands shown at the top of Figure 6-81 are fairly standard. Although the wording may change from BBS to BBS, you will always have the option to scan, read, and enter messages from this menu.

TBBS automatically capitalizes the information in the message header entered by the BBS user. (Rcvd) next to Thad Juenger's name in message 477 shows that the message has been read by the addressee. TBBS also used the subject of the Thad's message as the subject for Jane Ferguson's reply.

## Entering Messages

To enter a message on your own, enter *E*. TBBS will prompt you for the message header and then the message, as shown in Figure 6-82.

```
Who is the message to? Jane Ferguson
What is the subject? What about other computers?
Is the message private(Y/N)? n
To: JANE FERGUSON
Subj: OTHER COMPUTERS?
Is this correct(Y/N)? y

Enter text of message.
<CR> by itself ends input.

01: Jane: You are speaking only about MS-DOS computers.  What about UNIX or
02:   XENIX computers?
03:

<L>ist, <V>iew, <C>ont, <E>dit, <R>cpt, <F>ile, <S>ave, or <Q>uit? s

Saving message to disk...
```

*Figure 6-82. Entering a Message on TBBS*

The Rcpt message entry command is a "return receipt" function. When you send a message addressed to someone, TBBS sends you a message telling when the message was read.

## Getting Help

Like everything else on TBBS, the online help is likely to be a little different on each BBS. Generally, you enter *H* at the main menu to get into the help system. TBBS then provides you with choices on the types of help you can get. Figure 6-83 shows a sample set of help menus and some typical online help.

```
GROTTO DE BLOTTO Help Files

<1>Messages
<2>Files
<3>Conferencing
<4>General System Info
<P>revious Menu
<B>ack to Main Menu

Command: 4

THE LIBRARY  HELP FILES
General Help Information
<1>System Options
<P>revious Menu
<B>ack to Main Menu

Command: 1
Type P to Pause, S to Stop listing

 GROTTO DE BLOTTO HELP FILES System Options Explained


Option S from the main menu brings you to a submenu with nine different
choices.  This file explains what each choice is for.

1.    Terminal Settings
Use this option if you need to change things like your screen display width,
whether or not you need line feeds, and so on.  When you select this option
you will have an opportunity to change all your screen display options.
```

*Figure 6-83.  Online Help on TBBS*

TBBS tends to use *H* as the only way to get help.  Unlike most other linear BBSes, you can't usually get online help by entering a question mark.

## Downloading Files

The procedure for downloading a file on TBBS is slightly different from other BBSes. When you enter *D* to download a file, TBBS will  show you a directory of the available files.  If necessary, set your transfer protocol and start the download.  A typical download appears in Figure 6-84.

```
GROTTO DE BLOTTO File Subsystem
General Files Directory

<U>pload Files to Here
<D>irectory and Download
<W>ho has uploaded which files
<T>ime on System
<P>revious Menu
<B>ack to Main Menu

Command: d
Type P to Pause, S to Stop listing

DAYHIKE.ZIP      7936   A checklist for dayhiking with details. (05/12/90)
SORTEDPREFIX     3072   Local phone prefixes, sorted into 1 list (04/03/90)
AIDSINFO        19072   Info on AIDS. (01/27/90)
SORTEDPREFIX     2688   Location of local phone prefixes. (12/12/89)
HYDROPOWER      18304   this is a file on hydroelectric power! (03/09/90)
ANTARCTC.TTY    18432   Antarctica Treaty w/signatories (02/26/90)
ACROSTIC.TXT    23826   Double Acrostics (04/02/90)

<D>ownload, <P>rotocol, <E>xamine, <N>ew, <H>elp, or <L>ist
Selection or <CR> to exit: p
Select from the following transfer protocols:

1 - TYPE file to your screen
2 - ASCII with DC2/DC4 Capture
3 - ASCII only, no Control Codes
4 - XMODEM
5 - YMODEM/YMODEM-g
6 - YMODEM/YMODEM-g Batch
7 - SEAlink
8 - KERMIT
9 - SuperKERMIT (Sliding Windows)

Choose one (Q to Quit): 4

<D>ownload, <P>rotocol, <E>xamine, <N>ew, <H>elp, or <L>ist
Selection or <CR> to exit: d

File Name? sortedprefix

Protocol=XMODEM   File SORTEDPREFIX,   24 records
Est. Time:     0 mins, 30 secs at 1200 bps

Awaiting Start Signal
(Ctrl-X to abort)

<D>ownload, <P>rotocol, <E>xamine, <N>ew, <H>elp, or <L>ist
Selection or <CR> to exit:
```

*Figure 6-84. Downloading a File on TBBS*

TBBS allows files to have filenames of up to 12 characters. This is distinctly different
from almost all other BBSes, which only allow MS-DOS style filenames of up to eight

characters, and optionally, a period and up to three more characters. Macintosh users will probably appreciate the expanded filename space, as Mac file names frequently do not conform easily to the MS-DOS style.

**Note:** Many TBBSes are set up with one primary file area for uploads and downloads. Other file areas are available after your account is verified. Check with your sysop for more information.

## Uploading Files

Uploading files on TBBS is straightforward. Figure 6-85 demonstrates the procedure for uploading a file.

```
GROTTO DE BLOTTO File Subsystem
General Files Directory

<U>pload Files to Here
<D>irectory and Download
<W>ho has uploaded which files
<T>ime on System
<P>revious Menu
<B>ack to Main Menu

Command: u
Enter 1-12 char full file name: LICENSE.FUN

Description (40 chars max)
1---5---10---15---20---25---30---35---!
Fun software license for real software.

Select from the following transfer protocols:

1 - Prompted ASCII
2 - ASCII, XON after <CR> rcvd
3 - ASCII, XOFF/XON flow control
4 - XMODEM - Checksum
5 - XMODEM or YMODEM - CRC
6 - YMODEM Batch
7 - SEAlink
8 - KERMIT
9 - SuperKERMIT (Sliding Windows)
A - YMODEM-g Batch

Choose one (Q to Quit)? 5

Protocol=X/YMODEM

File open, ready to receive
(Ctrl-X to abort)
```

*Figure 6-85. Uploading a File on TBBS*

## Utilities

You saw a typical utilities menu for TBBS earlier in the "Setting Options" section. Besides setting your display options from this menu, you can terminate this session and log on again without having to dial back in, see who else is on the system, look at the user log, and so on. Figure 6-86 demonstrates how to check the user log.

```
GROTTO DE BLOTTO System Options

<1>Terminal Settings
<2>Password
<3>Terminate and Logon Again
<4>Time on System
<5>Prompt Level
<6>Who Else is on the System
<7>Userlog (Database Search)
<8>Chat with Sysop
<9>Statistics
<B>ack to Main Menu

Command: 7

GROTTO DE BLOTTO User List Selective Searching

Please enter the name of the user that you wish to search for.  Partial name
descriptions (if you are not sure of the exact name) are allowable.

Type search key or <CR> to quit: rich
Grotto de Blotto Userlog Listing Report

P to Pause, S to Stop

User Name              Log    Last On   Total Total              Total   Total
                       Number           Calls Time               D/l     U/l

RICHARD PATTERSON      217    2-04-90    83    7hrs  6mins        567kb    0kb
RICHARD MERRIS         316    4-30-90     2    0hrs 21mins         22kb    0kb
GINA PETRICH           528    4-15-90    17    4hrs 19mins        932kb    0kb
RICH WILLIAMS          633    3-05-90     2    0hrs 24mins        115kb    0kb
HEINRICH MUELLER       876    2-15-90     1    0hrs  7mins          0kb    0kb
RICHARD SMITH          888    4-16-90    50    3hrs 15mins          0kb    0kb
RICH HALLER            902    4-18-90   201   22hrs 25mins       1266kb   63kb
WILLIAM ULRICH         914    4-20-90    23    9hrs 27mins        498kb    0kb
RICHARD STECK         1070    3-07-90    10    0hrs 45mins         22kb    0kb
```

*Figure 6-86. Checking the User Log on TBBS*

Note that when you enter a partial name to search for, TBBS (and most other BBSes) will list *every* user whose name contains that partial name. Entering *rich* lists the names in Figure 6-86 including <u>Rich</u>ard Merris, Gina Pet<u>rich</u>, and Hein<u>rich</u> Mueller.

## Other Interesting Features

TBBS has very extensive facilities for chatting with other users, either privately or in public forums. When you log on to a TBBS, see if you have access to conferencing. If not, leave a message for the sysop to find out how to join.

TBBS has *smart menus*. If a menu is displaying and you press a key for a command, TBBS immediately stops displaying the menu and performs the action you requested.

Don't forget: you can pause any display by entering *P* and resume it by pressing [ENTER]. You can stop any display by entering *S*.

## Logging Off

Logging off of a TBBS is usually done by entering *G* (for Goodbye) or *Q* (for Quit). Depending on how the sysop has set up the BBS, you may be able to log off from any menu, or just from the main menu. Figure 6-87 shows a typical logoff procedure.

```
Command: g

Logged on at 20:40:14
Logged off at 20:47:50

Thank you for calling Grotto de Blotto
Please Hang Up Now
Rî6ç £HÀ6┤┐9´b
NO CARRIER
```

*Figure 6-87. Logging Off of TBBS*

## Comments

TBBS is a fast, effective, multi-line BBS with an impressive array of features and options. Because the phone and equipment costs associated with running a large multi-line BBS are high, many TBBSes are likely to require a small subscription fee for full access to all of the BBS's features.

Individual TBBSes tend to differ more in appearance and organization than any of the other types of BBS listed in this chapter. To identify a TBBS, look for standard features like the menu of computers and terminals used to set the display options and the single-letter commands in angle brackets. Once you are familiar with the basic TBBS features, you can move from one customized TBBS to another without having to relearn how to use the BBS.

## OTHER LINEAR BBSES

There are many other good linear BBSes currently available that cannot be covered in detail in this chapter because of considerations of space and time. Some of these are clones of BBSes mentioned in this chapter; others are designed to run on computers other than the IBM, and will consequently take advantage of special features of those computers. Check Appendix C, "BBS Software," for names and addresses of other manufacturers and distributors of BBS software.

There will be many new BBSes appearing over the next few years that take advantage of newer, faster, and cheaper features in computers. Watch for more multi-user BBSes. New online games are likely to take advantage of the average BBS user's hardware and monitor by using more color or graphics. And, as mass-storage devices continue to get cheaper, BBSes will have larger message and file systems.

## BECOMING AN EXPERT

There are dozens of types of linear BBSes being used today. Although there are many features that they all have in common, they each have unique features that will make a particular type of BBS easier or more difficult for you to use.

Experiment with a number of different BBSes to see which types you prefer. You should also check new BBSes to see what changes may have been made in existing BBS software—a feature you found annoying may have been changed to something you like.

When you become familiar with a number of the BBSes in your area, you may find there is a local preference for one kind of BBS over another. If you prefer using a type of BBS that is in the minority in your area, you may have to look elsewhere for other BBSes running your favorite software. Chapter 8, "Extending Your Reach," gives some ideas on how to avoid excessive long-distance charges when dialing BBSes in other parts of the country.

Finally, try out new types of BBSes whenever you can. There is always something new that can be done with BBS software.

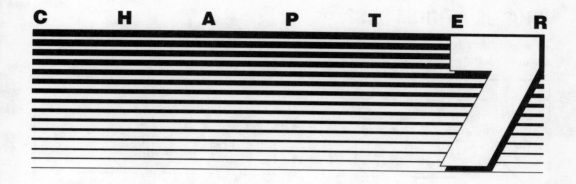

C H A P T E R

7

# ROOM BBSes

This chapter will explain how *room BBSes* work and how they are different from linear BBSes. You will also learn how to use one of the most common types of room BBS, TurboCit.

# WHAT IS A ROOM BBS?

In its simplest form, a room BBS is like a hallway with a lot of rooms coming off of it. Figure 7-1 shows a picture of a simple room BBS.

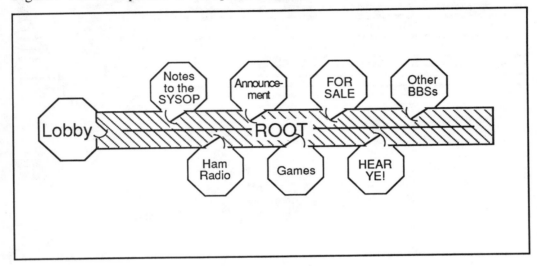

*Figure 7-1. Structure of a Simple Room BBS*

Imagine that you are standing in the room named "Lobby." As you look through the door of the Lobby into the hall, you can see that there are a number of doors leading to other rooms off of the hallway. Each door has a sign that identifies the room such as "Notes to the Sysop" or "Announcements."

## Understanding Rooms

The Lobby is generally the entry point for most room BBSes. Suppose that you want to go see what's happening in "Notes to the Sysop." You can leave the Lobby, walk down the hall, enter "Notes to the Sysop," and find the area for chatting with the sysop. You can continue from room to room, sending and receiving messages as part of discussions on each topic, according to the name of the room.

Rooms are not just separate message areas. The first distinction between a room BBS and a linear BBS is that *you can perform all of the BBS functions in a single room.* In other words, you can send and receive messages, upload and download files, and even change your display options and your password, all from within a room—they are almost like one-topic BBSes all by themselves.

Commands on a room BBS are *global;* you can enter a command at any prompt in the BBS and it will always do the same thing. For example, entering *G* on a linear BBS may mean "Goodbye," "Games files," or "Go back to main menu," depending at which prompt you enter *G*. On a room BBS, you can enter *G* at any prompt and it will always mean the same thing: "Go to the next room with new messages." This ability to use commands globally is the other distinction between room and linear BBSes.

## Hallways and Window Rooms

Many room BBSes have more than one hallway and several different *window rooms*, rooms connecting to one or more hallways. Imagine that you're standing in the Lobby again. Now, instead of just seeing one door leading out to a single hallway, you see many doors, each of which leads to a different hallway. You can only have one of these doors open at a time. When you open one door, you can walk down the hallway beyond that door and enter any of the rooms down the hallway. When you return to the Lobby, you can close the door to the hallway you just explored and open the door to the next hallway. You are then looking at an entirely new hallway with a different set of rooms.

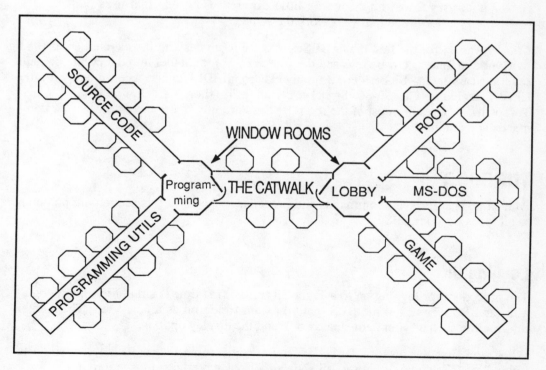

*Figure 7-2. Room BBS with Multiple Hallways*

The term "door" is already used to describe a program that you can run as part of the BBS. In order to avoid confusion with the existing term, the developers of most room BBSes chose instead to call the entry points to hallways *windows*. Unfortunately, although this term made sense to the developers, it is difficult for most people to think of a window as a logical place from which to enter and exit a hallway, unless you are a cat burglar. You should therefore remember that the entry points to a hallway are called windows, but that you can think of them acting like doors. A room that connects to more than one hallway is called a *window room*.

The advantages to these structures is that information can be grouped in different areas of the BBS. Although the structure shown in Figure 7-2 is fairly typical of room BBSes, room BBSes may have several different window rooms, each of which has several hallways. Access to window rooms can also be restricted, allowing only special groups of BBS users to enter the hallways connected to that room. For example, if BBS users aren't able to enter the "Programming" room, they won't be able to get at the rooms along the Source Code and Programming Utils hallways.

**Note:**   Some room BBSes call hallways *floors*. Although a drawing of a BBS that uses floors might look a little different from one that uses hallways, floors and hallways work the same.

*Citadel* was one of the first major BBSes to use a room design. It was released in 1981 by Cynbe ru Taren. Cynbe released the source code for Citadel into the public domain several years later. Since then, a number of room BBSes have been modelled after Citadel, including Citadel-86, Stonehenge, DragCit (short for "Dragon Citadel"), and TurboCit. As a result, most of the room BBSes currently in use have very similar commands and features.

# TURBOCIT

Almost all the TurboCit commands and procedures shown in this section are common to all types of room BBS.

## Logging On

The procedure for logging on to a TurboCit for the first time is similar to logging on to a linear BBS. First, tell the BBS that you want to log on as a new user. Then, enter information such as your name, password, and the display options.

When you first log on to a TurboCit, you are in a room that is usually called "The Lobby" or "Welcome." Figure 7-3 shows the first screen of information you will see after connecting with a TurboCit BBS.

```
Welcome to Grotto de Blotto, Seattle
Running TurboCit ver 4.00.03 (TurboC)
Alpha Test Site

Friday March 23, 1990, @ 11:03:09 PM (PST)
  40 messages

Lobby >>
```

*Figure 7-3. Initial Logon Screen on TurboCit*

At the Lobby >> prompt, you enter *L* (for Login) to tell the BBS you want to log on.

**Note:**  Single-letter commands on room BBSes are automatically processed as soon as you type them, just like turbokeys on RBBS-PC.  You don't have to press [ENTER] after a single-letter command.

When you enter a command on a TurboCit (and almost all other room BBSes), the BBS replaces each letter of the command with the appropriate word.  For example, when you type *L*, the BBS displays the full command name—in this case, Login.

At the logon prompts, enter your initials and password.  Room BBSes usually use both your initials and a password to double-check your identity, providing an added level of security.  Figure 7-4 shows you this procedure.

```
Lobby >> Login

Enter your initials: 012

Enter password: 0123456

No record: Request access? (Y/N) [Y]: Yes

<J>ump <N>ext <P>ause <S>top

Greetings.

Welcome to Grotto de Blotto.  As a new user, you will have limited access to some
areas of the BBS until I can verify you.  Many thanks for your patience.

Your sysop,

Michael Dispater
```

*Figure 7-4. Entering Initials and Password on TurboCit*

The BBS does not display the characters when you enter your initials and password, but instead shows numbers or random characters. This prevents someone from reading over your shoulder and discovering your logon information.

Press *P* to pause the display and *S* to stop the display and return to the menu.

Next, enter your username, as shown in Figure 7-5.

```
<J>ump <N>ext <P>ause <S>top

Enter the name or pseudonym you would like.

Enter full name: Sam Spade

 nm: Sam Spade
 in: ss
 pw: gumshoe

OK? (Y/N/A)[A]: Yes
```

*Figure 7-5. Entering Your Username on TurboCit*

Pressing *A* will abort the process and return you to the `Enter your initials?` prompt. Type *Y* and press [ENTER] to accept the information as it is.

TurboCit automatically sets your display options when you first log on. You can change them at any time. Figure 7-6 shows the options you can change.

```
Screen <W>idth....... 79
Lines per <S>creen... 23
<U>ppercase only..... Off
<L>inefeeds.......... On
<T>abs............... On
<N>ulls.............. Off
Terminal <E>mulation. Off

<H>elpful Hints...... On
l<I>st in userlog.... Yes
Last <O>ld on New.... Off
<R>oom descriptions.. On
<A>uto-next hall..... Off

<Q> to save and quit.

Is this OK? (Y/N)[Y]: Yes
```

*Figure 7-6. Setting Display Options on TurboCit*

Most of the display options are similar to those in linear BBSes.  When you first log on, it's probably safest to accept the default settings by pressing [ENTER] at the prompt.  You can change the display options later as you get more experienced with the BBS.

The last part of the registration process is entering your real name and phone number, as shown in Figure 7-7.

```
Enter your REAL name: Sam Spade

Enter your phone number [(xxx)xxx-xxxx]: (800)626-8257

 <J>ump <N>ext <P>ause <S>top

 Messages are formatted to each caller's screen width.  To defeat this
 formatting, start each line with a space.
 You have up to 1024 characters.
 Enter message (end with empty line).
    03/23/90 11:05:49 From Sam Spade To Sysop
Hi.  I'd like to request access, please.  Phone me any time.

 Entry cmd: Save buffer
```

*Figure 7-7.  Entering Verification Information*

Save the message by pressing *S,* just like any other BBS.  The BBS may log you out at this point, or you may be given limited access privileges until the sysop verifies your account.

TurboCits (and room BBSes in general) do not have a menu of bulletins that appears after you log in.  You generally see the unread messages in the Lobby, followed by a display of the rooms with unread messages, the rooms that do not have unread messages, and whether or not you have mail.  Figure 7-8 shows an example of this.

```
 Rooms with unread messages:
Lobby>>              For Sale>           Upload]:
Statistics>
 No unseen msgs in:
Letters>             NEW ITEMS!]         Notes to the Sysop>
Protocols]:
 : => group only room
 ] => directory room
Lobby>>
```

*Figure 7-8.  Initial Room Display on TurboCit*

This display shows that the rooms "Lobby," "For Sale," "Upload," and "Statistics" all have messages that you haven't yet read, and that the rooms "Letters," "NEW ITEMS!," "Notes to the Sysop," and "Protocols" do not have unread messages.

Room names can be one or more words and can contain punctuation and numbers. Each room name is also followed by one or more characters that tell you what the room can be used for.

- *A single angle bracket (>).*
  Rooms followed by a single angle bracket (>)—such as `Statistics>`—are rooms that are used exclusively for messages. You can think of these rooms as having exactly the same purpose as message areas on a linear BBS.

- *Two angle brackets (>>).*
  Rooms followed by a double angle bracket (>>)—such as `Lobby>>`—connect to more than one hallway.

- *A bracket.*
  Rooms followed by a bracket—such as `NEW ITEMS!]` and `Uploads]`—contain files for uploading and downloading. You can read and enter messages and upload and download files in these rooms.

- *A colon.*
  Rooms followed by a colon—such as `Protocols:]`—are *group only* rooms, with limited access. On a room BBS, the sysop can assign BBS users to membership in one or more *groups*. These groups have names like "General Access," "Downloads," "Adults," and so on. The sysop can set up rooms so that only members of certain groups can enter them.

- *More than one character.*
  A room name can be followed by more than one character. For example, `Protocols]:` is followed by both a bracket and a colon. These symbols mean that not only can you read and enter messages as in any other room, you can also upload and download files (denoted by the bracket), and that access to this room may be restricted (denoted by the colon).

Entire hallways can also be restricted to members of a certain group. For example, the sysop might set aside a hallway for the exclusive use of a group of BBS users called "Seniors."

**Note:** If you are not allowed access to a room, you won't be able to see it in the list of rooms. If you are not allowed access to a hallway, you won't be able to list that hallway.

## Reading Messages

The Lobby>> prompt at the bottom of Figure 7-8 shows you that you are currently in the Lobby. The display also shows that the Lobby has unread messages. Reading unread messages in a room is extremely simple: just press *N* (for Read New); you don't even have to press [ENTER]. The BBS starts displaying the new messages, as shown in Figure 7-9.

```
Lobby>> Read New

<J>ump <N>ext <P>ause <S>top
    90Mar23 From Edgar Katz
Aha!  I made it on the first call!  Heh-heh.  Normally it takes me
half an hour of redialing to get in.

    90Mar23 From Jane Ferguson
Jeepers!  I guess we should strike a medallion or something, eh?  :)

    90Mar23 From John Johnson
Hi guys... how's the gang?

Lobby>>
```

*Figure 7-9. Reading New Messages on TurboCit*

The message header shows the date and, on some BBSes, the time the message was entered, as well as the BBS user who entered it. Unlike linear BBSes, however, room BBSes do not have an entry for the message subject.

Room BBSes have two very handy features for reading messages. If you enter *N* (for Next) in the middle of a message, the BBS will skip the rest of that message and start displaying the next message. Entering *J* (for Jump) skips to the next paragraph *within* a message.

You can read messages from the first message in the room by pressing *F* (for Read Forward) or from the newest message back by pressing *R* (for Read Reverse). You can even read the "old" messages—the messages you have already read—by pressing *O*.

## Entering Messages

Entering a message in a room is similar to entering a message in a message area on a linear BBS. First, press *E* ( for Enter Message) at the room prompt. The BBS automatically provides the message header. You can then enter your message. Press [ENTER] only when you want to start a new paragraph; the BBS will automatically wrap your words to the next line for you. Figure 7-10 shows the entry of a typical message.

```
<J>ump <N>ext <P>ause <S>top
Messages are formatted to each caller's screen width.  If you wish to defeat
this formatting, start each line with a space.
 You have up to 1024 characters.
 Enter message (end with empty line).
    Friday 90Mar23 From Sam Spade
Hello.  I am new to room BBSes and I'm still looking around.  Is there anyone
out there who has recently made the transition from linear to room BBSes?

  Entry cmd:
```

*Figure 7-10. Entering a Message on TurboCit*

At the `Entry cmd:` prompt, you can save the message by pressing *S*. There are a number of typical message entry commands. Pressing a question mark (*?*) at the `Entry cmd:` prompt displays the command list shown in Figure 7-11.

```
  A-bort
  C-ontinue
  F-ind + Replace
  P-rint formatted
  R-eplace text
  S-ave message
  W-ord count
  ?- this list
```

*Figure 7-11. Message Entry Commands on TurboCit*

Use the Print Formatted command to see what the message will look like to other BBS users. TurboCit does not format the message as you enter the text, as some linear BBSes do.

One command you probably haven't seen before is *W* for Word Count. Press *W* at the `Entry cmd:` prompt to tell you how many lines, words, and characters are in your message.

Entering and replacing message text on a TurboCit is the same as on a linear BBS. Be sure not to confuse the absence of line numbers on the screen with a full-screen message editor such as the one in OPUS. Press *S* to save your message and return to the room prompt.

# Using Dot Commands

The most common commands in room BBSes are single-character commands like those on a linear BBS, such as *G, N, P,* and *S*. However, there aren't enough single letters for all the commands. Most linear BBSes solve this by using menus, so the same command letter can mean several different things. Some linear BBSes such as PCBoard use single-letter commands where possible and then use several characters or a whole word when they run out.

Room BBSes solve this by putting a period, or "dot," at the start of the command. These commands are known as *dot commands*. The dot at the front of the commands tells the BBS not to act on the command as soon as you press the key, but rather to wait until you press [ENTER]. This lets you type the command and add information such as a room name.

The commands you will use on any room BBS most of the time are single-letter commands. You use dot commands most frequently when working with files, when sending mail to another person, and when going to a specific room.

# Changing Rooms

Changing rooms in a room BBS requires two simple commands: the Known Rooms command and the Goto command.

### Listing the Rooms in a Hallway

Press *K* for Known Rooms at the prompt to list the rooms in the current hallway. The BBS will list all the known rooms in the hallway and show the status of each room for unread messages. Figure 7-12 shows the Known Rooms command.

```
Lobby>> Known Rooms

 Rooms with unread messages:
Lobby>>             For Sale>            Upload]:
Statistics>
 No unseen msgs in:
Letters>            NEW ITEMS!]          Notes to the Sysop>
Protocols]:
 : => group only room
 ] => directory room
Lobby>>
```

*Figure 7-12. Using the Known Room Command*

## *Going to a Room with Unread Messages*

You can change from one room to another in several ways.  The most common is to press *G* for Goto.  This moves you to the next room with unread messages, as shown in Figure 7-13.

```
Lobby>> Goto For Sale
  32 total
  32 messages
  32 new
For Sale>
```

*Figure 7-13.  Changing Rooms on TurboCit*

When you press *G,* TurboCit displays `Goto` followed by the name of the next room with unread messages, such as "For Sale."  It also displays the number of messages in the room and how many are new.  You can then read the messages in For Sale by pressing *N.*

Each time you press *G* at the room prompt, you will go to the next room with unread messages in the order the room appeared in the room list (shown earlier in Figure 7-11).  If there are no more rooms with unread messages, pressing *G* will take you to the window room.  Figure 7-14 demonstrates this.

```
For Sale> Known Rooms

 Rooms with unread messages:
For Sale>              Upload]:                Statistics>
 No unseen msgs in:
Lobby>>                Letters>                NEW ITEMS!]
Notes to the Sysop>    Protocols]:
 : => group only room
 ] => directory room
For Sale>  Goto Upload
 20 total
 19 messages
 19 new
Upload]: Goto Statistics
 3 total
 3 messages
 3 new
Statistics> Goto Lobby
 15 total
 13 messages
Lobby>> Known Rooms

 Rooms with unread messages:

 No unseen msgs in:
Lobby>>                For Sale>                Letters>
Upload]:               NEW ITEMS!]:            Notes to the Sysop>
Protocols]:            Statistics>
 : => group only room
 ] => directory room
Lobby>>
```

*Figure 7-14. Using the Goto Command on TurboCit*

You can also press a plus sign (+) to go from room to room, whether they have unread messages or not.

**Warning:** If you are using a Hayes or Hayes-compatible modem, pressing the plus sign (+) three times in a row without any intervening characters will hang up your modem. For this reason, it is probably safer to press the minus key (-), which moves you through the rooms in reverse order.

Figure 7-14 also demonstrates that when you leave one room and go to another, the BBS assumes that you have read the messages in the previous room. It then removes the room from the list of rooms with unread messages. If you go back to that room, pressing *N* (for Read New) won't display anything. You will instead have to read the messages by pressing *F* (for Read Forward) or *R* (for Read Reverse).

### *Going to a Specific Room*

The most common way to go to a specific room is to type *.G* followed by the room name. An example of this appears in Figure 7-15.

```
Lobby>> .Goto notes
 17 total
 17 messages
Notes to the Sysop>
```

*Figure 7-15. Using the .Goto Command on TurboCit*

TurboCit displays .Goto as soon as you type *.G* You don't have to put the complete room name after the command, just enough to uniquely identify the room. For example, you could go to the Upload room by entering *.GU*. The Upload room is the only room on this hall that starts with the letter U.

## Changing Hallways

To change to another hallway, go to a window room (one that is connected to more than one hallway) such as the Lobby. Then press the greater than key (>). This is the Next Hallway command. The BBS will switch you to the next hallway, as shown in Figure 7-16.

```
Lobby>> Next Hall: IBM/MS-DOS
Lobby>> Known Rooms

 Rooms with unread messages along IBM/MS-DOS
IBM Misc]            IBM Communications]    IBM Utilities]
 No unseen msgs in:
Lobby>>              IBM Graphics]
 ] => directory room
Lobby>>
```

*Figure 7-16. Switching Hallways on TurboCit*

When you press the greater than key, the BBS displays the words Next Hall: followed by the name of the hall. The example in Figure 7-16 shows you switching to the IBM/MS-DOS hallway. As you can see, the rooms off this hallway are different from the rooms in the previous hallway.

Each time you press the greater than key, you switch to the next hallway, until you finally come back to the hallway you started from. (The starting hallway is frequently named Root or General.) You can also switch to the previous hallway by pressing the less than key (<).

**Note:** You can also press the bracket keys ] and [ for the Next Hallway and Previous Hallway commands.

A room BBS can have many different hallways. Figure 7-17 shows the hallways on a typical room BBS.

```
Lobby>> Next Hall: C Programming
Lobby>> Next Hall: General Programming
Lobby>> Next Hall: Citadel BBS Stuff
Lobby>> Next Hall: Cooking
Lobby>> Next Hall: Writers and Freelancers
Lobby>> Next Hall: Conventions
Lobby>> Next Hall: Games
Lobby>> Next Hall: Root
```

*Figure 7-17. Hallways on a Room BBS*

## Sending Mail

Sending mail is simpler on TurboCit and other room BBSes than it is on linear BBSes. To send mail, you use a dot command: *.EE* (for Enter Exclusive message). The procedure for entering mail appears in Figure 7-18.

```
Letters> .Enter Exclusive message

Enter recipient: Jane Ferguson

 <J>ump <N>ext <P>ause <S>top

 Messages are formatted to each caller's screen width.  To defeat this
formatting, start each line with a space.
 You have up to 8192 characters.
 Enter message (end with empty line).
    03/23/90 11:36:21 From Sam Spade to Jane Ferguson
Jane: Give me a call at the office before next Tuesday.  I'd like to ask
you some questions about BBSing that would take too long to type.
Maybe we could meet for lunch somewhere?


 Entry cmd: Save buffer

Letters>
```

*Figure 7-18. Sending Mail on TurboCit*

The BBS prompts you for the recipient's name. You must enter the name *exactly* as it appears in the userlog, or the BBS won't be able to find the person. If you don't know precisely how someone has logged on, look at the userlog by entering the dot command *.RU* (for Read Userlog). The BBS then uses that information as part of the message header. Later, when Jane Ferguson logs on, she'll see something like Figure 7-19.

```
  Rooms with unread messages:
Lobby>>                 For Sale>              Letters>
Notes to the Sysop>
 You have private mail in:
Letters>
 No unseen msgs in:
Upload]:            NEW ITEMS!]:           Protocols]:
Statistics>
 : => group only room
 ] => directory room
Lobby>>
```

*Figure 7-19. Room List with Mail Waiting on TurboCit*

The known room list now shows mail waiting for Jane Ferguson in the Letters room. When she goes to the room and reads the new messages, she'll see the message from Sam Spade. At the end, Jane will be asked if she wants to reply to the message. If so, TurboCit automatically prepares to send mail to Sam Spade. Jane can now enter a message, as shown in Figure 7-20.

```
    03/23/90 11:36:21 From Sam Spade to Jane Ferguson
Jane: Give me a call at the office on Tuesday.  I'd like to ask you some
questions about BBSing that would take too long to type up.  Maybe we
could meet for lunch somewhere?


Respond? (Y/N)[Y]: Yes

 <J>ump <N>ext <P>ause <S>top

 Messages are formatted to each caller's screen width.  To defeat this
formatting, start each line with a space.
 You have up to 8192 characters.
 Enter message (end with empty line).
    03/23/90 18:14:54 From Jane Ferguson to Sam Spade
I'll be glad to.  George gave me your new number.  Talk to you soon.


 Entry cmd: Save buffer

Letters>
```

*Figure 7-20. Sending a Reply on TurboCit*

When Sam logs on again, he will see [reply] after the message header on his original message to Jane. This shows that Jane has read Sam's message. Jane will also be able to tell when Sam has read her reply: [received] appears after the message header of Jane's reply. This is very similar to the way many linear BBSes show that messages have been read and replied to.

**Note:** Mail on a TurboCit is always private. Only the sender, the recipient, and the sysop can read mail. General messages entered with the message entry command, *E,* are always public.

## Setting Options

To change an option, enter the dot command *.EC* (for Enter Configuration) at a room prompt. The BBS will display a list of options (shown in Figure 7-21) for you to change.

```
Lobby>> .Enter Configuration

Screen <W>idth....... 79
Lines per <S>creen... 23
<U>ppercase only..... Off
<L>inefeeds.......... On
<T>abs............... On
<N>ulls.............. Off
Terminal <E>mulation. Off

<H>elpful Hints...... On
1<I>st in userlog.... Yes
Last <O>ld on New.... Off
<R>oom descriptions.. On
<A>uto-next hall..... Off

<Q> to save and quit.

Change: Tabs Off

Change: Save changes
```

*Figure 7-21. Changing Options*

When you enter the single letter for a specific option, TurboCit fills in the appropriate text for you. In Figure 7-21, the tabs had been set to "on"—use tab characters instead of spaces. Pressing *T* at the  Change:  prompt changes tabs to "off"—use spaces instead of tabs. Pressing *Q* at the prompt saves the changes and returns you to the room prompt.

## Getting Help

TurboCit has several levels of help. The first level of help is a list of common commands. You can see this list by pressing a question mark (?) or a slash (/) at any room prompt, as demonstrated in Figure 7-22.

```
Lobby>> ?
 <J>ump <N>ext <P>ause <S>top

        Single-Key Commands:
 B-ypass           C-hat
 D-ownload         E-nter message
 F-orward          G-oto
 H-elp!            I-ntro
 J-ump Back        K-nown rooms
 L-ogin            N-ew
 O-ld              R-everse
 T-erminate        U-pload
 X-clude Room
 ~ - Ansi On/Off   ? or / - this menu
 + - next room     - - prev. room
 > - next hall     < - previous hall
        Multi-Key Commands:
 .B-ypass          .E-nter
 .G-oto            .H-elp
 .K-nown           .L-ogin
 .R-ead            .T-erminate
 .Xpert (on/off)
 .(D, E, H, K, R, T, U) ? for extended help
```

*Figure 7-22. List of Commands on TurboCit*

You can also get general help on commands by pressing *H* at the room prompt. Figure 7-23 shows the general help on commands.

```
   HELP

   Commands work two ways:  single-key and multiple-key.  To enter a
single-key command, simply press that key.  To enter multiple-key commands,
press the '.' key, the key for that command, and any parameters.

   Most single-key commands are default forms of multiple-key commands. For
example, typing G will goto the next room with new messages, while
.G(roomname) will go to the room (roomname).

   Typical commands commonly used include:

   L — Will login to the system.
   N — Will read new messages in a room.
   E — Will let you enter a message.
   G — Will go to the next room with unread messages.
   T — Will log you off and hangup.

 .EE — Will let you enter a private message.
 .ER — Will let you create a new room.
 .EC — Will let you change your terminal configuration.
 .TS — Will log you off without hanging up, someone with you can
        login without having to call back.

   To get a list of options for each command, you can use the following
conventions:

 .E? — Lists options for the Enter command.
 .H? — Lists options for the Help command.
 .K? — Lists options for the Known command.
 .R? — Lists options for the Read command.
 .T? — Lists options for the Terminate command.

   For more information, type .H? to get a list of additional help topics.
```

*Figure 7-23. General Help on Commands on TurboCit*

The help shown in Figure 7-23 lists some of the common single-letter and dot commands. At the bottom, you can see that you can get specific help on the options you can use with each command. Figure 7-24 shows an option list for the Read command.

```
Lobby>> .Read ?
 <J>ump <N>ext <P>ause <S>top

 .RB-y User
 .RC-onfiguration
 .RD-irectory
 .RE-xclusive
 .RF-orward
 .RH-allways
 .RI-nfo file
 .RL-imited
 .RN-ew
 .RO-ld
 .RP-ublic
 .RR-everse
 .RS-tatus
 .RT-extfile
 .RU-serlog
 .RV-erbose
 .RZ-IP-file
 .R?- this list

Lobby>>
```

*Figure 7-24.  Help on the Read Options on TurboCit*

You can enter any of the dot commands shown in the list. Unfortunately, this list doesn't explain much; you just see a lot of commands, some of which may be unfamiliar. To get extended help, enter *.H* followed by the subject you want more help on. Figure 7-26 shows the list of extended help topics usually available on room BBSes.

```
Subject             What It Tells You
========================================================================
BYPASS              information on changing rooms and reading messages
DOWNLOAD            how to read, upload, and download files
EDIT                how to edit messages
ENTOPT              a detailed description of display options
GOTO                how to go to the next room and next hallway
GROUP               how to enter a message for a specific group of users
HALLWAY             how to change from one hallway to another
HELP                how to use the help command effectively
INTRO               general system information
KNOWN               using the Known Room, Known Hallway, Known Group, and
                       Known Windows commands
LOGIN               how to log in and change your configuration
MAINOPT             what options you can perform from a room prompt
MESSAGE             how to enter and read messages
NODES               how to send mail to a user on another BBS
OPTIONS             a list of help topics available on the system
POLICY              the BBS policy statement
READOPT             how to read messages, file directories, and so on
ROOM                general information about rooms
SPECIAL             how to use miscellaneous special features
USERCFG             how to change your display options and default settings
```

*Figure 7-25. Extended Help Topics on room BBSes*

You can see the "INTRO" topic by entering *I* (for Introduction) at the room prompt. This file usually contains statements about the BBS and its policies. In addition to the topics shown in Figure 7-25, many sysops will add help files of their own. You can get a list of topics that TurboCit offers extended help on by entering *.H?*.

## Downloading Files

To download a file on a room BBS, you must first go to a directory room that contains files. Directory rooms have a bracket after the room name. A directory room is like a separate file area on a linear BBS. From the directory room prompt, you can list the files in the room with the *.RD* (for Read Directory) or the *.RVD* (for Read Verbose Directory) command. Figure 7-26 shows what both of these commands would look like for a typical directory room.

```
Graphics & Pictures]  .Read Directory

picnic.zip   pih.exe      skater.zip   wristwch.zip  sandy.zip
Graphics & Pictures]  .Read Verbose Directory

 Filename      Date      Size    D/L Time
 picnic.zip    90Jan26   40048     2.78
 pih.exe       90Mar05   15360     1.07
 skater.zip    90Feb22   26573     1.85
 wristwch.zip  90Feb18   42750     2.97
 sandy.zip     90Mar21  110310     7.66
        5 Files     286720 bytes free
Graphics & Pictures]
```

*Figure 7-26. List of Files in a Directory Room*

Like a file area on a linear BBS, a single directory room can contain dozens of files. After you choose the file you want to download, you enter the appropriate download command at the room prompt, specify the file to download, and begin. Figure 7-27 lists the download commands and demonstrates downloading a file.

```
Graphics & Pictures]  .Download ?

 .D C>RC-Xmodem
 .D X>modem
 .D R>LE-Zmodem
 .D Y>-Batch
 .D Z>modem
 .D 1>K-Xmodem
 .D 4>K-Zmodem
 .D ? - this list

Graphics & Pictures]  .Download 1K-Xmodem

Enter filename: skater.zip

File Size: 26 blocks, 26573 bytes
Transfer Time: 2 minutes

 <J>ump <N>ext <P>ause <S>top

   You must have the specified protocol to use this function. If you are
using Zmodem or Batch-Ymodem you may use wild cards ('*?') and specify
multiple files.

Ready for file transfer? (Y/N)[N]: Yes

Graphics & Pictures]
```

*Figure 7-27. Downloading a File on TurboCit*

As with a linear BBS, you must start receiving the file with your communications program immediately after telling the BBS to start the file transfer. When the transfer is done, TurboCit returns you to the room prompt.

## Uploading Files

You can upload a file to almost any directory room. Go to the directory room appropriate to the file you want to upload and enter the appropriate upload command. Figure 7-28 shows the upload commands and a sample file being uploaded.

```
Graphics & Pictures] .Upload ?

 .U C>RC-Xmodem
 .U X>modem
 .U R>LE-Zmodem
 .U Y>-Batch
 .U Z>modem
 .U 1>K-Xmodem
 .U 4>K-Zmodem
 .U ? — this list

Graphics & Pictures] .Upload 1K-Xmodem

Enter filename: beach.gif

Enter comments: GIF picture file.

 <J>ump <N>ext <P>ause <S>top

 You must have the specified protocol to use this function.

Ready for file transfer? (Y/N)[N]: Yes

Graphics & Pictures]
```

*Figure 7-28. Uploading a File*

## Other Interesting Features

Room BBSes have many interesting capabilities and features. Many room BBSes allow users to create their own rooms. For example, a BBS user might create an Education room to start a discussion about local school board policies.

Rooms can be "hidden"—that is, they will not appear on the list of known rooms. There are two ways to get to a hidden room. The first is to be a member of a group that has access to the room (in which case the room is not hidden from you). The second is to enter *.G* followed by the *complete* room name. For example, if a hidden room were called "Sysops Only," you could go to it by entering *.G sysops only* (capitalization is not important), but just entering *.G sys* is not sufficient. Once you have "found" a hidden room, you will be able to see it in the known room list.

**Note:** There is a game on room BBSes called the "Hidden Room Game." The sysop creates a room called "Starting Place" and a hidden room with the name of an object of some kind in a separate hallway. The sysop then posts clues about the name of the hidden room in Starting Place. The BBS users try to guess the exact name of the hidden room from the clues. The first person to correctly guess the hidden room's name gets to create the next hidden room, posting the clues in the hidden room that was just discovered. An otherwise empty-looking hallway can actually contain a dozen or more hidden rooms in sequence, each packed with clues about the identity of the next one.

One very convenient command is the *.EO* (Enter Old Message) command. If you are in the middle of entering a message and you realize that you are entering the message in the wrong room, you can abort the message, change rooms, and then enter *.EO*. TurboCit (and most other room BBSes) will then ask if you want to use the aborted message. When you reply *Y,* the BBS will display the message header and the text as it was before you aborted it. You can then continue entering text and save the message.

You can scan for messages to or from a specific user with the *.RB* (Read By-User) command. When you enter this command, the BBS asks for the user name to look for. You can enter a complete name, or part of a name using wildcards. The BBS will then display all the messages to or from any user with a matching username.

Some alternative commands have been added to TurboCit specifically for disabled users. For example, you can press the bracket keys [ or ] instead of the greater or less than signs (< and >) to change to the previous or next hallway. Pressing a slash (/) gives help just like pressing a question mark (?). These alternative commands are all unshifted keys, which are much easier for users who must using typing sticks.

## Logging Off

To log off of a room BBS, press *T* at any prompt. Figure 7-29 shows the typical log off procedure.

```
Lobby>> Terminate Quit-also

Confirm? (Y/N)[N]: Yes
 Sam Spade logged out
 .⅂d|⅂-↔iˆ
NO CARRIER
```

*Figure 7-29. Logging Off a Room BBS*

# OTHER ROOM BBSES

TurboCit is only one of a number of room BBSes. MiniBin, Stonhenge, STadel, and 128BBS are all room BBSes running on a variety of computers. Most room BBSes are closer in their design than most linear BBSes. Of the commands on one room BBS, 80 to 90 percent will work on any other room BBS. Information on ordering TurboCit appears in Appendix C "BBS Software."

# BECOMING AN EXPERT

Room BBSes have many advantages over linear BBSes. Room BBSes are fast and easy to use for sending and receiving messages; you can read all the messages on an entire room BBS without using more than three commands. Room BBSes are also extremely flexible. Hidden rooms and hallways can be used as entertainment or a security feature. BBS users can create their own rooms as needed.

One disadvantage to room BBSes is that there are currently no multi-user room BBSes. As a result, room BBSes have no features for chatting (other than with the sysop). Games that allow several players at the same time are also not available on room BBSes. Another disadvantage is that some BBS users prefer having a list of commands in a menu on the screen. Although room BBSes will display a list of commands when you press a question mark (*?*), there is no menu for novice users comparable to those on a linear BBS.

The biggest disadvantage to room BBSes may well be that there aren't many of them. Only about 10% of the BBSes you are likely to encounter are room BBSes. Part of this may be due to the lack of BBS software that uses a room structure; it is easier to write a good linear BBS than a good room BBS. Another factor may be the way BBS users perceive the differences between the two types of BBS—many users of linear BBSes simply don't like the way room BBSes look.

Despite their rarity in the BBS world, room BBSes are a fascinating way to exchange information. They can make a very pleasant counterpoint to linear BBSes.

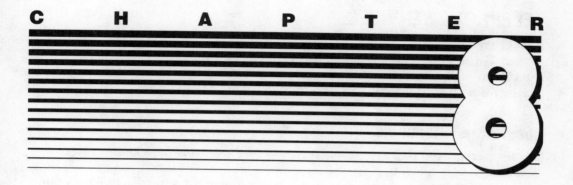

# EXTENDING
# YOUR REACH

This chapter discusses long-distance phone services, networks, and amateur radio BBSes. It will help you to extend your reach to other parts of the country and even other parts of the world.

Use this chapter to learn how to access BBSes outside of your local calling area with long-distance services, while keeping telephone charges down. It also shows you how to exchange mail and files with other BBSes through international networks and how to communicate through shortwave BBSes.

# TELEPHONE SERVICES

As you explore BBSes, you are likely to hear about a BBS in another part of the country and will be interested in trying it. However, logging on to BBSes around the country adds to your long-distance phone bill. Fortunately, there are several inexpensive alternatives to dialing directly to a BBS outside your local calling area.

## Local Area Extensions

The first service you should look into is a *local area extension* (also known as a *phone linking service* or a *call transfer service*). Local area extensions let you call to people long distance—but within your area code—while paying but a fraction of the cost normally associated with a call to that area.

Dialing a number directly from one city to another city is usually a toll call. However, many towns or areas in between the cities can dial both cities as local calls. You could make a local call to a friend in that town, have the friend dial the number in the second city, and hold the phones up to each other. This would be a bit awkward, but you would save the long distance charges.

Many major metropolitan areas now have local area extensions that use computers as the "person" in the middle. To use these services, you dial a general access number for the computer. You then enter an access code followed by the number you want to phone. The computer bills your account a nominal fee for the call—generally around 25 to 50 cents—and dials the second number.

Most local area extensions let you talk as long as you like without charging for more than the initial connection. The type and availability of service depends on local and state phone regulations as well as the way your local phone calling areas are determined. Some phone companies have also successfully petitioned utility commissions in some states to classify the local area extensions as "long-distance services," which requires the local area extensions to charge for each minute of connect time. Check with your local area extension company to see what areas they service and what they charge.

## Packet-switching Networks

Local area extensions usually don't extend outside an area code region. To make inexpensive long-distance calls to a different area code, use *packet-switching networks*.

When you communicate with a BBS over a packet-switching network, the network splits the information you and the BBS are sending each other—such as keystrokes, menus, files, and messages—into *packets,* each of which contain up to 1000 characters. The network then sends these packets from one place to another over very high speed data-transmission lines.

**Note:**    Packet-switching networks can only be used for data transmission and will not work with voice calls, because voice calls are not *digital.* That is, they are not composed of tones representing simple "on" or "off" bits.

To access a packet-switching network, you would first dial its local number, then enter a user ID (for billing purposes) followed by the number that you want to dial. The network takes care of creating the packets and routing them. It will look like you are connected directly to a BBS.

Because packet-switching networks use very efficient high-speed data transfer equipment, they can offer you long-distance data calls at less than half the cost of dialing directly. Some packet-switching networks also offer discounted service in "off-peak" hours—6 P.M. to 7A.M., weekends, and holidays—when you pay $30 to $50 per month for a minimum of 20-30 hours of long-distance data calls anywhere in the U.S. The same amount of directly dialed long-distance calls could easily cost you $300 or more.

Furthermore, packet-switching networks usually provide a cleaner data signal than regular telephone lines, reducing occurrences of data-transmission errors.

Unfortunately, packet-switching network service may not be available if you live outside a major metropolitan area or are trying to reach a BBS that is outside a metropolitan area. This is because only populous areas generate enough business for the packet-switching service to cover the data-transmission equipment.

### *PC Pursuit*

PC Pursuit, operated by US Sprint Communications Co., is the best-known packet-switching network service for BBS users. To register, you can phone 800-835-3638 and talk to a customer service representative, or phone the PC Pursuit BBS at 800-835-3001 (1200 baud, 7 bits, even parity, 1 stop bit) and leave your name, address, and credit card number. PC Pursuit is part of the SprintNet data network (formerly known as the Telenet Public Data Network).

To get a current list of US Sprint Communications Co. local access numbers from the BBS dial, 800-546-1000 (also 1200-7-E-1). Enter three carriage returns, then enter your area code and local *exchange* (the first three digits of your phone number) at the prompt. At the "@" prompt, enter *MAIL.* Then enter *PHONES* as both the user name and as the password (the characters do not appear when you type the password). The BBS displays a menu of the information you can examine. This procedure and a sample menu appear in Figure 8-1.

```
TERMINAL=

YOUR AREA CODE AND LOCAL EXCHANGE (AAA,LLL)=206,782

@MAIL

User name?  PHONES
Password?




JANUARY 1990

WELCOME TO TELENET'S ONLINE U.S. ACCESS TELEPHONE NUMBERS DIRECTORY.

TELENET'S DIAL ACCESS SERVICES PROVIDE YOU ACCESS TO THE TELENET PUBLIC
DATA NETWORK 24 HOURS A DAY FOR RELIABLE DATA TRANSMISSION ACROSS TOWN
AND WORLDWIDE.  YOU CAN ACCESS THE TELENET PUBLIC DATA NETWORK NATION-
WIDE WITH A LOCAL PHONE CALL FROM THOUSANDS OF CITIES AND TOWNS OR BY
USING TELENET'S IN-WATS SERVICE.  THE NETWORK IS ALSO ACCESSIBLE FROM
OVER 85 INTERNATIONAL LOCATIONS.

DEPEND ON TELENET'S DIAL ACCESS SERVICES FOR:

   -- DIAL UP FLEXIBILITY WITH ACCESS ON DEMAND
   -- ERROR PROTECTED NETWORK TRANSMISSION
   -- 24 HOUR CUSTOMER SERVICE SUPPORT AND NETWORK MANAGEMENT

FOR CUSTOMER SERVICE, CALL TOLL-FREE 1-800/336-0437.  FROM OVERSEAS
LOCATIONS WITH NON-WATS ACCESS, CALL 703/689-6400.



                         TELENET'S ONLINE
              U.S. ACCESS TELEPHONE NUMBERS DIRECTORY

              1. ASYNCHRONOUS DIAL SERVICE
              2. X.25 DIAL SERVICE
              3. NEW CITIES AND RECENT CHANGES
              4. TELENET SALES OFFICES
              5. TO EXIT THE PHONES LISTING

 PLEASE ENTER YOUR SELECTION (1-5):  1
```

*Figure 8-1. PC Pursuit Online Information*

### BT TYMNET

BT Tymnet and the TYMNET network are owned and operated by British Telecomm. The TYMNET network was founded in 1966 by TYMSHARE, Inc. to sell computer time on large computers.

You can get information from BT TYMNET by logging on to the Tymnet Information Service through a local BT TYMNET access number.  If you don't know the local access number for BT TYMNET, you can talk to customer service representatives through BT TYMNET's 24-hour customer service line at 800-336-0149. Be sure to tell the customer service representative what speed modem you will be using, as there are different access numbers for different communications speeds.

After obtaining a local access number, set your parameters to the appropriate speed, 7 bits, even parity, and 1 stop bit. Dial the access number. At the `please type your terminal identifier:` prompt, enter *A*. Then, at the `please log in:` prompt, enter the word *information*. BT TYMNET will then display a menu of options. You can select a menu option by entering the appropriate number, get help by entering *HELP*, or return to the login prompt by entering *QUIT*. After you enter *QUIT* and you see the `please log in:` prompt, you can hang up. Figure 8-2 shows the logon procedure and a sample BT TYMNET menu.

```
please type your terminal identifier
-2703:01-011-
please log in: information



                    TYMNET INFORMATION SERVICE


Welcome to TYMNET's Information Service!  TYMNET is the world's largest Public
Data Network, with local access in over 850 U.S. and Canadian cities and access
to and from over 80 foreign countries.



                             MAIN MENU


    1.   Direct Dial & Outdial (R) Access
    2.   Data Base and Timesharing Services
    3.   International Access
    4.   Certified Products
    5.   Computers Interfaced to TYMNET (R)
    6.   Sales Office Directory
    7.   Technical and User Documentation
    8.   Special offers

If you need assistance, type 'HELP'.  When you are finished, type 'QUIT'.

Type the number of the desired menu item at the prompt.

YOUR SELECTION:
```

*Figure 8-2. BT TYMNET Online Information*

For current information on registering to use BT TYMNET, phone 800-872-7654 and ask to speak to a marketing representative.

### Other Packet-switching Networks

In addition to SprintNet data network and BT TYMNET, some areas have other packet-switching networks. For example, Canadian BBS users can use DataPac, run by Bell of Canada. Check with the sysops in your area to find out which long-distance services they use.

# FIDONET

There are a number of networks of BBSes through which you can route messages and files. The largest and best-known of these is *FidoNet,* a worldwide network of over five thousand BBSes of all types. FidoNet started in 1984 as an experiment. Tom Jennings, the author of the Fido BBS software, lived in San Francisco and was working on software with John Madill, who lives in Boston. To communicate, they added code that would let Jennings' BBS dial Madill's BBS and exchange messages and files automatically, in the middle of the night, when the rates were low.

Automated message and file routing is now a very popular BBS feature. Although the network started between two Fido BBSes, Fido, RBBS-PC, PCBoard, OPUS, WILDCAT!, TBBS, and many other types of BBSes are now part of FidoNet and can exchange information with other BBSes in the network.

## How FidoNet is Organized

FidoNet identifies BBSes by dividing the world into zones, regions, networks, individual systems, and points. Each *zone* is a continental area. North America is zone 1, Europe is zone 2, Oceania (Australia, New Zealand, and the Pacific Islands) is zone 3, and South America is zone 4.

Each zone is then divided into smaller areas called *regions*. Regions have a two-digit number. For example, the Northwest region (region 17) contains Alaska, Washington, Oregon, Idaho, Montana, British Columbia, Alberta, Manitoba, and Saskatchewan. According to Ken Kaplan, co-founder of the International FidoNet Association, the original areas for the regions were based more on basketball conferences than anything else.

Regions themselves are divided into *networks*. A network is a relatively small, usually metropolitan, area, such as Greater Seattle (network 343). Finally, individual systems are the BBSes themselves, each of which is identified with a *node number*. The node number is a unique number in the network.

*Points* are FidoNet addresses for single users who get lots of network mail, but don't have their own BBS. A sysop can set up a point on the BBS so the user can call in and pick up mail sent via the network from a mailbox on the BBS. The sysop's BBS can also transfer messages to the BBS user's computer.

The easiest way to understand how FidoNet addresses work is to think of them as phone numbers. The zone is the same thing as the country code, the network is the area code, and the node number is the actual telephone number. FidoNet addresses are written as *zone:network/node* (with a point address, *zone:network/node.point*). For example, Seattle is in zone 1, region 17, network 343. A BBS with a node number of 21 in Seattle would have a FidoNet address 1:343/21. If the BBS had points, they would have addresses like 1:343/21.1, 1:343/21.2, and 1:343/21.3.

Region numbers are not part of the FidoNet address; they serve as administrative divisions only, set up to coordinate the list of nodes for an area, particularly for BBSes too far away to be part of a network. Regional coordinators now are responsible for keeping track of the BBSes in a region, assigning node numbers to independent BBSes, and network numbers to new networks.

## Netmail

*Netmail* is mail addressed to someone at another BBS with a FidoNet address. The addition of the FidoNet address is about the only difference between sending mail on your own BBS and sending netmail.

There are two ways in which you can send netmail. The first is known as *direct* mail. Direct mail is sent directly from one BBS to another. Each BBS has a list of BBSes that has the FidoNet addresses and BBS phone numbers. When you enter a message addressed to someone on another FidoNet node, the BBS looks up the phone number for the BBS in the list, dials the number, and transfers the message. If you are sending messages from one BBS to another across town, this won't cost anything, but if you are sending it long distance, the line charges will mount up. Many sysops set up a prepaid account for your long-distance charges. The BBS automatically charges the cost of each call to your balance.

**Note:** Not all FidoNet BBSes send direct mail immediately. Some wait until the lowest dialing rates take effect, usually 11:00 P.M. Check with your sysop to find out what restrictions apply to sending direct mail.

The second way to send netmail, *routed* mail, is not as fast as direct mail, but it is less expensive. This method involves routing the message through the network of BBSes. After you enter a message addressed to a BBS, the BBS transfers the message to a BBS that serves as the *host* for the local area. The host BBS will either phone a local BBS (if the message is addressed locally) or transfer the message to another host closer

to the addressee's BBS. The second host will transfer the message to either the local
BBS the message is addressed to, or hand it off to yet another host, until the message
finally arrives at its destination. Messages sent this way usually arrive within 24 hours,
although they can occasionally take a couple of days for long or difficult network
routes. This method of routing mail is not used much because of its lack of delivery
speed.

When using either method to send netmail on a FidoNet BBS, go to the FidoNet message area. This will have a name like "FidoNet," "Netmail," or "Matrix," depending
on what kind of BBS you are using and how the sysop has set the message areas up.
After entering the normal message header information, you will be asked to enter the
FidoNet address for the message. If you don't know the address, ask the BBS to list
the network numbers. Figure 8-3 shows an example of this.

```
Type the MATRIX address.
  To list areas, type `/' by itself.
  To list nodes in net 343, type `#' by itself.

Matrix address: /

Matrix areas

NETWORK 1      Intl FidoNet Co     Scottsdale A
NETWORK 10     Calif Nevada        Tustin C
NETWORK 102    SoCalNet            Los Angeles C
NETWORK 103    Orange Co CA        Anaheim C
NETWORK 119    ChicoNet            Chico C
NETWORK 125    SF Bay Net          San Francisco C
NETWORK 143    Silicon Valley      Sunnyvale C
NETWORK 161    SF EAST BAY\VALLEY  Novato C
NETWORK 202    San Diego Co CA     San Diego C
NETWORK 203    SacraMetro Valley N Sacramento C
NETWORK 204    SF Peninsula Net    San Mateo C
NETWORK 205    Fresno/Central Vall Fresno C
NETWORK 206    1000 Oaks Net       Thousand Oaks C
    More [Y,n]? n

Matrix area (network): 343
```

*Figure 8-3. Partial List of Networks*

After you have selected the network number, you can then list the nodes within the network. A partial node list appears in Figure 8-4.

```
NETWORK 343    Lesser Seattle Oper   Washington
      343/100  Central Hub           Seattle WA
      343/1    BECS TandyOpus        Seattle WA
      343/101  BECS Fido             Renton WA
      343/11   Puget Sound TBBS      Edmonds WA
      343/111  Seattle Echos         Edmonds WA
      343/31   SEA/MAC               Seattle WA
      343/200  East Seattle Hub      Bellevue WA
      343/3    Glacier Peak Rainbo   Bellevue WA
More [Y,n]? n
```

*Figure 8-4. Partial Node List for Network 343*

After selecting the node number, enter the addressee's name, followed by your message.

When you save your message, the BBS will tell you the payments you have made to your FidoNet account on the BBS, the charges already levied against your balance for calls, the cost of the message you just sent, and your balance. The status display Figure 8-5 shows a starting balance of $10.

```
Saving your message (#252)...
Payments           1000
Charges              26
This message         26
Balance             948
```

*Figure 8-5. FidoNet Account Balance*

# Echomail

Where netmail is the ability to address messages to a specific BBS, *echomail* lets you enter a message on one BBS and have that message eventually appear on all the other BBSes in the network. Echomail as it is used on FidoNet was first developed by Wynn Wagner III (who wrote OPUS) as a way for the Dallas sysops to communicate without sending direct mail back and forth. He sent a copy of the program to someone else, and national echomail conferences blossomed on FidoNet within a few months.

Here's how echomail works: you join an echomail conference, known as an *echo,* on a BBS. Echomail conferences look just like message areas on other BBSes, and in fact, that's just what they are. To send a message to the other BBSes in the conference, you simply enter the message. Unlike netmail, which requires you to enter a network and node address, echomail requires no special addressing.

Later that evening, the BBS transfers the message to the host BBS for the local area. The host BBS then calls all the BBSes in the area and transfers your message along with all the other messages the host has accumulated to the other local BBSes. The host BBS then calls up a host BBS in another area and transfers the messages to it. The second host BBS then routes the messages to the BBSes in its local area, and calls yet another host BBS. This process continues until your message has been routed to all of the BBSes in the network. When someone then reads your message on another BBS in the echomail conference, the name, phone number, and FidoNet address of the BBS the message was entered on appear at the bottom of the message. This provides enough information to let someone reply to you directly via netmail if they wish.

There are echomail conferences on virtually any topic you can think of. Your BBS will almost certainly support only a small portion of them. When you join a conference by entering *J* for Join Conference or *A* for Area Change, you can usually list the conferences available on that BBS. Leave a message for your sysop if you'd like to participate in an echomail conference on a particular topic that isn't currently offered on the BBS.

Echomail conferences frequently have a moderator, whose job is to keep the discussion alive and adhering to the topic.

Participating in an echomail conference is much like taking part in a discussion on a local BBS. You will be using the same general message entry commands and procedures you would for reading and entering local messages. When entering echomail, you should follow the same general rules you would in any local message area:

- *Stick to the topic.*
  People read an echomail conference to find out more about the topic that interests them, not about your trip to the dentist.

- *Be polite and courteous.*
  The effects of flame mail, rudeness, and generally obnoxious behavior seem to multiply as the distance from the sender increases. Keep your messages civil.

- *Don't waste time on trivialities.*
  Refrain from putting messages like, "Naw, I don't think so," on an echomail conference. They add little to the conversation and sysops have to pay to transfer your message from one place to another. Be considerate of their phone bill.

- *Don't use echomail to send personal messages.*
Any message you enter in an echomail conference is going to be routed to every BBS participating in that conference, even if the message is private. (The message would be addressed to the recipient if she or he logged on to any BBS carrying that echomail conference). A message sent through echomail will be transferred several thousand times to get to every other node in the net. This can add up to a lot of long-distance charges for someone.

- *Don't include control characters or ANSI graphics in your messages.*
Not every BBS user on the echo will have the same computer and communications package you do. If you embed a lot of control characters or ANSI graphics in your message, a lot of the readers will only see mangled message text. For the same reason, use spaces instead of tabs in all echomail.

- *Allow for the time delay.*
Don't expect an instantaneous response. Even under the best circumstances, there can be as much as a week between when a message is posted on one BBS and when a reply wends its way through the hosts back to you. When you reply to a previous message, quote the original message; giving the context helps the recipient to identify what you are responding to and gives extra information to other readers who haven't been involved with the conversation.

## Using Netmail with Echomail

Netmail and echomail can be combined very effectively. For example, suppose you are looking for information on how to solve a programming problem. You can enter a message on an echomail conference that describes your problem and requests help from other users on the conference. The message will then circulate through the BBSes in the conference. A BBS user in another town, seeing your message, may then send you netmail about how she solved the problem with a small program she wrote, and may ask if you want a copy.

When you receive the reply, you can send a *file request* to the other BBS. A file request is the same as direct mail: the BBS phones another BBS directly and then downloads the specified file. This will probably only take a few minutes of download time, and will cost you very little in long-distance charges.

FidoNet also helps distribute shareware. Authors of shareware can upload a file to regional shareware distribution nodes within FidoNet. The regional coordinators then make a list of the current software available to the FidoNet sysops in the area. The shareware distribution network allows shareware to travel quickly from the source throughout the country.

Every BBS in the FidoNet has a set time (usually in the middle of the night) known as *zone mail hour,* when the BBS is unavailable for calls from BBS users. During this time, the BBS sends and receives netmail, echomail, and files.

## Comments

The terminology for many of the procedures described in this section is different depending on the type of BBS you are using. There will also be some variation in the network features available to you from BBS to BBS. Talk to your sysop about the options that are available to you on your BBS.

FidoNet is supported by the hundreds of volunteers across the world that comprise the International FidoNet Association (IFNA). Ken Kaplan incorporated IFNA in July 1986. IFNA is a continually evolving organization that helps coordinate the networking for thousands of BBSes. IFNA can provide more information on FidoNet, IFNA, and FidoNet BBSes in your area. You may also want to ask about FidoCon, a convention of FidoNet users and developers held annually. Contact the International FidoNet Association, P.O. Box 41143, St. Louis, MO 63141, 314-576-4067 (voice), or send mail over FidoNet to 1:1/10.

# OTHER NETWORKS

FidoNet is not the only network for passing messages and files. Several other computer networks also pass messages and files from one place to another. These networks, while not running on BBSes themselves, can connect with BBSes to send and receive mail and files through them. These networks offer the same advantages as FidoNet—such as the chance to discuss ideas and exchange files with people around the world—but they reach a different and larger group of people than FidoNet does.

## The UUCP Network

The UUCP (Unix to Unix CoPy) network is very much like FidoNet. You can send netmail over the UUCP network directly from one UUCP node to another. However, unlike FidoNet, sending individual pieces of netmail over the UUCP network is not usually charged to the user, but to the organization funding the node.

The UUCP network is comprised primarily of computers using the *Unix* operating system, a powerful operating system used on multi-user computers. There are over 10,000 UUCP nodes at universities, software companies, and large corporations.

The UUCP network equivalent to FidoNet's echomail system is called *Usenet*. Usenet is a system for exchanging *news* (similar to FidoNet echomail) between computers on the UUCP network. You can read and participate in Usenet *newsgroups,* which are similar to echomail conferences.

**Note:** Although Usenet started on the UUCP network, it now runs on several other interconnected networks as well. "Usenet" specifically refers to the collection of computers and networks that exchange news.

The Usenet software was first developed in late 1979 by Tom Truscott and Jim Ellis of Duke University as a means of exchanging information with other Unix users. In 1981, the Usenet software was expanded and improved by Mark Horton and Matt Glickman at UC Berkeley. Rick Adams, then at the Center for Seismic Studies, has been coordinating improvements to the Usenet software since 1984.

### Using Usenet

You use Usenet for many of the same reasons you use FidoNet. Like FidoNet, you can exchange netmail with other users around the country and in many parts of the world. You can also take part in discussions on virtually any topic. Experts and specialists in every field participate in Usenet newsgroups. You can take advantage of the expertise of the participants in the newsgroups by asking questions and communicating directly with netmail.

There are two ways you can use Usenet. The first is to log on directly to a Unix computer that is part of a network that has access to Usenet. This allows you to send and receive mail and to participate in Usenet newsgroups. There are UUCP computers at most major universities and many private corporations throughout the U.S. Even if you are not part of a university or corporation with a UUCP node, you may still be able to qualify for UUCP access. Check with your university's or company's computer department to find out how to register directly to use the network.

**Note:** Not all UUCP computers have access to Usenet newsgroups.

The second way to use Usenet is through a FidoNet BBS connected to a UUCP node with special software. Although Usenet is not part of FidoNet, you can route mail to UUCP through FidoNet. Tim Pozar, Garry Paxinos, and John Galvin wrote a collection of programs known as *UFGATE* that allow FidoNet BBSes to send and receive UUCP mail and netnews. A connection between FidoNet and Usenet is known as a *gateway*.

It is possible for you to use a FidoNet-UUCP gateway even if your local FidoNet BBS does not have one. You can send mail to a gateway BBS from another FidoNet node and include the UUCP address in the first line of the message. The gateway BBS will translate the message into UUCP format and send it to the local UUCP node. From there, the message will be routed through the UUCP network until it reaches the UUCP addressee.

Many FidoNet BBSes will feature Usenet newsgroups among the available conferences. Although the particular format for displaying Usenet newsgroups varies from BBS to BBS, they generally appear as standard echomail conferences. The primary difference is that each newsgroup entry will have a UUCP message header at the start of the message text.

### Understanding UUCP Addresses

To send mail to someone on the UUCP network, you need to know their UUCP address. Every UUCP user at a UUCP node has a *username*. A username is simply a name that mail can be sent to: Sam Spade might be just *sam* or *sams*. A user's username is typically the name they use to log on. The username will have as many characters as necessary to be unique—most are at least three characters long, but some are as long as 10 or 12 characters.

The original UUCP addressing method, still used at some UUCP nodes, requires you to enter a *bang path*. Bang paths are UUCP addresses that are really complete routing paths separated by exclamation points. (Exclamation points are known as *bangs* in typography, and Unix users have picked this up). For example, a technical writer at Apple Computer named Jon Singer has the UUCP address *apple!jon*. The bang path to send a message to him from Sam Spade in Seattle would look something like this:

*tikal!beaver!sun!apple!jon*

The first four words are the names of the computers in the path the message will take. The message will first be transmitted from Sam Spade's UUCP node to a Unix computer named *tikal* in the Seattle area. The message will then be transferred to *beaver*, a computer at the University of Washington that serves as a *backbone site*. Backbone sites are like host computers in FidoNet. They connect to many other computers in the local area as well as to other backbone sites in other areas. The message is next transferred to *sun*, a computer operated by Sun Microsystems, Inc., that serves much of the San Francisco Bay area and the San Jose peninsula. From *sun*, the message is finally transferred to Apple's computer and arrives in Jon's mailbox.

As you can see, bang paths require you to understand how to get from the starting node all the way to the destination. You can usually find out the path from any place to any other place without too much difficulty. Many Unix computers have a program called *uupath* that will help you plan your message routing.

Not surprisingly, many people think the computer, not the user, should take care of the message routing. As a result, more and more UUCP computers are using "smart" mailing and routing programs that have replaced bang paths with *ARPA-style addresses* or *at-sign syntax* addresses.

ARPA-style addresses were developed as part of *ARPANET,* one of the first private networks. ARPANET (also known as DARPANET) was created by the Advanced Research Projects Agency of the U.S. Department of Defense (ARPA). ARPA funded research on computer networks in a number of university computer science departments and several private corporations. This led to the development of a small private network in the late 1960's and has since grown to include hundreds of computers throughout the U.S. and Europe. Much of what is known today about networking and packet-switching came from development of ARPANET.

ARPA-style addresses have the username followed by an at sign (@), followed by the *domain*. A domain is the formal name for a computer or group of computers that share a common purpose or function, even though they may not be in the same geographical area. Jon's address in this format is

*jon@apple.COM*

In this format, the first word (*jon*) is the username and *apple.COM* is the domain. There are can be one or several computers that are identified collectively as *apple.COM*, but Jon will be the only user on all of them with the username *jon*. The extension COM shows that this is a commercial domain. Other extensions you might see include EDU (educational), GOV (government), and ORG (miscellaneous organizations).

UUCP addresses and mail routing systems are currently being changed from the older bang path addresses to ARPA-style addresses. Until this process is complete, it may be necessary to use bang path addresses at some UUCP nodes, and consequently, some FidoNet gateways. If you are sending UUCP mail to someone, make sure that they have given you their UUCP address in a format you can use at your network node. Check with either the sysop of your UUCP node or the sysop of a FidoNet BBS with a Usenet gateway to find out more about the current formats for addresses.

The UUCP mail routing system isn't perfect. Mail occasionally gets "lost" and never arrives at its destination. There may be unforeseen delays in transmission, and a piece of mail may take several weeks to arrive.

### Connecting to Usenet through FidoNet

To send a message from FidoNet to UUCP through a gateway, you need to address the FidoNet message to a FidoNet BBS running the UFGATE gateway. The addressee should be *uucp*. The first line of the message must be *To:* followed by the UUCP address. The *To:* tells UFGATE that the information that follows is the UUCP address. Figure 8-6 shows a sample message ready to route to the FidoNet gateway BBS.

```
To: Uucp

Subject?  Test

1: To: jon@apple.COM
2:
3: Jon: Good to talk to you again.  I wanted to try routing you a message via
4: FidoNet.  Please send me a UUCP message so I can see how it looks.
5:
6: Sam Spade
7:
Command: s
Saving message #253
```

*Figure 8-6. Sending UUCP Mail from FidoNet*

It is also possible to send mail from a UUCP node to someone on FidoNet.  The message is routed to the UUCP side of the gateway, where it is translated into FidoNet format, sent to the FidoNet node, then routed through FidoNet to the FidoNet addressee. The domain name for FidoNet is *fidonet.org*.  You must include the node, network, and zone number as part of the UUCP address, as well as the name of the recipient.  A typical address from the UUCP node to FidoNet will look like this:

recipient@f<*node*>.n<*netnumber*>.z<*zone*>.fidonet.org

If you are sending mail to a FidoNet point, the format would add a point number as follows:

recipient@p<*point*>.f<*node*>.n<*network*>.z<*zone*>.fidonet.org

As an example, if you wanted to send a message from UUCP to Sam Spade on a FidoNet BBS with an address of zone 1, network 343, FidoNet node 8, the address on the UUCP message would be:

sam_spade@f8.n343.z1.fidonet.org

Although this may look a little complex, you'll soon get used to sending messages between UUCP addresses.

### Sending Binary Files

Usenet sends and receives messages using seven-bit ASCII characters.  As you may remember from the discussion of ASCII characters in Chapter 1, this is fine for written messages and text, but you can't send programs which use eight-bit ASCII, or binary, characters.  However, you can use a program called UUENCODE to translate a program into ASCII text so you can then send it over Usenet as a message.  When the addressee receives the message, a second program called UUDECODE translates the ASCII text back into a program.

UUCP also doesn't let you attach files to a message, as FidoNet does. An enhancement to the UFGATE gateway software is due out soon that will use UUENCODE to automatically translate a program attached to a FidoNet message into ASCII text and insert it into the message text. You can usually download UUENCODE and UUDE-CODE from a FidoNet BBS with a gateway.

## Summary

There are many networks in addition to FidoNet and the UUCP network: BITNET, a network for educators, MILNET, a network for military projects, CSNET, the Computer Science net, and NSFNET, a network sponsored by the National Science Foundation, just to name a few. Each of the networks has a specific focus or audience. FidoNet is certainly the easiest network to participate in: all it takes is setting up an account with a FidoNet BBS for long-distance charges.

Other networks cater to different audiences. Because of the number of UUCP nodes at universities and major corporations, Usenet has a high percentage of college students and technical and professional people. BITNET is populated largely by professors and researchers. MILNET is almost exclusively for people involved in projects funded by the Department of Defense. If all your friends or colleagues are using a particular network, you'll probably want to use that network, too.

If you are not able to obtain access to a UUCP node through a local university or corporation, you can sign up with one of several public access UUCP nodes. One of the best is the WELL (Whole Earth 'Lectronic Link) in Sausalito, California. The WELL is run jointly by Whole Earth and Network Technologies. It can handle several dozen callers simultaneously and has over 100 conferences. One of the WELL's advantages is that it has very modest monthly membership fees. You can arrange to pay for all charges by entering a credit card number as part of the registration process; otherwise the WELL will also bill you on a monthly basis. For more information on the WELL, see Chapter 9, "Online Information Services."

## BBSing ON THE AIR

You can also extend your reach with amateur radio. This section introduces you to some of the ways you can use amateur radio to extend your reach and where to get more information.

## Amateur Radio

*Amateur radio* (also known as *ham radio*) is two-way radio transmission on a specific set of noncommercial shortwave radio frequencies. You can communicate in many ways with amateur radio. You can send and receive Morse code, voice, and many forms of *digital* communication using computers.

**Note:** You may already be somewhat familiar with citizen's band (CB) radio. CB is also a two-way radio transmission on a specific set of shortwave radio frequencies. However, CB is restricted to transmitting and receiving your voice only, and there are very specific regulations limiting the power you can use and the distance you can communicate.

Amateur radio offers some exciting options to BBS users. An amateur radio station performs the same function as a telephone, except that there are no limitations on the distance you can communicate and no long-distance charges. You can communicate with the space shuttle and send and receive messages from satellites 23,000 miles above the surface of the Earth. Amateur radio operators even bounce radio signals off of the moon regularly—a round trip of about half a million miles! How about that for extending your reach?

## Shortwave BBSes

A BBS's computer and modem can be connected to an amateur radio station to create a *shortwave BBS,* a BBS without phone lines. The major advantage of shortwave BBS is that shortwave radio signals can travel around the world fairly easily. You can talk to other shortwave BBS users in Australia, Russia, or Brazil with less power than it takes to run a single incandescent light bulb.

Shortwave BBSes are usually fairly simple linear BBSes. If you are familiar with Fido or RBBS-PC, you will have no problems understanding a typical shortwave BBS.

Logging on to a shortwave BBS is about the same as logging on to a BBS over the phone. You enter your logon information on the computer connected to the amateur radio transmitter and receiver, and read the information the BBS sends back to you. However, if the BBS is busy with another user, you don't get a busy signal. As a matter of fact, you can see what the other user is doing simply by monitoring the frequency. The modem will translate the signals into characters and display them on your screen.

Shortwave BBSes do not usually operate faster than 1200 baud, and many operate only at 300 baud. This is because the faster you send information, the "wider" your radio signal becomes. There is only a limited amount of space available for amateur radio signals in the shortwave frequencies. A 2400- or 9600-baud signal would take up too much space, sort of like only being able to tune in one FM radio station on the bottom third of the FM band.  However, 9600 baud is becoming popular in the VHF and UHF portions of the amateur radio bands, where there is more room for a signal.  1200 baud is the current practical limit for amateur radio BBSes in the lower shortwave frequencies.

You can send information using 300 or 1200 baud ASCII (just like you would over a phone line), or you can use any of several other forms of digital communications, such as *RTTY* (radioteletype, the communications method used by teletype machines) or *AMTOR* (Amateur Teleprinting Over Radio).  All of these forms of communications are done by the computer and the transceiver.  All you have to do is type on the keyboard and watch the screen.

Another difference between a shortwave BBS and a phone-line BBS is that shortwave BBSes use call signs for user IDs.  Call signs are combinations of letters and numbers that identify from which country an amateur radio operator is transmitting.  They are issued with one's amateur radio license by the Federal Communications Commission, the Canadian Department of Communications, or the equivalent organization in other countries.  For example, call signs that start with K, W, N, or A—such as KA7NYB or W1AW—are issued to operators in the U.S.  Other call sign prefixes are G for Great Britain, F for France, D for Germany, and U and R for the U.S.S.R.  Call signs for other countries may start with two letters: VE for Canada, VK for Australia, and EA for Spain.

Call signs are unique—no two people have the same call sign.  You can buy a directory of amateur radio operators that lists the operator's call sign, full name, and address.  Because it is a federal offense to use another person's call sign, it is not considered necessary to use passwords on a shortwave BBS.

## Packet Radio

Packet-switching networks (discussed earlier in this chapter) route packets of information from one location to another.  *Packet radio* is very much like a packet-switching network: routing information is attached to a block of data of up to 256 bytes, and the entire packet is transmitted.  Like a packet-switching network that uses phone lines, there can be several intermediate stations that route the packets between the originating station and the destination.  The intermediate stations simply look at the routing information and send the packet to the next appropriate station.

When you enter a message for someone, the packet radio BBS will route it to a packet-radio BBS nearer to that person.  That BBS will in turn hold it for the addressee or pass it on once again to another BBS even nearer.  This continues until the message arrives at a packet radio BBS the addressee logs in on.

Routing messages on packet radio is a little like sending routine netmail messages and echomail over FidoNet, except there is more handing off of messages between packet radio BBSes than there is between FidoNet BBSes. The reason for this is that packet radio tends to use radio frequencies that are fairly high—about the same as some broadcast television frequencies. As a result, these radio signals are mostly *line of sight*: you must be able to see from one packet radio station to the next in order to send and receive information. Many packet radio relay stations are built on tops of mountains or tall buildings to give them a better "view."

Like shortwave BBSes, packet radio BBSes are linear BBSes that use call signs for the user ID. Figure 8-7 shows an amateur radio operator Bob, KD7NM, logging on to a packet radio BBS and listing the last nine messages entered on the BBS.

```
cmd:c kd7ws
cmd:*** CONNECTED to KD7WS
cmd:ll 9

Msg# Stat Size  To     From   @ BBS  Date/Time Subject
 390 PF    840 KT7H   N8GNJ  KE7OM  0106/2349 hi speed discussions
 389 P     939 KD7NM  N8GNJ         0106/2342 fast
 388 B     917 ALL    WA6PGP ALLUSA 0106/2318 Attention: College Radio Clubs
 387 B     680 ALL    WS7M   ALLUSA 0106/2219 AST Memory
 381 PY    792 N8GNJ  KD7NM         0106/1650 Speech Synthesizers
 380 PY    610 N8GNJ  KD7NM         0106/1636 High Speed routing
 378 P    1146 N7KIY  NA7P          0106/1618 I'M GETTING YOURS...
 376 B    9478 ALL    VE7DIE LAN80  0106/1419 LAN80 MAP JAN 16/90
 373 B    3898 ALL    K4NGC  NWGB   0106/0821 World Wide Packet Stats
```

*Figure 8-7. Logging on to a Packet Radio BBS*

In the first line, Bob has entered *C* followed by the call sign of the BBS. This tells the packet radio BBS that he wants to *connect,* to log on to the BBS. The BBS responds with the message `*** CONNECTED to KD7WS`, which says that Bob is now connected to the KD7WS packet radio BBS. Now that he is logged on, Bob enters *ll 9* (list the last 9 messages on the BBS). The BBS responds with a list of the messages. The message number is assigned by the BBS. The status shows that a message is a bulletin (B) or personal mail (P), whether the mail has been forwarded (F), and if the addressee has read it yet (Y for Yes). The size is the size in bytes. To and from are the call signs of the addressee and the sender. @ BBS is forwarding instructions—how to route the message through the packet radio network and which BBSes or areas to send it to. Message 390 is sent to KE7OM's packet radio BBS and is personal mail. Messages 388 and 387 have a designation of "ALLUSA," which means that they are to be routed to every packet radio BBS in the U.S.

Bulletins (such as messages 388 and 387 in Figure 8-7) are handled very much like echomail. Each BBS passes the message on to all other BBSes the message is designated for: ALLCAN for all of Canada, PUGET for the Seattle and surrounding Puget Sound area, or ALLCA for all of California.

While packet radio BBSes may seem similar to shortwave BBSes, there are a couple of major differences. One advantage packet radio BBSes have over shortwave radio BBSes is better file handling capabilities. Most shortwave BBSes focus on messages and announcements. Another advantage of packet radio is the ability to connect from one relay station to another to extend your reach beyond the immediate area. This is very much like being your own telephone operator, routing your call from one central office to the next. You build a route of connections from relay station to relay station. Only the "ends" are active—your station and the last station in the chain of relay stations and BBSes you have assembled. The intermediate stations automatically pass information back and forth.

Packet radio BBSes can be single-user or multi-user. Software is available that allows one *terminal node controller* (the computer interface that connects to the radio) and radio to serve several users. It can automatically work for several radio/terminal node controller combinations, switching packets from one radio to another, as well as running several copies of the BBS.

There are packet radio BBSes in every populated area in North America and in many cities around the world. Many amateur radio operators are working to build a global packet radio network using packet radio BBSes, relay stations, and satellites. This network would be similar to FidoNet in many ways. You could use a packet network to exchange messages and files with other packet radio operators anywhere on the planet within a few days.

## Communicating via Satellites

Another exciting possibility in amateur radio is sending and receiving information via orbiting satellites. There are satellites devoted exclusively to amateur radio. OSCAR 1 (Orbiting Satellite Carrying Amateur Radio) was launched in 1961. Since then, the U.S. and the Soviet Union have launched more than a dozen satellites exclusively for the use of amateur radio operators. You can use amateur satellites to send and receive messages, upload and download files, and act as relay stations from one point to another (just like commercial communications satellites).

Like packet radio, communicating with a satellite involves radio frequencies that are line of sight: you must be able to see the satellite to send and receive information. Amateur radio satellites use low-earth and elliptical orbits, about 100 miles up. These satellites can be seen by the entire planet twice a day. The current planned launch of four amateur radio satellites will allow intercontinental messages to be picked up eight times per day and delivered within 12 hours.

You can communicate with other amateur radio operators directly via satellites. To do this, both of you would have to point your antennas at the satellite. You would then be able to send Morse code, talk, or transfer information with computers.

Satellites can also be used as part of a land-based packet radio system to skip over large distances that don't have packet radio BBSes. Packet radio BBSes can use satellite *uplinks* and *downlinks*—special transmitting and receiving equipment that allows the BBS to use an amateur radio satellite to bridge large areas where line of sight communications would be impractical. Figure 8-8 shows KD7NM in Seattle connecting first to a packet radio station in Alberta (VE6PAC-1), then to the Calgary satellite uplink (CGYSAT), then to the satellite downlink in Ottawa (OTTSAT), then to another packet radio relay station in Ottawa (VE3OCR), and finally to a packet relay station in Western Quebec (VE2RM), 3000 miles away from the starting point.

```
KD7NM>YTHNET:C VE6PAC-1
YTHNET>KD7NM:LBY:W7HGM-8> Connected to LBG:VE6PAC-1
KD7NM>YTHNET:C CGYSAT
YTHNET>KD7NM:LBG:VE6PAC-1} Connected to CGYSAT:VE6PAK-1
KD7NM>YTHNET:C OTTSAT
YTHNET>KD7NM:CGYSAT:VE6PAK-1} Connected to OTTSAT:VE3RWJ-1
KD7NM>YTHNET:C VE3OCR
YTHNET>KD7NM:OTTSAT:VE3RWJ-1} Connected to OTTAWA:VE3OCR
KD7NM>YTHNET:C WQC
BCYTHNET>KD7NM:OTTSAT:VE3RWJ-1} Connected to WQC:VE2RM
KD7NM>YTHNET:I
YTHNET>KD7NM:WQC:VE2RM> Rigaud, Quebec
Owned by the Western Quebec VHF/UHF club, VE2RM Inc. 145.01
LOCATED 30 MILES WEST OF MONTREAL NEAR ONTARIO BORDER.
```

*Figure 8-8. Packet Switching on Packet Radio*

Figure 8-8 shows KD7NM calling from YTHNET (pronounced "Youth-Net"), a packet radio network node provided for Novice amateur radio operators in the Seattle area. Most Novices on YTHNET are junior high school students. The "Novice" class license is the simplest amateur radio license to obtain.

After connecting to the packet relay station in Western Quebec, KD7NM asks the relay station for information about itself by entering *I*. The BBS responds with information about its operators, the frequency it is operating on (145.01 megahertz), and its location. From here, KD7NM could continue making connections to other stations, leave a message on a BBS, or chat with another packet radio user who had also logged in to the Western Quebec relay station.

Besides being used as orbiting linear BBSes and relay stations in packet radio networks, many satellites carry sensors, cameras, and similar equipment. One amateur radio satellite launched recently contains a TV camera that looks at about a 350-

kilometer square of the Earth. Images are then stored, processed, and broadcast for anyone to receive.

## Summary

Amateur radio, in existence since 1914, is an exciting hobby that offers a wide range of opportunities for BBS users to extend their reach. There are amateur radio operators in every country, over a million around the world, with whom you can communicate without government interference. Amateur radio is a hobby that helps break down international barriers.

Becoming an amateur radio operator is very easy. Amateur radio clubs in most cities sponsor regular classes on how to become a radio amateur. The names and addresses of several books and magazines focusing on amateur radio also appear in the bibliography. For more information on meeting radio amateurs in your area and how to get involved with amateur radio, write to:

American Radio Relay League
225 Main St.
Newington, CT 06111

# BECOMING AN EXPERT

There are many different ways to extend your reach without incurring large phone bills. Local area extensions can cut your phone costs when phoning within your area code or state, and packet-switching networks can do the same when phoning to major metropolitan areas across the country.

BBSes can operate by themselves or as part of a network. FidoNet, the main BBS network, is the most accessible of all computer networks. You can use FidoNet to send mail directly to BBS users almost anywhere. You can also participate in discussions on virtually any topic with BBS users around the country and around the world.

In addition to FidoNet, there are dozens of other networks that run on all kinds of computers. One of the most popular of these is the UUCP network. This network works much like FidoNet: messages and news are forwarded from computer to computer until they reach their destination. There are UUCP nodes in every major metropolitan area in the U.S. and Canada, and there are dozens of UUCP nodes throughout Europe and other parts of the world.

Perhaps the most dramatic way to extend your reach is through amateur radio. You can use shortwave radio to log on to and participate in BBSes anywhere on Earth, route messages through the packet radio network, and even send and receive information via satellite, all at no cost.

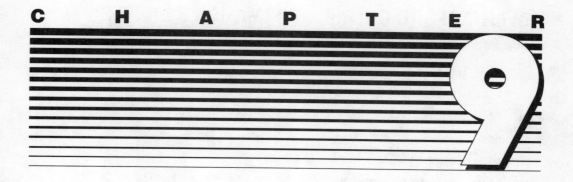

C H A P T E R

9

# ONLINE INFORMATION SERVICES

This chapter describes some of the most popular *online information services*, multi-user telecommunication systems that provide a variety of services accessible through computers. These services act as a "super-BBS," allowing you to exchange messages and files, chat with other users, participate in conferences on hundreds of subjects, shop electronically, and make airline reservations. They also provide *information databases,* collections of specialized information or data available online.

# ADVANTAGES TO ONLINE INFORMATION SERVICES

Online information services have the following general features in common:

- extensive files for downloading
- fairly sophisticated mail facilities
- many conferences, forums, and round-tables
- at least one information database
- a number of online games for multiple players
- a selection of online services, such as online travel services and shopping

Many of these features can be found on local BBSes that are made available to users free-of-charge. Since online information services charge for access, why would you want to use an online information service instead of a BBS in your area? The most obvious advantage is that they are *big*: tens and hundreds of thousands of people all over the world tap into online information services. Experts in a number of fields are regular participants and contributors to forums and conferences. If you have a question about something, you can easily find any number of people who can give you professional advice on any topic.

Due to the sheer numbers of people involved, you can usually find more files on online information services than on any BBS. No matter what type of file you are looking for—general utilities, special fonts, templates for a spreadsheet, or games—online information services will have entire areas devoted exclusively to files and programs for your type of computer.

Many online information services offer extensive chatting—often known as *CB* or *Citizen's Band* conference—because of the similarity to people chatting informally on CB radio.

You can also run dozens of games through doors in the online information service. One advantage to the games offered on online information services is that many are designed for simultaneous multiple players. For example, you can climb into your starship and do battle with other users (you can also send comments to the other players assuring them of their imminent demise), or take part in a team effort exploring a dungeon. Each of the characters, being run by a real person, will react differently—and unpredictably—adding excitement to the game.

But online information services offer a great deal more than a wider range of files, messages, and games. Most maintain databases of information on a variety of specialized subjects. As a matter of fact, many online information services exist solely to provide specialized information through one or more databases.

Online information services also can be used for shopping. Many companies offer goods for sale in an area of the service with a name like "The Mall" or "Merchant's Corner." Selecting items is usually done by checking off the item on a menu and specifying the quantity you wish to purchase. Paying for your selections is usually done by entering a credit card number, although some merchants will also allow you to mail a check or even debit your checking account directly. Your purchases are then mailed to you.

Several online services offer check-free transaction processing from the CheckFree Processing Center. This service lets you pay your bills electronically by debiting your checking account and crediting the payee's account. You don't need to write and mail a check—the service takes care of the paperwork for you. Check-free transaction services even provide you with an updated check register showing your account status.

Many software companies are using online information services for customer support. For example, you can participate in a conference about almost any Microsoft product on online information services. Product support conferences are frequently moderated by representatives from the software companies, allowing you to enter your questions and comments directly to the company. You can also swap sample files with support representatives and other users.

Conducting online support conferences on a service is a good idea for the companies as well, as the conferences promote the free exchange of ideas between users and advertises the features of the product. Users will also solve other users' problems, thereby reducing the overall support load.

In general, online information services are usually a combination of a BBS and a source of specialized information and goods. The next section explains ways to look for and use online information services effectively.

# USING AN ONLINE INFORMATION SERVICE

Online information services support themselves by charging a fee for the *connect time*—the time you spend actually connected to the online information service. Many services also charge you a one-time membership fee for setting up your account. This cost usually includes a set of manuals and a credit for online time.

The cost for connect time can vary depending on the speed of the modem you are using (most services charge less for 300-baud modems than they do for 2400-baud modems) and the time of day. Charges are frequently higher for normal business hours (*prime time*) than for evenings and weekends. You may also have to pay extra to use special information databases or services. These charges are most often billed to your credit card number, although some online information services will debit your checking account if you prefer.

## Choosing an Online Information Service

Choosing an online information service requires a little planning on your part. To begin with, make a list of all the things that you'd like to accomplish with an online information service, such as uploading files and software or participating in professional conferences.

Once you form an opinion of what you would like to do with an online information service, you should examine several of the online information services to see which one best fits your needs. Several of the largest and most popular of the online information services are profiled later in this chapter.

If you are going to subscribe to an online information service to get information on a particular topic, ask fellow members of special interest groups or professional organizations which services offer the best materials. In addition, dozens of books have been written on online information services; a selection of titles appears in the bibliography.

Many online information services offer *starter kits* that include introductory materials, registration information (usually containing a certificate good for online credit), tutorials on how to get started with the service, wall charts, and user's guides on the service. Many starter kits even offer communications software designed specifically for that online information service.

Finally, if you feel like you don't have enough information to choose an online information service, pick one, become a member, and use it for a while. After a few months, if you don't feel like you're getting what you want, try another online information service. You'll discover the differences between the two services and be able to make an informed decision. If there is no monthly minimum fee for using the services, you might even choose to stay on both.

## Keeping Your Costs Down

As you may have already guessed, the primary disadvantage to online information services is that you can spend a lot of money using them. Rates vary from a few dollars an hour (for just looking around or leaving messages at 300 baud) to several hundred dollars an hour (for accessing some specialized information databases). Obviously, the best way to keep your costs down is to use an online information service effectively, with a minimum of wasted time.

Study the service manual to get an idea of the things you can do with the service before you go online. The few hours you spend reading and developing a search strategy will be abundantly repaid in savings of online time.

Find out how to use shortcuts that bypass menus or that let you stack commands to speed up getting to another part of the service. Most services have names for areas and conferences that permit you to jump directly to the conference of your choice.

If you consistently use a certain portion of the online service, set up a script or macro in your communications software that takes you to that area automatically. For example, you could set up a script to take you to your favorite online game.

You can also minimize your expenses by taking advantage of the online information service's billing policies. For example, a service may charge different rates for different speed modems. If you just want to chat with people or read messages, you probably don't need to communicate at 2400 baud; most people don't read faster than 1200 baud. As a matter of fact, you may find that 300 baud is acceptable for straight chatting. By telling your communications program to dial your 1200 or 2400 baud modem at 300, you could save up to half of your regular access charges without really slowing down the conversation.

If you want to access a special information database, though, use your modem at its fastest rate. Many information databases cost several times the normal connect time for an online information service. The few dollars you saved on the base rate for connect time by communicating at 1200 or 300 baud would be gobbled up by the additional connect charges.

Similarly, use the fastest modem setting you can for uploading and downloading files. Most online information services structure their connect charges to give you a break the faster you go.

## Tips and Techniques

Online information services tend to have a number of commands and features in common. This can make exploring different online information services easy. Naturally, each service has its own commands and features that make it unique; however, online information services have similar linear designs that are easy to follow.

Most online information services use BT TYMNET, SprintNet, or another packet-switching network to route calls from users around the country. You can find out local access numbers by dialing the service's customer support number. Online information services offer extremely helpful customer support. They can tell you a great deal about almost any part of the service and if the service offers specific features you are looking for. You can register on a service over the phone with the help of the support representative, or you can do it yourself online. You can also purchase books and starter kits for the service through the support line.

Before signing up, call the support line and ask the representative if there is a demonstration account for the online information service. With a demonstration account, you can log on to the online information service and tour some of the general features allowing you to become comfortable with the service's commands. Also ask which areas of the service can be used free of charge. Activities that typically aren't charged for include setting display options, checking on rates and current billing, and filling out online questionnaires.

Limit yourself the first time you're on an online information service. Ask for help about the general commands, look at the main menu and submenus, get a list of the conferences, and then log off. You should capture all of the information displayed on your screen so you can examine it later. Examine the material you've captured. It is a good idea to print out the list of commands and post it near your computer for quick reference. Continue to take short trips to explore small areas of the service until you feel comfortable with its organization and commands.

While exploring a service, you can press [CTRL-S] to stop the online information service from displaying information on your screen and [CTRL-Q] to resume the display. Many of the online information services also allow you to press [CTRL-C] to cancel the current command and return to the previous menu or prompt. Pressing [CTRL-O] stops a menu from displaying and immediately gives you the prompt, letting you skip over menus with which you are familiar.

Most online information systems are set up in *pages*. A page is a menu or a screen. Find where the page identifier appears on the menus and screens. This identifier may be a number (such as 925) or a section header (such as GAMES-1). You can use this page identifier to jump from anywhere in the service to any other place by entering a command followed by the appropriate page identifier. This command will probably look something like GO [page number]—for example, GO 197—or M [page number] (for Move to)—such as M 197. Areas of special interest will often have a name assigned to them that is easy to remember. You could enter *GO SHOPPING* or *M MALL* to move directly to the online merchants. The page identifier for the main menu is usually called MAIN or TOP. By entering *MAIN* or *TOP* at the prompt, you are usually returned to the main menu.

Logoff commands differ from service to service. On some online information services, you enter *BYE*; on others, you may enter *EXIT, OFF, GOODBYE,* or *QUIT*. However, when these commands are entered at a submenu within a service, you may just be taken to the previous menu. They may only log you off when you are on the main menu. When in doubt, check the online help files or read the manual.

Finally, *never give your password to anyone!* No authorized representative of an online information service should ever, under any circumstances, ask you to give them your password. If someone gets your password, they can log on under your account, rack up several hundred dollars of charges, and you will have to pay for it. Therefore, be extremely careful with your password, and change it frequently. If you demonstrate the service for someone, change your password afterwards.

# COMPUSERVE

CompuServe is the largest and probably the most famous of all the online information services. It started in 1968 as Compu-Serv, a computer processing center for Golden United Life Insurance Company. Compu-Serv became an independent company in 1975 and changed its name to CompuServe three years later. InfoPlex, a commercial electronic mail service, was added in 1978.

Up until 1979, CompuServe was aimed at providing commercial computer service. In 1979, CompuServe started MicroNET, a nighttime service aimed at the rapidly growing home and hobby computer market. It merged with H&R Block, the tax preparation company, and went to 24-hour access in 1980. Over the next few years, MicroNET developed into what is now the CompuServe Information Service (CIS). CompuServe expanded into Japan in 1987 and Europe in 1988. By 1990, CompuServe had over 500,000 users.

## Logging On

To log on to CompuServe, you will need to get a local CompuServe number. You can phone CompuServe's Customer Service representatives at 800-848-8990, or 614-457-8600 inside Ohio or outside of the U.S. Local numbers are also listed in the CompuServe membership starter kit.

CompuServe offers an online demo account for you to experiment with. You don't need to be a member of CompuServe to use it. Figure 9-1 shows a typical logon screen for CompuServe.

```
   03SEC

 Host Name:  CIS

 User ID: 77770,101
 Password:


 CompuServe    DEMO         DEM-94

  Welcome to CompuServe and the world of videotex information!
   This demonstration of the CompuServe Information Service will give you an
 overview and description of many of the over 600 services available to you
 through a regular CompuServe subscription.
   The pages that follow are structured as a menu-choice system. For additional
 information on any item, just type and enter the appropriate number into your
 terminal.  To move back to previous menus, type and enter the command M at any !
 prompt.  The command T will return you to the "top" or the beginning of the
 Demonstration, page DEM-1.  To disconnect from the Service, enter the command
 OFF or BYE.
   The regular CompuServe Information Service uses these commands and ones
 similar to them in addition to word-search capabilities in designated areas.

 Press <CR> for more !

 CompuServe    DEMO         DEM-8

   Regular subscriptions are available from microcomputer retailers throughout
 the United States and Canada.  For additional information on obtaining your
 CompuServe Information Service subscription, select "Subscriber Information" on
 page DEM-1 and check out "The Starter Kit" and "Your Local Dealers."

 Last page !
```

*Figure 9-1.  CompuServe Logon Screen*

When you connect with the local number, you will be prompted for the host name. Enter *CIS* (for CompuServe Information Service).  CompuServe then prompts you for the user ID and password.  Enter *77770,101* for the demonstration user ID and *FREE-DEMO* for the password.

**Note:** User IDs on CompuServe are two numbers separated by a comma.

You are then taken on a guided tour of the CompuServe Information Service. Press [ENTER] to get the next page of information when prompted. When CompuServe displays `Last page!` at the bottom of a screen, it means that there is no more information on a topic. You are then returned to the menu. Figure 9-2 shows the menu for the demonstration account.

```
CompuServe   DEMO           DEM-1

  1 Tour of the Service
  2 Sample Menus of the Service

  3 What's New

  4 Subscriber Information
  5 Find a Topic

Last page, enter choice !
```

*Figure 9-2. CompuServe Demonstration Menu*

The page identifier, DEM-1, is in the upper right corner of the figure. You can enter *GO DEM-1* at any prompt to return to this menu.

## Looking Around

From the main demonstration menu, you can select menu options 1 and 2 to look at CompuServe. Select menu option 3 to see what has been added, changed, or expanded on CompuServe recently. Option 4 will get subscriber information; option 5 will list the conference topics. Figure 9-3 shows a few sample menus.

```
CompuServe   DEMO          DEM-100

  1 Subscriber Assistance
  2 Find a Topic
  3 Communications/Bulletin Bds.
  4 News/Weather/Sports
  5 Travel
  6 The Electronic MALL/Shopping
  7 Money Matters/Markets
  8 Entertainment/Games
  9 Home/Health/Family
 10 Reference/Education
 11 Computers/Technology
 12 Business/Other Interests

Enter choice !3

CompuServe   DEMO          DEM-103

COMMUNICATIONS/BULLETIN BOARDS contains the EasyPlex Electronic Mail service, a
"real-time" CB Simulator, the National Bulletin Board, many discussion forums,
clubs and special interest groups, and a FEEDBACK feature that lets you leave
messages for Customer Service. The following page shows the various sections of
this area.

Press <CR> for more !

CompuServe   DEMO          DEM-11

COMMUNICATIONS/BULLETIN BOARDS

 * EasyPlex Electronic Mail
 * CB Simulator
 * Forums (SIGs)
 * National Bulletin Board
 * Directory of Subscribers
 * Ask Customer Service
 * CB Society
 * Access (Public File Area)
 * Hallmark Color Mail

Last page !
```

*Figure 9-3. CompuServe Sample Menus*

CompuServe has many conferences and forums.  You can list the topics by selecting option 5.  Figure 9-4 demonstrates the procedure and shows a partial list of topics.

```
CompuServe Index (FREE)   INDEX

FIND A TOPIC

 1 Search for Topics of Interest
 2 List ALL Indexed Topics
 3 Explanation of Index

Enter choice !2

CompuServe Index (FREE)

ALL INDEXED TOPICS - 524 TOPICS

 1 44 Cakes                     DS
 2 A Help Store                 AH
 3 AAMSI Communications         AAMSI
 4 ABC CompuLease               DU
 5 ABC Worldwide Hotel Guide    ABC
 6 AEJMC Forum                  AEJMC
 7 AI EXPERT Forum              AIEXPERT
 8 ALDUS Forum                  ALDUS
 9 AM/PM Music & Video          AM
10 AP Datastream (E)            ENS

Enter choice or <CR> for more !

CompuServe Index (FREE)

ALL INDEXED TOPICS - CON'T

11 AP Sports ($)                NEWS
12 AP Videotex, Business        APV
13 AP Videotex, Entertainment   APV
14 AP Videotex, Politics        APV
15 AP Videotex, Weather         APV
16 AP Videotex, World News      APV
17 Academic Amer. Ency ($)      ENCYCLOPEDIA
18 Access Phone Numbers (FREE)  PHONE
19 Adobe Forum                  ADOBE
20 Adventures in Travel         AIT

Enter choice or <CR> for more !
```

*Figure 9-4.  Listing Topics on CompuServe*

The word FREE at the top of the figure shows that the index is free—that is, you are not charged for your access time while you are using the index, even if you are using a regular CompuServe account.

The list in Figure 9-4 is in alphabetic order by topic. You can go directly to any forum or conference by entering *GO* followed by the conference name at the prompt. For example, to go to the list of CompuServe access phone numbers—which is also free—you would enter *GO PHONE*.

## Logging Off

Logging off of CompuServe is done by entering *OFF* or *BYE* at any prompt. Figure 9-5 gives an example of logging off of CompuServe.

```
CompuServe    DEMO           DEM-1

 1 Tour of the Service
 2 Sample Menus of the Service

 3 What's New

 4 Subscriber Information
 5 Find a Topic

Last page, enter choice !bye


Off at 23:23 PDT 12-Mar-90
```

*Figure 9-5. Logging Off of CompuServe*

The demonstration account gives you an excellent opportunity to experiment with your CompuServe commands and to get a feel for the service without having to pay for it.

## The Executive Option

The CompuServe demonstration account shows features of the CompuServe Information Service (CIS). If you sign up with CompuServe as an individual, you will get a CIS account. CompuServe also offers accounts for people interested in business through the Executive Option.

The Executive Option gives you access to financial and news databases and features that a regular CIS account doesn't have access to. These services and features include:

- the Executive News Service (a news "clipping" service)
- capsule summaries of current market performance
- financial and SEC reports for specific information about a company
- a broker's estimating and forecasting database for forecasting earnings
- security screening, for identifying securities
- a demographic database

The Executive Option also gives you a 50% increase in the online storage space and additional discounts on database access. There is a monthly minimum for this service, but the usage charges are the same.

## Summary

CompuServe is a good all-around service for people who have a number of different interests and who only want to use one service. CompuServe has been described as being like a big city: if you're looking for anything, you can usually find it, although it might take you a little while to do so.

For more information on CompuServe, call 800-848-8990 (voice), or 614-457-8600 (voice) inside Ohio or outside of the U.S. You can also write to CompuServe at 5000 Arlington Centre Boulevard, P.O. Box 20212, Columbus, OH 43220.

# GENIE

GEnie, a service of General Electric Information Services, began operation in October of 1985. GEnie is aimed at the personal computer enthusiast; its average subscriber tends to have personal computers at home and office. GEnie is second only to CompuServe for the number of registered users, with about 180,000 at the beginning of 1990.

## Logging On

GEnie uses General Electric Information Services' packet-switching network, so you can't get hold of them through SprintNet data network or BT TYMNET. To register as a GEnie user, set your communications for half duplex (local echo on) and call 800-638-8369. Figure 9-6 shows the initial logon procedure.

```
CONNECT 2400
HHH
U#=◄XJM11701,GEnie

 *** WELCOME TO GEnie (tm) ***

     The General Electric
Network for Information Exchange

 GEnie, the information service
 for Micro-computer enthusiasts
 and professionals...like you!

GEnie international availability

          1) U.S.A.
          2) Canada
          3) Public Data Net
          4) Japan NEC

Enter # of country where
you are located ?1

Genie features include:

*  World News, Weather, Sports
*  Business & Financial Information
*  Travel, Airline & Tour Information
*  Electronic Encyclopedias
*  GE Mail (TM) electronic mail
*  RoundTable (TM) Bulletin Boards
*  Real-Time Conferencing
*  RoundTable (TM) Software Libraries
*  LiveWire (TM) CB Simulator
*  PC Newsletters and Information
*  Multi-player Games

GENIE SERVICE AVAILABILITY:
GEnie Services are available 24 hours
every day. Occasional outages are
scheduled.
```

*Figure 9-6. GEnie Initial Logon Screen*

When you are first connected, enter *HHH*. This lets the GEnie network know that you're logged on. It will respond with a U#=◄ prompt. The first time you log in, you enter *XJM11701,GENIE*. The first half (XJM11701) is the account and the second half (GENIE) is the password.

GEnie responds with some basic information about features and leads you through the registration procedure. When you have entered your registration information, GEnie tells you that the information you entered will be verified shortly and logs you off.

You will be contacted by a GEnie representative within about one business day, after which you will be issued your own user ID and password and will receive a GEnie user's manual.

## Looking Around

Once you have your user ID and password, you can log on to GEnie by dialing the local access number for your area. Local access numbers are displayed as part of the registration procedure. The main menu is shown in Figure 9-7.

```
   ** Thank you for choosing GEnie **

   The Consumer Information Service
        from General Electric
        Copyright (C), 1989

GEnie Logon at: 23:58 EDT on: 900318
Last Access at: 01:21 EDT on: 900317

*  Can police confiscate repeat DUI  *
   offenders' vehicles...Type "ALERT"

*  Cats...Dogs...Birds...Ferrets...  *
   Pet-Net RT has it ALL! Type "PET".

* Free Connect Time -  Free Shopping *
  at 6 GEnie Mall Stores! See "MALL"

You have no letters waiting.

GEnie           TOP            Page  1
       GE Information Services

  1. GEnie Users' RT  2. Index - Info
  3. Billing/Setup    4. GE Mail & Chat
  5. Computing        6. Travel
  7. Finance          8. Shopping
  9. News            10. Games
 11. Professional    12. Leisure
 13. Reference       14. Logoff

Enter #, or <H>elp?4
```

*Figure 9-7. GEnie Main Menu*

At the top of Figure 9-7, you can see that GEnie displays one and two-line blurbs about some of the topics available. An RT is a RoundTable, GEnie's name for a special interest group or conference. You can also see that GEnie uses numbers for page identifiers and that the main menu is TOP . You can move directly to a page by entering *M* (for

Move) followed by the page number. You can also select a menu option by adding a semicolon and the number of the selection. For example, if you want to move to the main menu (page 1), and select the games option, enter *M 1;10* at any prompt.

One of the first places you should take a look at is the index of services (option 2 on the main menu). Here you can get a listing of the topics on GEnie, as well as valuable tips and online help on using GEnie. Figure 9-8 shows the index menu and the tips and information menu.

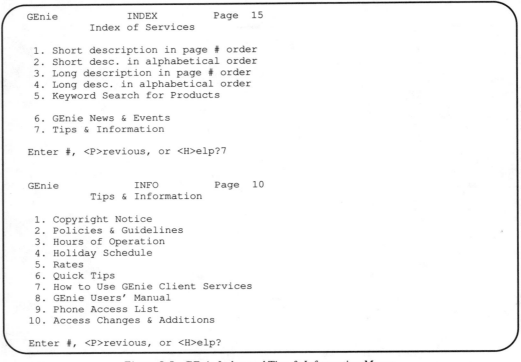

```
GEnie           INDEX          Page  15
        Index of Services

1. Short description in page # order
2. Short desc. in alphabetical order
3. Long description in page # order
4. Long desc. in alphabetical order
5. Keyword Search for Products

6. GEnie News & Events
7. Tips & Information

Enter #, <P>revious, or <H>elp?7


GEnie           INFO           Page  10
        Tips & Information

1. Copyright Notice
2. Policies & Guidelines
3. Hours of Operation
4. Holiday Schedule
5. Rates
6. Quick Tips
7. How to Use GEnie Client Services
8. GEnie Users' Manual
9. Phone Access List
10. Access Changes & Additions

Enter #, <P>revious, or <H>elp?
```

*Figure 9-8. GEnie Index and Tips & Information Menus*

The online manual (selection 8) is well written and easy to use. The sections are organized like the categories on the main menu. You may want to capture sections of this manual and print them out for later reference. Figure 9-9 shows a partial list of the leisure interests you can pursue on GEnie.

```
GEnie          LEISURE          Page 520
     Hobbies & Leisure Interests   BA

  1. Genealogy RT
  2. Photography RT
  3. Scuba RT
  4. Science Fiction & Fantasy RT
  5. Spaceport RT
  6. CINEMAN Entertainment Information
  7. Hollywood Hotline TM Movie Reviews
  8. Rainbo Electronic Reviews
  9. GEnie Banner Maker
 10. MIDI/WorldMusic RT
 11. Soap Opera Summaries
 12. Writers' RoundTable
 13. Aviation RoundTable
 14. Radio & Electronics RoundTable
 15. Rocknet Entertainment News

Item #, or <RETURN> for more?
```

*Figure 9-9.  Partial GEnie Leisure Menu*

Most of the options are labled with RT to indicate they are RoundTables.  Some options, on the other hand, simply provide users with information. Figure 9-9 is only a partial list.

GEnie also supports a wide variety of business services and RoundTables.  Figure 9-10 shows the GEnie financial menu.

```
GEnie          FINANCE          Page 600
     Business & Financial Services

  1. About Financial Products
  2. Dow Jones News/Retrieval
  3. $GEnie Quotes Securities Database
  4. $VESTOR 24-Hour Investment Advisor
  5. GEnie Loan Calculator
  6. NewsGrid Headline News
  7. Investment Software
  8. GEnie QuikNews
  9. NewsBytes News Service
 10. Schwab Investors' RT
 11. Home Office/Small Business RT

Enter #, <P>revious, or <H>elp?1
```

*Figure 9-10.  GEnie Financial Menu*

Two of the options on the menu in Figure 9-10 are preceded with a dollar sign. This means that there is an additional charge for using these services. Enter *RATES* at a menu prompt to find out more about the additional charges for any service.

The menu of professional services lists RoundTables and services for people in various professions. The professional services menu appears in Figure 9-11.

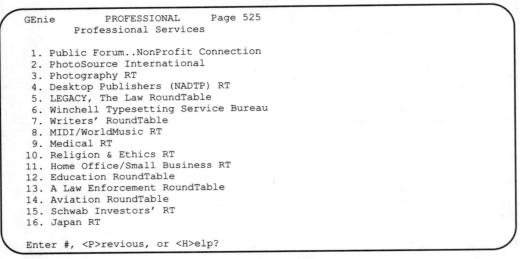

```
GEnie         PROFESSIONAL      Page 525
        Professional Services

  1. Public Forum..NonProfit Connection
  2. PhotoSource International
  3. Photography RT
  4. Desktop Publishers (NADTP) RT
  5. LEGACY, The Law RoundTable
  6. Winchell Typesetting Service Bureau
  7. Writers' RoundTable
  8. MIDI/WorldMusic RT
  9. Medical RT
 10. Religion & Ethics RT
 11. Home Office/Small Business RT
 12. Education RoundTable
 13. A Law Enforcement RoundTable
 14. Aviation RoundTable
 15. Schwab Investors' RT
 16. Japan RT

Enter #, <P>revious, or <H>elp?
```

*Figure 9-11. GEnie Professional Services Menu*

In addition to the features shown in this section, GEnie has several online reference services, including Grolier's Encyclopedia and the NewsBytes News Service. NewsBytes is an online weekly news magazine reporting on developments in computers and computing.

## Logging Off

To log off of GEnie, you can select option 14, Logoff, from the main menu, or type *BYE* at any menu prompt. Figure 9-12 shows a typical logoff procedure from the computing menu.

```
GEnie          COMPUTING          Page 510
               Personal Computing

 1. Apple RoundTables
 2. Atari RoundTables
 3. Commodore & Amiga RTs
 4. IBM PC & Compatibles RoundTables
 5. Product Support RoundTables
 6. Personal Computer News
 7. BBS RoundTable
 8. CP/M RoundTable
 9. Laptops RoundTable
10. Tandy RoundTable
11. TI & Orphans RoundTable
12. Programming Language RTs
13. NewsBytes News Service

Enter #, <P>revious, or <H>elp?bye


Thank you for choosing GEnie.
Have a nice day!

Online: 9 minutes, 23 seconds.


OFF AT 00:07EDT 03/19/90
```

*Figure 9-12. GEnie Logoff Procedure*

## Summary

GEnie focuses on the personal computer user a little more than CompuServe, but it also offers a wide range of services that will make it attractive to general and business users. GEnie does not have a demonstration account at this time.

GEnie has a $29.95 one-time sign-up fee. This charge includes a $10.00 usage credit, a subscription to LiveWire magazine, and your GEnie User Manual. Usage rates vary depending on when you are phoning and your baud rate. For more information on GEnie, call 800-638-9636, or write to GEnie, 401 N. Washington Street, Rockville, MD 20850.

# DELPHI

DELPHI opened for business in October of 1981. Wes Kussmaul, a Boston consultant, set up an online encyclopedia and other materials for DELPHI that became available for public access in February 1983.

One of the first things you notice about DELPHI is that it is very informal. For example, you get to pick your own user name; your user ID doesn't have to be a number or your first initial and last name.

## Logging On

You can log on DELPHI directly at 617-576-0862 (for 3/1200 baud) or 617-576-2981 (for 2400 baud), or you can log on through a local SprintNet data network or BT TYMNET number. (Information on obtaining SprintNet Data Network and BT TYMNET numbers appears in Chapter 8, "Extending Your Reach.")

If you already have a SprintNet data network or BT TYMNET account, you may want to log on to DELPHI that way. Talk to DELPHI's member service representatives at 800-544-4005 for information on logging on through a particular packet-switching network. There are slight differences in how you tell the packet-switching network you are logging on to DELPHI depending on the network you are using, your baud rate, and your modem settings. Once you reach the `Username` prompt, you use the same logon procedure, as illustrated in Figure 9-13.

```
Username: JOINDELPHI

ENTER YOUR PASSWORD: signup

WELCOME TO DELPHI !!!

It is a pleasure for us at DELPHI to
welcome you to our outstanding,
worldwide information and communications
network and to the exciting world of
telecommunications.

Shortly, you will be prompted to
register for your no-risk  signup, which
entitles you to a lifetime DELPHI
membership, a copy of "DELPHI: The
Official Guide" (a $19.95 value), plus
More?
a $14.40 usage credit for only $49.95.

Thanks for joining DELPHI.  We
appreciate having you as a member.

Welcome to DELPHI.
Copyright (c) 1987
General Videotex Corporation

ABOUT DELPHI, OUR DEMONSTRATION AND
ONLINE SIGNUP

Please remember, the time you spend
touring and joining DELPHI is free. The
following brief demo is intended to show
you our state-of-the-art system. You
don't have to know how to type and you
don't need to know a lot about
computers.
```

*Figure 9-13. Sample Logon Procedure for DELPHI*

After a few more screens of information, you will see the interactive demonstration menu (shown in Figure 9-14).

```
INTERACTIVE DEMONSTRATION Menu:

DELPHI Main Menu
ACCESS Phone Numbers
RATES and Prices
NO RISK Signup Policy
SIGNUP for Membership
EXIT (Signoff)

DELPHI>What do you want to do?
```

*Figure 9-14. DELPHI Demonstration Menu*

Continue to explore some of DELPHI's features by entering *DELPHI* or sign up as a new user by entering *SIGNUP*. This demonstration is also available after you register with the service.

## Looking Around

The main demonstration menu appears in Figure 9-15.

```
DELPHI MAIN (Demo) Menu:

Business & Finance    News-Weather-Sport
Conference            People on DELPHI
DELPHI Mail           Travel
Entertainment         Workspace
Groups and Clubs      Using DELPHI
Library               HELP
Merchants' Row        EXIT

MAIN>What do you want to do?
```

*Figure 9-15. Main Demonstration Menu for DELPHI*

You can see in Figure 9-15 that there are no numbers in front of the menu options. To select an option from the demonstration menu (or anywhere else on DELPHI) is very simple. All you need to do is enter the first letter or two of the option you want to select. For example, you simply enter *L* to select the library menu. The library menu is shown in Figure 9-16.

```
DELPHI's Library contains the Kussmaul
Encyclopedia (more than 20,000 entries),
CAIN (Computerized AIDS Information
Network), Dialog's Research Library and
Grolier's Encyclopedia.

The Library also contains information on
food and cooking.  The Online Gourmet
lists hundreds recipes, including
vegetarian and special holiday meals.

Library Menu:

CAIN
BOS-DELPHI/Boston
KC-DELPHI/Kansas City
Grolier Encyclopedia
HealthNet
Hearing Impaired Forum
Kussmaul Encyclopedia
Librarian
MetroLine City Search
Online Gourmet
Personal Advisor
Research Library (Dialog)
Terra Nova
WordLine Country Search
Dialog-Help
Help
Exit
```

*Figure 9-16. Library Menu for DELPHI*

DELPHI's library contains a number of interesting services, such as the Computerized AIDS Information Network (CAIN) and the Grolier Academic American Encyclopedia, as well as more typical services such as Dialog.

Another interesting section of DELPHI is the News-Weather-Sports area, shown in Figure 9-17.

```
DELPHI's News-Weather-Sports provides
continuously updated news and sports
from United Press International, weather
reports, a complete financial news
package, news summaries, movie reviews
and much more.

News-Weather-Sports Menu:

        Newsbrief
        Accu-Weather Forecasts
        UPI News Service
        Astro Predictions
        Financial News
        Movie News and Reviews
        Press Releases: Business Wire
        Sports
        Help
        Exit
```

*Figure 9-17. DELPHI News Menu*

The News menu lets you look at news from the United Press International wire service, the latest sports scores, weather reports, and reviews of current movies.

Despite the relaxed and informal feeling of DELPHI, there are a number of areas and features of interest to business users. Figure 9-18 shows the business menu.

```
DELPHI's Business and Finance Services
let you calculate mortgage payments,
make transactions via an online
brokerage service and obtain stock and
commodity quotations.  You'll also find
the Dow Jones Averages and the UPI
Financial NewsWire.  Some of these
services, such as the commodity and
stock quotes and VESTOR may carry an
additional charge, which is stated online.

Business and Finance Menu:
UPI Business News
Business Forum
CD Infoline
Commodity Quotes
Donoghue's Money Fund Report
Dow Jones Averages
Financial and Commodity News
Futures Focus
Investment Software
Mortgage Calculator
Press Releases: Business Wire
Security Objective Service
Stock Quotes
Trendrest Ratings & Portfolio Analysis
VESTOR - 24 Hour Investment Advisor
Help
Exit
```

*Figure 9-18. DELPHI Business Menu*

As you can see in Figure 9-18, DELPHI offers a range of business news services and stock reports. You will have to pay an additional charge for some of these services.

## Logging Off

You log off of DELPHI by typing *bye* or *exit* at the main menu. Figure 9-19 shows what this looks like.

```
MAIN>What do you want to do?bye


SAMSPADE off at 18-MAR-1990 00:39:11
Session time: 18 minutes.


Thank you for using DELPHI.
```

*Figure 9-19. Logging Off of DELPHI*

You also type *exit* to exit from areas of DELPHI and return to the preceding menu. Be careful not to enter too many Exit commands, or you may accidentally log yourself off DELPHI.

## Summary

DELPHI has a lot of personality. Most other online information services have numbered menus from which you select the option you want. DELPHI gives you the feeling that you are merely choosing something from a list. As a result, DELPHI is very easy to use for people who aren't used to selecting menus and options.

For information on registering with DELPHI, phone 800-544-4005 or 617-491-3393, or write to General Videotex Corporation, 3 Blackstone St., Cambridge, MA 02139.

## BIX

BIX (short for the BYTE Information Exchange) was started in 1984 by the editor and several other staff members of BYTE magazine. It is an online computer service for the microcomputer professional. Unlike many of the other online information services, BIX has no information databases. Almost all the conferences are on computer-related topics. BIX's scope and purpose is to be the premier source of online information for enhancing your microcomputer performance. If you like BYTE magazine, you'll like BIX.

BIX is a little unusual in that it has no hourly rates and no sign-up fee. BIX currently costs $39 a quarter for unlimited access. The manuals are free with sign-up. There are BT TYMNET charges to get in to BIX, however: $2/hour for offpeak access and

$8/hour for peak access for 300 and 1200 baud. 2400 baud costs $3.50/hour for off-peak access and $10.50/hour for peak access. You can also sign up for unlimited off-peak BT TYMNET access at $15/month. If you use BIX a lot, it can be an exceptional bargain. BIX also has 9600 baud and MNP direct-dial lines in the Boston area. However, since there are no hourly connect charges for BIX itself, you probably don't have to worry about uploading and downloading data quickly as much as on some of the other online information services.

BIX does not have a demonstration account. You can, however, have BIX send you a free demonstration diskette in IBM, Macintosh, Amiga, and Apple IIgs formats that shows you BIX's mail functions, sample listings of files, several conferences, and samples of the MicroBytes Daily News, an award-winning daily news service.

## Logging On

You can log on to BIX through a local BT TYMNET number, or you can dial directly to BIX in Boston, 617-861-9767. At the `Please log in` prompt, enter *BIX*. After a moment, you will be connected to BIX. Figure 9-20 shows what this looks like.

```
  BIX: call connected
Welcome to BIX — ttyx7, 9448
= = BYTE/CoSy - BIX 3.5 = =

Welcome to BIX, the BYTE Information Exchange

McGraw-Hill Information Services Co.
Copyright (c) 1989 by McGraw-Hill Inc.

CoSy Conferencing System, Copyright (c) 1984 University of Guelph

Need BIX voice help...
In the U.S. and Canada call 800-227-2983, in NH and elsewhere call
603-924-7681 8:30 a.m. to 11:00 p.m. EDT (-4 GMT) weekdays
Name? new
```

*Figure 9-20. BIX Initial Logon Screen*

To register as a new user, type *new* at the name prompt. BIX will then lead you through the registration procedure.

## Looking Around

After you register with BIX, you can use the system right away without waiting to be verified. BIX will mail you your user manuals and the demonstration diskette in a few days. Figure 9-21 shows the BIX main menu.

```
      BIX Main Menu

   1  Electronic Mail
   2  Conference Subsystem
   3  Listings
   4  CBix
   5  MicroBytes - Industry News Briefs
   6  McGraw-Hill News
   7  Subscriber Information
   8  Individual Options
   9  Quick Download
  10  Command Mode (abandon menus)
  11  Logoff (bye)

Enter a menu option or ? for help:
```

*Figure 9-21. BIX Main Menu*

Most of the features on the main menu are fairly typical. Some things worth noting are CBix, BIX's CB simulator for multi-user chatting, and MicroBytes, an online computer magazine and news service. BIX also has an "expert" mode option (option 10). You can turn off the menus and enter specific commands.

Figure 9-22 shows the conference menu, which reflects the technical nature of BIX.

```
      Conference Groups Menu

   1  bytebix        Conferences and communications about BYTE and BIX
   2  ai             Conferences on artificial intelligence
   3  applications   Conferences on applications programs and programming
   4  chips          Conferences on chips and semiconductor technologies
   5  computers      Conferences about specific brands of small computers
   6  graphics       Conferences about graphics and small computers
   7  ibm.exchange   Complete information about IBM Computers
   8  igx            The Interactive Game Exchange
   9  languages      Conferences about specific programming languages
  10  mac.exchang    Everything you want to know about the Macintosh
  11  op.sys         Conferences concerning different operating systems
  12  regions        Conferences for BIXen from various geographical areas
  13  technology     Conferences about new technology
  14  telecomm       Conferences on telecommunications
  15  user.groups    User Group conferences
  16  writers.ex     The Writers Exchange
  17  other          Conferences on technology and society
  18  vendor.support Conferences run by vendors (NOTE: These conferences
                     are run entirely by vendor staff and not by BIX
                     personnel. Opinions expressed in these conferences
                     are those of the vendor and participants and not
                     necessarily those of BIX, BYTE or McGraw-Hill.)

   p  Previous menu
  mm  Main menu

Enter a menu option or ? for help:
```

*Figure 9-22. BIX Conference Menu*

Each of the options on the conference menu is actually a category of topics.  For example, if you entered *3* for the applications category, you would see the following topics (shown in Figure 9-23).

```
        Join Conference Menu

    1   Show information about a conference

    2   o apps.digest       Selected items of interest in the Applications group
    3   o apps.386          Application programs for 80386-based computers
    4   o clipper           The conference on Nantucket's Clipper
    5   o dbms              The database management program conference
    6   o engineering       The conference on engineering programs
    7   o framework         Ashton-Tate's Framework
    8   o games             The games program conference
    9   o gem               The GEM interface
    10  o microsoft         Products from Microsoft
    11  o sciences          The conference on scientific programs
    12  o spreadsheets      Discussions on spreadsheets
    13  o telecomm.pgms     The telecommunications program conference
    14  o television        Working with video
    15  o ventura.pub       The Ventura Publisher
    16  o word.processor    The word-processing program conference
    p   Previous menu
    mm  Main menu

    (o=open,c=closed)

Enter a menu option or ? for help:
```

*Figure 9-23.  Topics in Applications Category on BIX*

# Logging Off

Enter *11* at the main menu or *BYE* at any menu prompt.  Figure 9-24 shows an example of logging off.

```
Enter a menu option or ? for help: bye
Goodbye..'sspade'
Off at Mon Mar 19 20:37:56 1990
Total connect time for this session was 9 minutes.
Thank you for using BIX!  Please come back soon.
```

*Figure 9-24.  Logging Off of BIX*

## Summary

BIX is an excellent place to go for technical information on computers. Because it does not have information databases or other online services, it feels much more like a local BBS than any of the other services featured in this chapter. BIX is the online information service for you if you are interested in something like a large, technical BBS.

For more information, call BIX 800-227-2983 (voice) or 603-924-7681 in New Hampshire, or write BIX at 1 Phoenix Mill Lane, Peterborough, NH 03458.

## THE WELL

The WELL (Whole Earth 'Lectronic Link) was mentioned in Chapter 8 as a public Usenet system. You may also want to consider joining the WELL for what it has to offer as an online information service.

The WELL is different from the other online information services mentioned in this chapter. First, as an outgrowth of the Whole Earth Catalog, the WELL has a strong orientation towards people rather than technology—members of the WELL are known as "Wellbeings" rather than users. Although there are conferences on computers and computing, there is a strong emphasis on connectivity and exchanging ideas on non-technical subjects such as philosophy, political thought, and writing. In addition, you can tap into Usenet through the WELL, which allows you to read and participate in the spectrum of Usenet conferences.

## Logging On

Dial 415-334-6106 at 3/12/2400-8-N-1 and enter *newuser* at the prompt to register. Figure 9-25 shows the logon screen for new users.

```
This is The WELL  - use lower case to login

DYNIX(R) V3.0.14 (well)
Type your user name or "newuser" to register
login:newuser

            WELL Registration **** Please READ CAREFULLY

    The WELL is a computer teleconferencing system running on a VAX 750
computer in Sausalito, California.
    Our conferencing program runs in the UNIX environment.  We offer our
users access to the UNIX operating system, to USENET and to UUCP mail.
    As a new user, you will receive a FREE MANUAL, so be sure
to enter your mailing address below where requested.

CHARGES (billed by calendar month):
        Monthly membership     $8.00/month
        Hourly useage          $3.00/hour regardless of time or baud rate.
        Disk storage over 500K $0.02/Kilobyte ($20.00/Megabyte)
        CompuServe Packet Net  $5.00/hr (call 800/848-8980 for local number)
            (Canadian, Alaskan and Hawaiian customers call us for instructions)

As each : prompt appears, simply type in the information requested, followed
by <return>.  If you make a mistake and want to fix your entry, you can use
the backspace key or <Control-h> and you can type it again.
    TO ABORT THIS REGISTRATION, type <Control-c> at any time.
```

*Figure 9-25. Initial Logon Screen for the WELL*

When you enter *newuser* at the `login:` prompt, information about the WELL and its current rates is displayed. It then takes you through a fairly standard registration procedure.

Your user ID is what you'll use to log on with. People will send mail to this ID, but they'll also be able to see your name. Most people either use their initials or their first name and last initial. You can't have the same user ID as someone else—the WELL will tell you during registration if someone already has chosen that user ID.

Unix, the operating system on which the WELL is run, is *case-sensitive;* that is, it makes a difference if you enter something in capitals or lowercase letters. Unless specifically told to do otherwise, you should always use lowercase letters on the WELL. The most significant exception to this is your password, which must be a combination of capital and lowercase letters.

Once you have entered the registration information, the WELL will log you out. If you entered a credit card number, your account will be activated within a couple of days. It may take a little longer if you are sending in a deposit for monthly billing. You can phone the WELL at 415-332-4335 (voice) 9:00 A.M. to 5:00 P.M. Pacific Time on weekdays for more information on billing.

## Looking Around

Once your account is activated, you can look around the WELL. Figure 9-26 shows the opening screens of the WELL.

```
Last login: Sat Mar 17 00:04:43 on ttyhb
DYNIX(R) V3.0.14 NFS  #3 (): Mon Mar 19 13:34:53 PDT 1990
Copyright 1984 Sequent Computer Systems, Inc.

   You have reached the WELL (Whole Earth Lectronic Link).  Material
   posted on the WELL is the sole property of its author.  Reproduction
   in any medium without the express permission of the individual author
   is strictly prohibited.
   Opinions of conference hosts do not necessarily reflect those of
   WELL management or ownership.

For voice phone support, call +1 415 332 4335, Monday through Friday,
       between the hours of 09:00 and 17:00 (5:00 PM) Pacific Time

-> For personal online help, type          support

-> For information on long-distance packet access to the WELL, type    cpn
       at a prompt.

PicoSpan T3.3; designed by Marcus Watts
 copyright 1984 NETI; licensed by Unicon Inc.

This is the Entry Conference, the WELL's "foyer" and a place to learn
how to use the WELL.  If you are new to the WELL type    s1<cr>   to see
the first topic: The Walkthrough.  This will show you how to go to different
conferences and look around.  Topic #2 is also recommended.  Type    b<cr>
For a listing of other topics in this conference.  Mail  tex  for more info.
                 \\\\  WELL Hot Spots  ////
                      for August 1
1. Telecom (g tele) topic 512: Universal BBS/CC Exchange Method?
2. Spirituality (g spi) topic 96: Free Rent
_____

For help at the OK: prompt type: ?conf - lists public conferences; commands
- lists WELL and Unix commands; support - for voice help; cpn - information on
long distance access; help - general advice; Billing questions - email to
accounts; picohits - most active conferences; menu - see the WELL manual;
manual - to download the WELL manual; anything else - mail tex

22 brandnew items
First item 1, last 121

Ok (? for help):
```

*Figure 9-26. Opening Screens for the WELL*

After login information and bulletins, you are in the "Entry" conference. Several topics are spotlighted. You can go to any conference by entering *g* followed by the name of the conference, such as *tele* for Telecommunications or *tec* for Technical Writers.

You can get online help at any prompt by entering *help*. You can also get extended help on a number of topics. Figure 9-27 shows the standard help screen.

```
Welcome to PicoSpan; a Unix-based Conferencing Program (version T3.3)
    PicoSpan Commands you can get help on:
Item commands:
        Read Enter Browse Remember
Other ways to communicate:
        Mail Send Who
General commands:
        Unix Stop Bye Help Join Next Display Set Define Source Echo
Other help keywords:
        INTRODUCTION morecommands system keys conferences
        etiquette editor fairwitnesses summary dates

To get more help on a specific topic, type HELP <topic>
where <topic> is one of the above keywords.  Note that most
commands can be abreviated; ie, "b a" for "browse all", "r5"
for "read 5"...

You can also type HELP at many points, including the "Respond, forget or
pass? " prompt, and the "Join, observe..." prompt, as well as at
the "Ok: " prompt.  Don't hesitate to ask somebody if you
still can't figure out something!

Ok (? for help):
```

*Figure 9-27. Online Help Screen*

Remember that the WELL is based on the Unix operating system. Unix is a powerful and effective multi-user operating system, but it can also be a little difficult to use at first. There are conferences just for getting answers to general questions about the WELL—General and Help. You can go to either of these by entering *g gen* and *g help,* respectively.

Conferences on the WELL are grouped into seven loose categories.

- *Business - Education* contains topics like Entrepreneurs, The Future, Homeowners, One Person Business, and Translators.

- *Social - Political - Humanities* is the largest category with over 30 conferences, including Emotional Health (with the appealing conference name of "bridges"), Dreams, Liberty, Nonprofits, Parenting, and Poetry.

- *Arts - Recreation - Entertainment* is almost as large, and has conferences such as Audio-Videophilia, Boating, Cooking, Flying, Gardening, MIDI, Motorcycling, and Pets.

- *The Grateful Dead* is an entire category unto itself, with topics like Feedback, Tapes, Tickets, and Tours.

- *Computers* has topics for most common computers, operating systems, and applications.

- *Technical - Communications* discusses ways to exchange information, including Packet Radio, Photography, Technical Writers, Usenet, and Video.

- *The WELL Itself* contains information about the system and how to use it in topics such as General, Help, System News, Deeper, and Entry.

For an overview of a number of different topics, you might also want to look at the Best of the WELL conference. It contains some of the most interesting material from the other conferences on the WELL. For a complete list of the conferences on the WELL, enter *help conferences* at the prompt.

## Logging Off

Logging off of the WELL is done by entering *bye* at the prompt, as shown in Figure 9-28.

```
Ok (? for help): bye
[][][][][][][][][][][][][][][][][][][][][][][][][]
To know all things is not permitted.  - Horace -
 . . . but you can still go Deeper . . .   - Hawkins -
User: samspade, charges added to your bill this session:
      Usage: 0.60 hours at $3 an hour,                      $1.80
p                             Thanks :-)

a
⌈å⊦
NO CARRIER
OK
```

*Figure 9-28. Logging Off of the WELL*

After a closing quotation, your charges for this session on the WELL are displayed and you are disconnected.

## Summary

The WELL is not a traditional online information service. It is designed to increase the connections between people by providing a forum for people to communicate and share ideas. Wellbeings, members of the WELL, are likely to be more interested in how to use a new technology than in the technology itself (although you can find yourself discussing technology with some of the most brilliant minds in Silicon Valley). The WELL only has conferences and files.

The WELL also has access to Usenet (described in Chapter 8, "Extending Your Reach"), and is strongly recommended as a public access Usenet node.

For more information on the WELL, call 415-332-4335 (voice) or write The WELL, 27 Gate Five Road, Sausalito, CA 94965.

# OTHER ONLINE INFORMATION SERVICES

This section briefly describes several other online information services and information databases. You should contact the service or database directly for more information about rates, local access, and specific services offered.

## Prodigy

Prodigy is a combination of a general information service (weather, headlines, games) and an electronic shop-at-home service. To use Prodigy, you need a personal computer with graphics capability; Prodigy screens have extensive graphics.

Prodigy is very inexpensive—currently $9.95 a month for unlimited usage. In fact, this fee doesn't cover the Prodigy's operating costs. The difference is made up by advertising revenue from companies such as J.C. Penney and Manufacturers Hanover.

Prodigy is aimed at the personal market rather than the professional market. The extensive graphics and menus make Prodigy fun to use and easy to understand even for people who aren't familiar with computers.

Prodigy is currently available only in metropolitan areas, but service areas are expanding rapidly. For more information on Prodigy, call 800-822-6922, or write Prodigy, P.O. Box 4064, Woburn, MA 01888-9961.

## PC MagNet

PC MagNet, the PC Magazine Network, was created to let readers download the programs that had appeared in the magazine and to upload messages or questions for the

PC Magazine staff. PC MagNet is part of CompuServe. If you have a CompuServe account, you can access PC MagNet by entering *go pcmagnet* at any menu prompt.

One of PC MagNet's big attractions is that you can download the utilities published in PC Magazine all the way back to 1985. You can also communicate directly with PC Magazine's editors and let them know what you liked or didn't like about a particular story.

If you aren't already a CompuServe subscriber, or you want to set up a separate PC MagNet account, you can follow the general log on procedure for CompuServe described earlier in this chapter. Enter a user ID of *177000,5000* and a password of *PC\*MAGNET*. When you are asked for an agreement number, enter *Z10D8907*. You will then be led through the registration process for PC MagNet.

PC MagNet is very interesting on its own, but is best if you are a regular reader of PC Magazine. A basic guide to PC MagNet appears in the April 11, 1989 issue of PC Magazine. For more information on PC MagNet, call 800-848-8990 (voice), or 614-457-8650 (voice) inside Ohio or outside of the U.S.

## Dialog

Dialog is a *gateway service*. A gateway service lets you access a number of information databases with the convenience of dialing one number and paying one bill. Dialog deals almost exclusively with information databases on a wide variety of topics, including agriculture, chemistry, education, law, patents, government, and medicine. For more information on the specific information databases available through Dialog, contact Dialog Information Services, 3460 Hillview Ave., Palo Alto, CA 94304, 800-334-2564 or 415-858-3785.

## Lexis and Nexis

Both Lexis and Nexis are gateway services. Lexis is for people doing legal research. Lexis currently has about 300 databases of statutes, regulations, codes, and legal analyses. Nexis is for people who need online full-text versions of over 350 magazines, newspapers, newsletters, and news services about current affairs, business news, medical and scientific information, and financial reports. Both Lexis and Nexis are available through Mead Data Central, P.O. Box 993, Dayton, OH 45401, 800-543-6862.

## Orbit

Orbit, another gateway service, provides access to approximately 75 million bibliographic records on scientific and technical topics. Orbit will be of particular interest to people working with technical patents and "hard" sciences such as electronics, chemistry, and engineering. You can find out more about Orbit from Pergamon Orbit InfoLine, Inc., 800 Westpark Drive, McLean, VA 22102, 800-45-ORBIT or 703-442-0900.

# INFORMATION DATABASES

Where an online information service tries to offer a full range of services and features to its users, an information database exists for passing on the information in a database. Information databases can be offered as part of an online information service, or they can be services of their own. Most online information services offer access to one or several information databases, such as an online encyclopedia, stock market figures, or news articles from selected publications.

Information databases that run on their own usually do not have as many features as most of the online information services. They are designed for people to log on, get the information they need from the information database, and log out.

There are currently more than 3000 information databases in this country on every conceivable topic from agriculture to zymurgy. The broad categories of information database you are likely to encounter are:

- *General information databases.*
  These include things like online encyclopedias and phone directories.

- *News databases.*
  These can be general, providing online access to everything that appears in a group of papers and magazines or one of the wire services; or specific, focusing on one type of news such as law or medicine. For an extra charge, most news databases can also provide "clipping" services, where you can set up the database to automatically send you a copy of every news article dealing with a particular person or subject.

- *General financial databases.*
  These list statistics on business trends and stock quotes and may contain profiles and other information about specific companies.

- *Specialized financial databases.*
  These deal with a smaller interest group than the previous category. Examples of databases in this category include databases that focus on specific industries, such as chemical producing, insurance, or coffee and tea trading.

- *Legal databases.*
  These contain legal-research information, sort of like an online law-library.

- *Scientific databases.*
  These almost always deal with one particular branch of science, such as medicine, chemical engineering, agriculture, and toxic waste management. For example, the National Aeronautics and Space Administration (NASA) has a database of the unclassified information on astronautics. There are also several very large multi-disciplinary scientific databases that list reports and pending research in different fields.

- *Other databases.*
  These are things like census statistics, educational materials, social sciences, and histories.

Some information databases are offered on a number of online information services. For example, EAASY SABRE and the Official Airline Guide (OAG), two excellent information databases for travel planning and flight reservations, are available through CompuServe, GEnie, and DELPHI, as well as other online information systems. Similarly, Dow Jones News/Retrieval, a source for business and financial news, current and back issues of the Wall Street Journal and other publications, stock quotes, and other information, is available on most major online information services.

If you have very specific information needs, you should be able to find the information database for you in a guide to information databases. Check the bibliography for some possible sources of information.

## MAKING AND SAVING MONEY ONLINE

There are several ways to make money with online information services. One of the most direct is to use online information services to advertise your own goods or services in the "Classified Ads" or "For Sale/Wanted" section. You can also set up your business as part of the service's online shopping mall and sell merchandise to other users via mail order, with the online information service providing the advertising medium and the order entry system.

If you have something to sell, advertising on a wide scale on an online information system can make you money. Author Jaron Summers made use of BBSes to advertise his high-tech murder/adventure story, *Safety Catch,* in an unusual way. Because the first month is crucial in determining subsequent book sales, Summers needed to get as many people to read the book in the first month as possible. His method was to upload the first chapter of the book to The Source and CompuServe. Summers then paid $5 to the first person to upload the chapter into BBSes, up to $50 per person. With users logging on to The Source and CompuServe from all over the world, Summers was able to reach tens of thousands of people with his advertisement. He sold 100,000 copies of *Safety Catch* within a month and a half.

Knowing where and how to find information is a salable skill in itself; you can use online information services to research almost any topic. Many large companies are retaining research specialists who know how to obtain information from information databases with the least cost. You may be able to sell your services as a researcher to companies who don't need a full-time information specialist.

For business users, an online information service can also be used to exchange mail and files with people in other offices. Although this is probably not as economical in the long run as setting up a private BBS for your company, there can be significant savings if you have offices on two or more continents. Many of the large services have local access numbers on several continents. It may be much cheaper to log on to an online information service for a few minutes and let the service route a file than to dial directly from one continent to a company BBS on another continent.

You can use the mail features of many online information service to send letters, faxes, and Telex messages, as well as the standard electronic mail. The advantage over a BBS here is that not everyone has to have a modem, nor know how to use it. Furthermore, you don't have to wait for someone to log on to the company BBS to pick up a message. The online information service gives you the speed of a direct phone call without the associated costs.

# BECOMING AN EXPERT

Online information services differ greatly. The handful of services covered in this chapter all offer unique combinations of services aimed at different classes of users. Take a little time to identify your goals and plan ways to accomplish those goals with a particular online information service before you log on. If you don't feel like your needs are being met on one service, you can probably find another service that suits you better, or you can subscribe to more than one service.

When you first register with an online information service, you will doubtless want to explore. Budget some amount of money and time for romping through the service. Be sure to capture the session using your communications program so you can look at the places you went in detail.

As a rule, the clock starts ticking when you log on. You should know why you're there, because it's going to cost you money. If you spend most of your online time flailing about trying to find out how a service works, you'll feel unhappy with the service because you don't think you're getting your money's worth. If you buy a couple of books or a starter kit, you'll be able to save a lot of time learning how a service works. Most starter kits also have a coupon good for online credit as well. Post the service's customer support phone number in a prominent place and don't be afraid to use it.

Be very careful when using information databases that have a large cost for number of entries retrieved or time online. A very common mistake is to specify too broad a set of information, such as asking a news clipping service for all the stories on the President in the last year. You may find that you've selected several hundred or thousand entries, each costing anywhere from a few cents to a dollar or more. Make your queries as specific as possible and run a limited test on the search criteria before performing the real selection. For example, restrict the allowable dates to a couple of weeks.

Another common mistake is to tell an information database to "print" something (that is, create a paper copy) instead of "typing" it (displaying it on the screen). If you print a large selection of information, you can generate a huge stack of paper that could cost you several hundred dollars for time online, printing charges, storage, and shipping.

The user who has learned to voyage into the online services can access more information than was ever thought possible. With a telephone and nominal fees, anyone can equip themselves with information on virtually any subject. Once you have acquired the static knowledge of facts, conferences and forums present opportunities for you to actively exchange ideas, sparking creativity and giving you new ways of looking at things.

Online information services and information databases represent the cutting edge of personal information retrieval. As these services develop their abilities to organize masses of material and put them at your fingertips, you will have more information power just a phone call away than most medium-sized companies.

Online information services represent a new way of sharing knowledge. They are also a new frontier of personal ability: the science fiction predictions of being able to tap into a large network of computers that have information on everything are coming true.

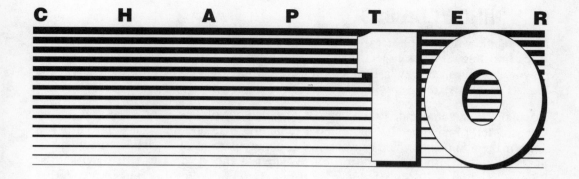

# 10

# SETTING UP
# YOUR OWN BBS

There are a lot of reasons for wanting to be a sysop. Being a sysop can be fun, challenging, and educational. But before you actually buy a computer and a modem, you should invest some time in planning what your BBS will be. This chapter explains how you can set up your own BBS. You'll see what it takes to be a sysop yourself.

# PLANNING YOUR BBS

Most people who set up their own BBS aren't ready for the real problems that happen. While most new sysops expect to have technical problems, such as hardware failures, power shortages, and even the occasional lowlife bent on crashing their BBS, the biggest problems are *ego* problems.

No matter how you decide to run your BBS, someone will leave you a message saying that you don't know the first thing about running a BBS and that you're a fool if you don't make a bunch of changes right away. Ninety percent of the BBSes that close in the first six months of operation close because the sysop can't deal with this. Remember that a BBS that doesn't offend somebody couldn't possibly interest anybody.

Decide what you want your BBS to be. Do you want to run the BBS as a business or to have fun? Will the general public be calling the BBS, or only a select group with special interests? Do you want to have downloads? Messages only? How much time will each user be allotted per day? How can they get more time? Will there be chatting and user conferences? Multiple incoming lines? Will you be tying into FidoNet or do you want to run the BBS just with the input from your users?

Clearly establishing the boundaries and the goals for your BBS before you set it up will shape every other decision you make about the form and function of the BBS: what hardware and software you use, what your user policies will be, and how you want the BBS to look. You will have fewer problems and waste less time if you know in advance what you want the BBS to be when you set about creating it.

Once you have set your boundaries and goals, the following steps will help you determine how to implement them:

1. Be logical and consistent when planning your message and file areas. If you have three message areas that deal with aspects of using IBM PCs, list them one after another. Don't make your users hunt for them.

2. The commands should be clear and easy to understand and take into account a user's assumptions. For example, most BBS users expect to be able to enter *H* for Help and *G* for Goodbye. By contrast, some badly designed BBSes have used *H* for Hang up and *G* for Get message. If you make this sort of mistake in planning your BBS, you won't be able to get people to call you more than once.

3. Write your BBS's policy (what you expect of your users, and what they can expect of you) before you have set up the BBS. Be clear and direct. Review the policy frequently before and after setting up the BBS to make sure that the policy is still an accurate reflection of what you want the BBS to be.

# CHOOSING BBS SOFTWARE

By the time you start making plans to set up your own BBS, you should be familiar with at least half a dozen types of BBS software. This knowledge lets you choose the features and options you want to emphasize on your BBS. Although most sysops set up the type of BBS they most enjoy using themselves, it is a good idea to carefully examine your alternatives before making a decision.

One common mistake new sysops make is to get BBS software that is easy for the sysop to set up rather than software that is easy to use. Although you, as a sysop, don't want to fight with your BBS software, be very careful not to make your BBS users work harder just to save you a little time. Evaluate BBS software as a BBS user first, then as a sysop.

There are a couple of advantages to using a public domain or shareware BBS package that lets you try before you buy. First, you will not be out a lot of money if the BBS fails to perform as expected. Second, your users are also likely to be already familiar with a public domain or shareware BBS; the faster you can get your users up to speed using the BBS software, the more likely they are to fulfill your goals for the BBS.

Whichever BBS you choose to run, you will always be able to attract some users who like that type of BBS. Most BBS users develop loyalties to one or two types of BBS, and will frequently explore a new BBS running their favorite BBS software just to see what it's like.

One factor in your choice of software should be what the users of a given type of BBS like. For example, if you want to set up an RBBS-PC BBS for the purpose of exchanging the latest files, and most users in your area use RBBS-PC BBSes for messages and discussions, you may have a hard time convincing the existing base of RBBS-PC users to come over to your BBS.

The following are many of the features that you should consider when choosing BBS software:

• good password and security features
• public and private message capability
• online help screens
• easily configurable menus and screens
• expandable message and file systems
• multiple user access levels
• doors
• multiple transfer protocols
• questionnaires
• availability of source code

- networking with other BBSes
- personal downloads
- system usage log
- multi-line capability
- upload/download statistics
- time accounting
- remote sysop capability
- good user and sysop documentation
- chatting between users in forums and in exclusive chat mode (on multiple user BBSes)

Get copies of public domain and shareware BBS programs or write to the BBS companies and ask for sales and marketing information about their products. Don't be afraid to ask other sysops if they recommend a certain BBS for the applications you have in mind. You may find that a BBS that is a joy to log on to is a pain to run.

Finally, always choose the BBS software *before* the computer and modem to run the software on. If you choose the computer first, you will eliminate some of your alternatives for BBS software.

## CHOOSING A COMPUTER

When selecting the computer to run the BBS on, remember that you don't need to run a BBS on any particular type of computer for exchanging messages and files. Seventy to eighty percent of the BBSes in operation today are running on some type of IBM clone because IBM clones are inexpensive, durable, and reasonably easy to work with. Parts—particularly hard disks—are cheap and plentiful. There are also a lot of options in IBM BBS software; the BBSes featured in Chapters 6 and 7 all run on IBM computers.

However, if you are planning to set up a BBS for users with a particular type of non-IBM computer, it would be a good idea to use the same type of computer for the BBS. For example, if you are setting up an Amiga BBS and want to have online games that use Amiga graphics, you will almost certainly need to use an Amiga for the BBS.

Whatever computer you choose, make sure your software can run on the computer and that you have enough hard disk storage. If you are running a message-only BBS with no files, 5-10 megabytes of hard disk space is probably adequate. If you are running a combination message and file BBS, you can get by with 20-40 megabytes. If you want your BBS to focus primarily on exchanging files, don't start with anything less than 60 megabytes of available hard disk space.

When you make plans to buy a computer for the BBS, don't plan on using the computer for anything else. Unless the BBS has restricted hours (which is not recommended for a public BBS), you won't be able to use the computer without taking the BBS offline.

# CHOOSING A MODEM

Ask the sysops in your area which modems they use and why. Some BBS software is tailored for a certain make of modem. Also find out how well a modem's auto-answer features work: many modems are superb at dialing out but are very poor at answering the phone and locking on to an incoming signal. Ask what the modem is like when operated on a noisy line. Finally, find out how dependable the modem is; it must be able to stand up to 24-hour usage for months at a time.

There are many good modems on the market today. Buy the best and fastest modem you can afford. This may not cost you as much as you think. Several modem manufacturers, including Hayes Microcomputer Products, Inc., and U.S. Robotics, Inc., have offered substantial discounts on their modems to sysops.

# SETTING UP PHONE SERVICE

It is still possible in many areas to get a second residential line installed in your home for the purposes of running a BBS as long as the BBS does not charge money; in other words, as long as it is noncommercial. If the phone company thinks that you are running the BBS for profit, they may demand that you switch to a business line, which will cost you a considerably greater amount per month as well as a charge for each incoming call.

*You must have at least one phone line in the house for the exclusive use of each BBS you are running. Never share a phone line with a BBS.*

When you set up the second phone line, buy an answering machine for your voice line. The answering machine intercepts and screens calls from users on your BBS. If your voice phone number appears in the BBS's logon display, people will call you at all hours of the night to ask questions, to tell you the BBS is down, or to complain.

You should also obtain a post office box. You will certainly want to list an address where people can send contributions, but listing your real address lessens your privacy and advertises where thieves can find several thousand dollars worth of computer hardware and software.

# DESIGNING YOUR BBS

Come up with a good name for your BBS. It should be easy to remember and reasonably short. Don't use trademarks in your BBS name—you'll get into trouble with the trademark's owner.

Put your name and P.O. box in the logon information and also in a bulletin. Making your name and address easy to find will make it easier for users to send contributions.

Your logon information should include the following:

- the BBS's name
- the BBS's phone number (with area code)
- the BBS's mailing address (your P.O. box)
- your name (or the name of your business)
- the hours the BBS is up
- baud rates and modem information
- file transfer protocols
- time limits
- type of BBS software
- number of incoming lines
- alternate phone numbers (if any)
- which line the user is on now
- FidoNet or other network ID
- the location of the BBS's policy statement

Although this sounds like a lot of information, it should fit easily into one or two screens. New users always read the logon screens when they log on for the first time. This information will make them feel more comfortable and tell them what they can expect of your BBS.

Be sure that your users always know where to find the BBS's policy statement.

# SETTING BBS POLICY

The policies you set will, in large part, determine the type of users you get. BBS policies differ from BBS to BBS. It can be a simple statement that you are only interested in receiving uploaded files archived in a certain format, or it can be a general purpose contractual statement of rights and obligations. BBS policies also tend to evolve. As a sysop, don't be afraid to change the policy if you can make it more workable; good BBSes should evolve with their users.

Make the BBS's policy easy to find, easy to read, and easy to understand. The BBS policy statement should also be required reading for new users as part of the initial logon procedure. Have them acknowledge that they have read the policy and agree to abide by its terms. Figure 10-1 is an example of policy statements that are designed to inform the user of legal rights and responsibilities.

```
===========================================================================
================ GROTTO DE BLOTTO BBS RULES & POLICIES ===================
Accessing this BBS at ANY security level constitutes an agreement by the
user to abide by ALL Rules & Policies outlined below as well as updated
rules, policies, and responsibilities that may come into effect in the
future.  In return, GROTTO DE BLOTTO will, at its convenience, provide
the named user access to its computer equipment and services via modem.

Rules, Policies, and Responsibilities:
~~~~~~~~~~~~~~~~~~~~~~~~~~~~~~~~~~~~~~~~

1.  The User does not and will not hold GROTTO DE BLOTTO or other users
responsible for fit or fitness of any files or programs downloaded from
this system, for any or all damage incurred while using said programs,
or time, damages, losses, either direct or consequential as a result of
connection to/with the BBS.  FURTHER, every user explicitly acknowledges
that all information obtained from GROTTO DE BLOTTO is provided "as is"
without warranty of any kind, either expressed or implied, including,
but not limited to the implied warranties of merchantability and fitness
for a particular purpose and that the entire risk of acting on
information obtained from GROTTO DE BLOTTO, including the entire costs of
all necessary remedies, is with those who choose to act on such
information and not the operator of this system.

2.  User's access to the BBS is solely at the discretion of the GROTTO
DE BLOTTO system operator.  Violation(s) of rules and policies set forth
herein may result in the user being denied access, temporary or permanent,
regardless of previous user subscription/security status.

3.  Pursuant to the Electronics and Communications Act of 1986, Title 18,
United states code, Section 2510, notice is hereby given that no
facilities are provided by this BBS for user to user sending/receiving
private, privileged and/or confidential electronic communications,
including, but not limited to: credit card numbers for telephone/
telegraph common carriers, bank numbers or codes, pirated software, etc.

4.  User will not upload any files/programs that are designed to hinder,
damage, or disrupt this BBS or other users' BBS(s) hardware/software
operation.  This includes VIRUS, TROJAN, or other malicious software.
Attempting to upload such a file/program to the BBS (even if no damage
has resulted) will result in immediate denial to BBS and direct legal
actions between GROTTO DE BLOTTO BBS and the user using all applicable
state/national/local laws.

5.  User will not allow any other person to use his/her name and password
to gain access to BBS.  Registered users will take full responsibility
for all actions, direct or indirect from said person(s).

6.  User will not attempt to mislead or defraud the GROTTO DE BLOTTO BBS
system operator by using aliases or providing misleading information
```

(phone number, address, etc.) to acquire higher BBS access or other privileges.

7. GROTTO DE BLOTTO BBS reserves the right to delete, set and/or change the status/security of any message left on the BBS. All user to user messages shall be deemed readily accessible to the general public. GROTTO DE BLOTTO BBS does not and will not guarantee privacy on any message left by the user. User understands that this BBS is/was not intended for any communication for which the sender intends only the sender and the recipient(s) to read! The GROTTO DE BLOTTO BBS system operator may/will review/delete any/all communications messages on the BBS.

8. User waives all claims against the GROTTO DE BLOTTO BBS, legal or otherwise, which may be incurred through the use and/or registration for use of the BBS(s).

9. User will not use offensive language on any part of BBS, including "private" messages. Definition of "offensive" is strictly that which the GROTTO DE BLOTTO BBS system operator deems is offensive.

10. Actively encourage and promote the free exchange and discussion of information, ideas & opinions, except when the content would compromise the national security of the United States; violate proprietary rights, personal privacy, or applicable state/federal and local laws and regulations affecting telecommunications; or constitute a crime or libel.

11. User will contribute, as well as receive, quality software so long as it does not violate proprietary copyright laws. Do not upload any software product unless it is either Public Domain, Freeware, or Shareware. Knowingly uploading a non-authorized commercial product without publishers written authority and permission of GROTTO DE BLOTTO BBS is a violation of United States copyright laws as well as a violation of the these Policies, Rules & Regulations of the GROTTO DE BLOTTO BBS.

12. It is each user's responsibility to report to GROTTO DE BLOTTO BBS any known violations of any of the above Rules and Policies. In addition, users should report to GROTTO DE BLOTTO/ BBS any information deemed useful to other users and/or the BBS concerning fit & fitness of any file/program located on this BBS.

*Figure 10-1. Sample Policy Statement*

The third item in Figure 10-1 is appearing on many BBSes these days. In effect, it states that this BBS is not to be used for transferring credit card or other access device information. This is a result of a new legal definition of a credit card which states that a credit card is now "a card, plate, code, or access device that can be used in conjunction with another card or access number if need be, to obtain cash, goods, or services." As a sysop, you should protect yourself should someone post such information on your BBS.

The BBS's policy is not just a strongly worded contract stating legal rights and responsibilities. You must also determine how many user levels you will have, what abilities to grant each level, how much connect time each user will have each day, and if you will grant extra connect time as a reward for uploading files. You should also think about what kind of activities you want the users to engage in—uploading files, entering messages, helping novice BBS users, using FidoNet—and how to encourage the users to perform the actions you desire. These general polices should also be written up in a bulletin that the users can find quickly and easily.

## Granting Access

Validating your users is one way to screen the people who will use your BBS. If you require your users to leave a phone number, try to get back to them within the next day or two. You should also not make your users jump through hoops for you. Don't quiz them about why they deserve to use your BBS. Once they're validated, they should have access to most of your BBS. Remember that most users are going to be fairly mundane. If you want to turn them into a tight group of quality users, you have to give them the opportunity to work with your BBS. In addition, the easiest way to find out if a user is a twit is to give the user free rein and see what happens.

Finally, if you are restricting portions of your BBS, don't let the restricted users know about the areas that they can't get into. It will only engender ill will and hurt feelings in the group that isn't allowed access.

## To Charge or Not to Charge?

You probably won't make any money with a public BBS. Only occasionally are BBSes self-sustaining, usually by offering something special to their users, such as online games, extended file privileges, or multi-user chatting. Most BBSes do, however, request voluntary contributions. Many of those encourage contributions by giving extra privileges for donating, such as more time online.

If you are going to charge for access, make it worthwhile. Don't just slap a surcharge on an otherwise ordinary BBS. You are asking people to pay you; therefore, you have an obligation to deliver something in return. State up front what the users will get in exchange for their fee.

In general, if you are setting up a BBS to have fun, don't plan to make a profit. If you are setting up a BBS to make a profit, don't plan to have any fun.

# LETTING THE WORLD KNOW YOU'RE THERE

Once you have your BBS set up and ready to go, you need to advertise. Put announcements on other BBSes. Figure 10-2 shows a sample message of this kind.

```
****************************************************
*                  Grotto de Blotto                 *
*              Sysop: Michael Dispater               *
****************************************************

      A new BBS, running 4 incoming lines on TBBS software.

  We specialize in shareware uploads and downloads for IBM and Macintosh,
   conferences on ham radio, job hunting, and commemorative space stamps.
                Multi-user chatting is also available.

              Call Grotto de Blotto 24 hours a day.
                          555-6789
                       3/12/24/9600-8-N-1
```

*Figure 10-2. Advertising a New BBS*

This message tells readers everything they need to know about your BBS: its name, your name, the type of BBS software, how many incoming lines you have (if you don't mention this, people will assume you only have one), the things that make your BBS unique, the times of operation, your phone number, and modem speeds. Repeat ads for your BBS on other BBSes at least once a month, but don't knock someone else's BBS to make your own look good. There is always room for another good BBS in the area.

You should also put ads in the newsletters of local computer clubs and special interest groups. Leave flyers about the BBS at computer stores in your area. On a larger scale, you can advertise in magazines like the *Computer Shopper,* the *Boardwatch Magazine,* and on *CompuServe* and other online information services.

If you are setting up a business BBS, advertise the BBS in the company newsletter. Put a notice on the cork bulletin board in the coffee room or cafeteria. Send a memo to supervisors and department managers that describes how the BBS will help them. Encourage them to find other ways to use the BBS—you'll be surprised at some of the innovative uses they come up with!

If your business BBS is for users outside the company, consider taking out ads in the newspapers, the yellow pages, Chamber of Commerce mailings, and the area's local commerce newspaper or daily business journal. Also, list the number for your BBS in trade journals and add your BBS number and modem information to your business cards and letterhead.

One of the hardest chores for a new sysop does is to wait for the first few callers. It usually takes three to six months before a BBS has a regular, devoted user base. Advertising can speed up this process, as will offering interesting or unusual features such as an extensive library of software downloads or online games.

If calls don't come pouring in right away, be patient and don't get discouraged. Keep spreading the word about your BBS and stay in good humor.

## DEALING WITH PROBLEM CALLERS

Occasionally, you will have the unpleasant task of having to talk to a user who is making trouble. If the person is really causing problems, don't let things roll along and hope that they'll get better. One idiot can embroil a whole BBS in pointless emotional turmoil. As soon as you spot someone getting out of line, send them private mail that outlines what they are doing and why you want them to stop. Do not make it a public issue and don't let them make it a public issue. Give them one chance to change their behavior. If they don't, kick them out. The sysop is the final judge of what is and is not appropriate behavior on the BBS.

Crashers and hackers have no excuse for existence on a planet that has discovered penicillin. However, in anticipation of the inevitable attempts to crash your BBS, you should enlist the help of your fellow sysops and try to crash the BBS on your own first. Test your BBS's security by logging in at the BBS computer and also over the phone. Once you are happy with the level of security on your BBS, be discreet. Hackers are not likely to be a problem unless you charge for access or you've been bragging about the impenetrability of your security.

## KEEPING YOUR BBS EXCITING

Building up a group of responsible, interesting BBS users does not happen up overnight. Your user base will take three to six months to develop. Expecting people to phone immediately is not realistic.

Cultivate the users you do have. First, offer as many help files as you can. If you get a whole bunch of new users involved and make them feel welcome, you'll soon have a large group of helpful, *experienced* users who are incredibly loyal to you and the BBS because of the support you have given them. You can't buy that at any price.

For the same reasons, be helpful and considerate to the users who are very new to telecommunications, even when they ask "dumb" questions. Remember that you didn't know much about BBSing at one time. Everyone needs a little help now and then.

Keep in touch with the users. Don't hide behind the BBS—come out and talk to your admiring audience! Answer messages whenever possible and participate in the conversations. Also, consider sponsoring BBS get-togethers at a pizza parlor, coffee shop, or local picnic ground. This lets BBS users meet each other (and you). Get-togethers can be very helpful for damping problem users; attaching faces to names makes it harder for people to be rude to each other on the BBS.

BBSes must change to continue to attract and keep users. Make sure that the BBS is continually exciting. Post bulletins about what's new. Make or change message and files areas as necessary to reflect the BBS users' current interests.

Be imaginative. Find things to add that are of interest to your users. For example, one BBS run by a newspaperman carried Dave Barry's columns in one of the message areas. Look for interesting new public domain software. You can also encourage your users to help you find good files by allowing them additional time or privileges in exchange for the amount of material they upload.

Offer things on your BBS that other BBSes don't. See if you can identify a type of file or program (Macintosh communications programs, EGA graphics programs, multi-player games) that is not readily available. If you build a better BBS, the world will beat a path to your door... or at least give you a call.

You can also subscribe to a number of *online magazines*. Online magazines are regular publications from a variety of publishers that are designed to be distributed on BBSes. Some online magazines are available in print and electronic formats, others are available in electronic format only. Some examples of online magazines are *InfoMat*, a weekly news service from BBS Press Service in Topeka, Kansas, and *Boardwatch Magazine* (also available in print), a high-quality monthly newsletter about BBSing and online information services, from Jack Rickard in Denver, Colorado.

Other online publications include the *USA Today Decisionline Update*, a summary of the day's events; *Boxoffice Magazine*, a trade magazine for the film and theater industries; and *Newsbytes Magazine*, a weekly dealing with the PC industry all over the world. These publications can be had through *Boardwatch* the address for which is in Appendix B, "BBS Numbers."

Finally, remember that the success of a BBS is not measured by the number of detractors it has, but by the number of users who call. Everything you do is bound to annoy someone.

# WORKING WITH OTHER SYSOPS

Talk to the other sysops in your area before, during, and after setting up your own BBS. They'll provide a mountain of advice on all topics. Fellow sysops can be very helpful in solving technical problems. They can also be a strong support network when you are facing a problem user.

Be considerate of other sysops, particularly those in your area. You're going to have to live with them for a long time. If a sysop in your area has spent a lot of time building an extensive library of downloadable public domain fonts, for example, it is extremely impolite to raid these files just so you can put them up on your BBS. Find other specialty files to offer on your BBS, or offer other sysops some unusual software in exchange for their software.

# DEALING WITH TECHNICAL PROBLEMS

The biggest technical problem you are likely to have is hard disk failure. While the failure of any other component in your computer may temporarily shut down the BBS, having your hard disk fail can cost you your messages, files, userlog, and BBS configuration.

Therefore, *back up your BBS regularly and often.* You should do a *full backup* (everything on the hard disk) about once a week, and *incremental backups* (everything that has been added or changed since the last backup) daily. If your computer malfunctions at some point, you will only lose at most a couple of days worth of activity. As a matter of fact, you could even restore the backed-up files on another, borrowed computer while yours is being fixed, and keep the BBS going.

**Note:**   If you have a hard disk bigger than 40 megabytes, seriously consider buying a tape drive to back up your BBS. Inserting 50 to 100 diskettes every week will become such a chore that you won't back up the BBS as often as you should.

If your BBS is shut down unexpectedly for a few days by a technical problem, try to get the problem identified and fixed as soon as possible. Should the problem look like it will keep your BBS offline for a week or two, post a message to that effect on some of the other BBSes. Your users will then know when to phone your BBS again, and they won't lose interest and go elsewhere.

# LEGAL CONSIDERATIONS

There are legal considerations for all sysops, even sysops of BBSes not used for business. For example, the sysop can be sued for libel if one BBS user enters a libelous message about another BBS user on a BBS. The sysop can also be held responsible for disseminating credit card numbers or illegally copied programs left on the BBS by a user.

The best defense against legal problems is to develop a good user base. As a sysop, you should also make it a point to review the messages and files uploaded on your

BBS. If this job becomes too big for you, consider enlisting some of the most responsible users to help you.

Jonathan D. Wallace, Esq.has written a book entitled *Syslaw: The Sysop's Legal Manual*. He is a lawyer and a sysop for LLM (212-766-3788), a BBS for law-related material. *Syslaw* is available for $25 from LLM Press, 150 Broadway, Suite 10, New York, NY 10038, 212-766-4198 (voice). Sysops who are particularly concerned with legal issues should buy a copy of this book. Ignorance is no excuse before the law.

## MAKING CHANGES TO THE BBS

Making changes to the BBS is necessary to keep the BBS exciting. The safest way to change the BBS is to first plan the change in detail. Discuss your idea with other sysops and see what they think about it. (Be prepared for vigorous disagreement.) Has anyone in the area done this before? What happened to their BBS when they did? Did the change draw more users or make the BBS more exciting?

Once you have determined what you want to do and how you want do it, make a copy of your BBS to experiment making the change on. *Never under any circumstances modify the only working copy of your BBS!*

Once you have made the change to a copy of your BBS, test the change to see if it works like you thought it would. You'll almost certainly find that you've overlooked something. Go back and correct any fine points.

When you're satisfied with the way the change looks, check your BBS's security with the change in place. Make sure that you haven't inadvertently created a hole through which someone can crash the BBS or gain unauthorized access.

If there are no leaks in your security, make another copy of the working BBS. Save this in your permanent archives. If the change doesn't work out, you can use the copy of the BBS you saved to restore the BBS to its unaltered state.

Now install the change in the working copy of the BBS and test the security again. The second test is because you may have done something just a little differently the second time that may have affected the BBS's security. Remember, if you don't test your BBS's security, your users will do it for you eventually.

Go back online. Make an announcement as part of the logon bulletins that you have implemented a change, and tell how the change will affect the users. Keep a slightly closer watch on the BBS for the first week or so to see how the change is working and how your users are reacting to it.

# MOVING OR CLOSING THE BBS

Everything has a beginning, a middle, and an end. BBSes are no exception. When you shut your BBS down, post notices on BBSes and notify other sysops in the area. Be sure to put notices on your BBS if you have enough advance warning. Spread the word to everyone who interacted with the BBS. If you just pull the plug and don't say anything, it will confuse a lot of people in the BBS community and tarnish your hard-earned reputation. Always respect your users.

Disconnect the phone you used for the BBS. Old BBS lists will circulate for some time with your BBS's number. Let the phone company know that the number shouldn't be reassigned for regular voice use for at least a year. If the number is immediately reassigned as a voice residential number, the new residents will be receiving phone calls at all hours from BBS users.

# MAKING MONEY WITH YOUR BBS

Most noncommercial BBSes are operated by people in their spare time more for fun than for profit. This is not to say that the sysops don't want their BBSes to make money; it's just that most noncommercial BBSes don't make money.

Only a handful of sysops even recover their operating expenses on a regular basis. Do not set up a BBS just because you think that hordes of users will jam the phone to you night and day at $35/year per person. Users won't usually pay for access to a typical BBS; there is just too much competition for the average BBS user's interest from free, public BBSes to make it worth anyone's while to pay for "just another BBS."

In order to successfully charge access fees, the sysop must have something special to offer the users. Some private BBSes offer an extensive array of files and online games. Others specialize in matchmaking and are able to charge a monthly or quarterly subscription for which the users receive unlimited time for chatting. If your BBS caters to an exclusive audience—for example, chemical engineers—you may make money by charging for advertising space from businesses that cater to your audience.

People who deal in rare items—such as books, guns, stamps, or antiques—may be able to make money running a BBS. Setting up a BBS and advertising the BBS number in national magazines related to that collectable may be a very profitable and low-cost method for buying and selling. Bulletins can be added about specials, announcements, and news items of particular interest.

## BECOMING AN EXPERT

There are two basic rules to remember before setting up and running your own BBS:

1. BBSes cost time.
2. BBSes cost money.

The corollary to these two rules is that BBSes will always cost you more time and money than you thought they would. Once you have made your best estimate of how much time and money setting up a BBS will take you, double it. If you're not a power user, you may want to triple this time estimate for the first six months. After the first six months, you'll either be a power user or you'll have given up.

Build a good relationship with the phone company representatives when you start a BBS. A positive relationship with the phone company is vital to your BBS's continued existence. You may also need to ask the phone company for help if someone ever tries to crash your BBS.

Establish clear, concise goals and limits for your BBS before going online. Tailor your policies to meet those goals. A good BBS does not just "happen"—it requires careful planning. Be prepared to spend a lot of time getting things the way you want them.

A BBS is not a democracy. Any power the users have is granted to them by you, the sysop. You must strike a balance between giving your users enough freedom to be creative on the BBS and keeping the BBS on track with its stated goals. As sysop, you have the absolute authority on the BBS. The most effective sysops never have to make this point to anyone.

Keep in touch and discuss ideas with the other sysops in your area. If there is a local sysop's association, consider joining it. Don't be afraid to ask other sysops for help, either. Every sysop makes spectacular mistakes now and then. Listening to sysops swapping stories about the history of the local BBS community can help you avoid making spectacular mistakes of your own.

Sysops are generally viewed by the users as a combination of genies and servants. Always consider your users and treat them with respect; after all, you work for them. Without users, the BBS would just be you and the computer. Don't make the BBS harder for the users to use just to make your job as sysop a little easier.

Listen to what your users say about other BBSes as well as your own. Log on to the BBSes of the sysops who get consistently favorable reviews, and incorporate the desirable parts of their BBSes into yours.

Finally, remember that good BBSes are exothermic: they generate heat, in the form of fun and enthusiasm, in everyone who uses them. Take pride and satisfaction in what you are doing and make sure that your BBS is a reflection of that.

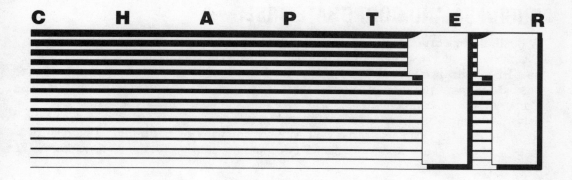

# WAYS YOU CAN USE BBSes

This chapter includes ways that you can use bulletin board systems for your business or office. It gives examples of different ways that a variety of business have put the power of BBSes to work for them. Concluding this chapter are ways you can use BBSes set up by the U.S. government and school systems around the country.

# BUSINESS AND CORPORATE BBSES

A business or corporation can use an online information service, as described in Chapter 9, to advertise and sell its products. However, a company may choose to set up a BBS of its own in order to customize the BBS to fit its product. Setting up a business BBS has a number of other advantages over online information services. Corporate BBSes can be used as a window to the public by directly advertising products, displaying price lists, disseminating public information, and acting as service representatives. They can also serve well within a company by performing a number of tasks, including acting as a messenger service and transferring files and other information.

Many BBSes allow different access levels to be set up; different access levels can be matched with different features on the menu. When BBS users log on, they see only those menu options that the sysop has authorized users with that level access to see; any other options will not show up on the menu. A sysop could use this feature to set up different menus of features for managers, sales people, executives, personnel reps, and support staff. Each group would be able to access only specific portions of the BBS.

While not as effective as restricting the menu options, many BBSes also allow sysops to set up passwords for files or messages. Other people can see that the files or messages are there, but they can't unscramble them. The most discreet method would be to combine the password protection with *personal downloads* or *private messages*.

Most BBSes require little actual maintenance and supervision, needing only an hour a day at most.

## Uses of Business BBSes

There are several applications for business BBSes. These applications include:

- exchanging information
- customer service and technical support
- mail and message systems
- telecommuting

These applications can benefit large offices in any industry.

### Exchanging Information

Businesses often effectively use BBSes as a central source of information. For example, one major company installed a BBS for sharing general information and announcements with all its divisions and uploading and downloading spreadsheets between divisions. Using the BBS cut the time people spent making long-distance calls from four hours a day to less than ten minutes.

Using a BBS also had some positive side effects that hadn't been predicted. Many managers and executives who had not used computers before the BBS was installed developed significant computer skills. Not only did they save time in finding out things directly from the BBS, the managers started to look at other ways in which computers could help them do their jobs. This increased their productivity dramatically in a number of areas not directly connected with the BBS.

Because the company had also mandated several specific software packages for use throughout the company, the BBS also became the focus for a company-wide software users group. The BBS users in the company exchanged tips on how to use the software in topic areas on the BBS.

### Customer Support

A business BBS can act as a 24-hour service representative, giving technical support and installation instructions, providing suggestions on ways to use products better, and taking customer complaints and suggestions.

One of the major advantages to using a BBS to augment the regular phone support is for handling frequently asked questions. A well-written answer to a question can be read by dozens or even hundreds of BBS users, preventing many extra phone calls to the support department. Users who have invented novel methods of solving problems will frequently tell other people how they did it. As a result, many support questions on the BBS are actually answered by other BBS users. This greater involvement by the users makes them like the product more.

Software companies may find a technical support line particularly useful. as it can be used to download programs and software patches quickly.

### Mail and Message Systems

A major advantage BBSes have over courier services is the speed with which information can be transmitted. For example, corporate officers at field locations can send copies of speeches to the corporate communications office for approval. Corrections, revisions, and clarifications can be made and returned in a few minutes. BBSes also have an advantage over faxes, as the actual file can be transmitted, edited, returned, and then printed out again at the field office. Similarly, many companies use BBSes to upload and download contracts and related files during negotiations when the participants are away from the main office.

### Forums and Brainstorming

The advantage of a BBS over a network email system is that everyone can see a forum on a BBS, but not everyone has to participate. In other words, the BBS is acting very much like a regular cork bulletin board on the wall near the coffee pot. Sending email to everyone with the latest addition to a discussion would hopelessly clog most networks, and everyone's time would be taken up reading and purging email from their mailboxes. Posting a discussion on a BBS allows both active and passive participation. Another advantage over email is that BBS users who stop in to look at a forum also can see where the discussion has come from simply by reading the messages that have gone before.

Forums on a BBS are a continuing source of inspiration for people who can't get together to brainstorm. Suppose half the people who want to get together are in one office and the rest are in another office several hundred miles away. Add to this the difficulties involved in clearing everyone's schedule just to have a phone conference. The solution is to start a forum and have everyone log on, post her or his ideas, then log on again a while later to see what other ideas their ideas have triggered. To see how the ideas have evolved, BBS users need only read the preceding messages in the forum. This process also allows people to join in the forum as their schedule permits. The entire "meeting" can take place over several days or weeks, with each participant checking the progress every day or two.

### Telecommuting

*Telecommuting* is working at home and using a BBS to send and receive projects and assignments. A wide variety of people—such as architects, word processors, programmers, clerks, documentation specialists, auditors, real-estate appraisers, editors, and actuaries—hold jobs related to the manipulation and transfer of information. The people who hold these jobs can benefit from telecommuting.

Telecommuting offers many advantages, both to businesses and to employees. One incentive for businesses is the direct cost-savings: employees who telecommute do not need an office or a parking space five days a week. Telecommuters usually show up at the office one or two days a week. Office space and facilities can be easily shared by several telecommuters.

Telecommuting reduces sick leave and absenteeism. Because employees are able to set their own schedules, they are less likely to call in sick just because they want to sleep a little later or run an errand. Transportation costs are also reduced. Employees don't have to fight traffic to get to the office. Handicapped employees or employees who have a particularly long commute find telecommuting very appealing.

Telecommuting is also very attractive to many people who have difficulty being tied to an office five days a week. For example, employees with children can be at home to take care of children after school gets out.

The best reason for businesses to set up telecommuting programs is that productivity and morale are dramatically increased. When the state of California tried a pilot telecommuting program with 200 state employees, they were able to save approximately nine times the cost of the program in increased productivity and reduced expenses. Giving employees more control over their own work schedules lets them set their own priorities and plan for their own best productivity. Treating employees like professionals who are able to make decisions about how to run their own lives makes them feel much better about what they are doing. This in turn leads to fewer stress-related illnesses, fewer sick days, lower insurance rates, and lower turnover of staff.

Telecommuting is not for every business. It is based on accomplishing a goal rather than warming a chair for eight hours. Managers must trust their employees and be able to identify and delegate assignments. Employees must be responsible, self-starting, and able to work well without a lot of interaction with other people.

If you think your business might benefit from telecommuting, try setting up a pilot telecommuting program that monitors the costs, the savings, and the employee satisfaction.

## Businesses That Use BBSes

This section will show examples of how other businesses effectively use their BBS.

### Banks and Financial Institutions

A number of banks and financial institutions have discovered that BBSes work more economically than bank messengers or delivery services for transmitting and receiving financial information. One major regulatory institution uses a BBS to receive information on mortgages and loans sent from its branches around the country to Washington, D.C.

### Hospitals and Clinics

Many hospitals and clinics have set up BBSes on which a patient can phone in and talk to a consulting nurse about general medical questions. These can provide a good source of basic information for people who don't have a regular doctor or need to ask a question late at night.

## Hotels and Resorts

People can phone a BBS at a resort to find out ski and weather conditions. The BBS can also serve to record and confirm reservations. Local businesses can buy ads directed at the traveller on the BBS for a low monthly fee. The ads are then entered as bulletins or included as part of the logon information.

## Insurance Agents

Selling the right insurance policy usually requires the insurance agent to run a number of different life and income projections for prospective customers. In addition, customers frequently ask general questions about their insurance. Full-service insurance agencies can set up BBSes to take orders from customers and provide a forum for insurance questions. By constructing doors in the BBS leading to actuarial and financial projection programs, customers can determine many of their insurance needs on their own.

## Job Shops and Contract Agencies

Many job shops and agencies maintain BBSes for candidates and clients. By selecting one or a series of questionnaires, new candidates can be screened for basic skills and routed to the account representative that handles that field without wasting anyone's time at the agency. Clients can call the BBS and leave messages to account representatives about new positions and candidate availability. Executive recruitment BBSes also let candidates and clients upload and download resumes and interview notes instead of relying on the post office—particularly effective when an immediate response is required.

One international association of contractors and consultants publishes a magazine of current job openings each week. Subscribers to the magazine can obtain a user ID and a password free of charge. They can then log on to the BBS and find out the jobs that are going to be published in the coming week's magazine. This gives them a jump on other contractors. BBS users can also enter up to 15 keywords with which to search through job openings. For example, a user could use this feature to list all the current openings for chemical engineering jobs in the Southeast U.S.

The contracting association could expand their BBS services by selling advertising on the BBS to clients its or by providing a routing service for candidate resumes and enquiries to clients who do not want to publicly advertise their needs. The association could also sell a "candidate matching" service to clients, where potential candidates pay to list their resumes and related information on the BBS. The clients could then review the resumes and select candidates.

## Lawyers

Lawyers use BBSes to pass information back and forth during cases. A BBS allows the clients a chance to see how things are developing and leave messages for the lawyers. Even if a lawyer is not available, the client can leave detailed questions, something that is not usually practical to do with an answering service. The lawyer can then review the client's question, compose an answer, and put it on the BBS for the client to examine later. In addition, the BBS provides a reasonably safe method of transferring encrypted files back and forth.

In addition, a forum lets lawyers and clients post messages that provide the history of a case. This can be very effective when there are a number of participants in a case who cannot meet regularly. The ability to brainstorm this way has led to the creation of good negotiating or defense strategies.

## Politicians

Many politicians install BBSes as a means of taking polls and surveys of constituents. This idea could be applied to a number of different fields where customer reactions need to be monitored. For such a BBS, extensive questionnaire, message, and multi-user capabilities are required, but chatting between users or sophisticated file transfers would not be as important.

## Publishers and Typesetters

Many publishers use BBSes to transfer files back and forth between authors, editors, and artists. BBSes are a fast, inexpensive alternative to express mailing manuscripts and diskettes. A BBS can also solve computer incompatibilities. For example, if a manuscript was prepared on an IBM, it can be uploaded onto a BBS and then downloaded and edited on a Macintosh.

## Radio Stations

Radio stations across the country operate BBSes to provide a forum for their listeners. These BBSes let people log on and enter their comments about the radio station and its music: what songs they like or dislike, what they think of the station's news reporting, the disk jockeys, or the commercials. In this fashion, the radio station's BBS has the same function as a "listener hot line."

In addition to receiving comments and feedback from listeners, the BBS can also be used for disseminating information. For example, upcoming musical events sponsored by the station can be featured as bulletins that include concert dates, times, and ticket information. The BBS can also have song lists for specific shows available for downloading.

### Real-Estate Agencies

For a real-estate agent, same-day or even same-hour information is the difference between making a sale and hearing about it. Many real-estate agents maintain private BBSes for clients that list the available properties and prices. Access to these BBSes is usually by subscription.

The main advantage to using a BBS in this industry is speed of communications. A choice property can be listed, shown, and sold in the time it takes for a letter to get from the real-estate agent's office to a potential client. By listing property information on the BBS as it becomes available, clients can find out about a property within a few hours of its becoming available.

### Software Companies

Online customer support is offered by more and more software publishers. The user posts messages, takes part in conferences on the uses of the products, receives updates for the download charges (if any), and voices suggestions for the development of future products. Users can also upload programs to technical support departments rather than mailing disks, saving time and money.

The BBS can alert users to known bugs quickly and can provide software patches to correct them. Users and distributors can phone the BBS and download patches and additional information. This level of responsiveness is very good for a company's public relations. For example, WordPerfect Corp. offers support for its word-processing program, WordPerfect, with a toll-free phone number. Their service has roughly 31 telephone lines that handle about 3000 calls a day.

### Stockbrokers

One stockbroker installed a BBS as a free service to current and potential clients. The BBS contains general information about the stock market in downloadable text files on topics such as over-the-counter stocks, IRA accounts, and recent developments in state and federal legislation. The BBS also has a library with information about new books about the stock market. In addition, there is an online glossary of terms used in the business.

Clients can request brokers to track a specific stock by setting up a file on the BBS. The brokers then enter the stock's daily closing price. BBS users can also use the BBS to set up brokerage accounts.

Furthermore, clients can upload and download orders, files containing company analyses, spreadsheets, and statistical information. By relegating some of the more routine requests for information to the BBS, the broker can service a larger number of customers effectively.

### Wholesalers and Direct-sales Organizations

A BBS can keep the company's field staff informed of the latest developments. In many businesses involving direct sales, such as the wholesale food industry, prices and inventory change constantly. Many companies have used BBSes as a way to let dealers and field representatives receive the latest price sheets. Sales orders can also be entered quickly by tailoring a questionnaire to ask for the appropriate sales information. With this system, a food sales representative can phone the company headquarters from a client's office on an 800 line, check the current price and availability of an item, use this information to close the sale, and then enter the sales information necessary to reserve the items in inventory and start processing the order.

One New York electronics parts distributor uses a BBS in place of a commercial email system to save on the cost of transmitting messages to dealers. General-interest news and advance information on new products and lines are handled by the BBS. Employee time is not taken up answering questions on the phone several dozen times, the information reaches dealers in a timely fashion, and the costs for running the BBS are minimal compared to those for creating new mailers and sending them out each time to the distributors.

# BBSES IN SCHOOLS AND COLLEGES

Public school systems have set up BBSes that service areas ranging from single districts to entire states. These BBSes provide a forum for education issues and a clearinghouse for news about state and federal grant programs. Most school BBSes also have educational software available for downloading. Other uses include exchanging information such as general policy statements, school board minutes, general announcements, and job openings.

For example, a senior high school in Pennsylvania has a BBS that is used by parents and students equally. The BBS lists information on cafeteria menus, upcoming school events, sports schedules, and exam times. Students can also look at lists of pen-pals, upload stories they've written, and send mail to each other. The school also prints a BBS newsletter.

There are also BBSes designed for teachers. The New Hampshire SpecialNet is a national network of BBSes based in Virginia for teachers and administrators involved in special education. SpecialNet BBSes focus on job opportunities and software and hardware developments related to special education.

## GOVERNMENT BBSes

Many city, state, and federal government offices operate their own specialized BBSes. Many of these BBSes are open to the public and are usually designed to provide information.

Government BBSes offer a fascinating array of information and can provide you with a handsome return for your tax dollars. Some examples of government BBSes at the federal level are:

- The Economic Bulletin Board, operated by the Office of Business Analysis, the Office of the Under Secretary for Economic Affairs in the U. S. Department of Commerce. This BBS provides economic news and information from the various economic affairs agencies within the Department of Commerce. This includes such news as press releases from the Bureau of Labor Statistics, economic indicators, and summaries of official news, reports, and studies from the Department of Commerce and member agencies. You can also use this BBS to find out how to obtain tapes of economic data from the Department of Commerce.

- The CMIC Electronic Bulletin Board, operated by the Census Microcomputer Information Center, Office of the Director, Bureau of the Census. This BBS carries news about microcomputers, reviews of software and hardware, and a number of public domain programs.

- The Microcomputer Electronic Information Exchange, operated by the Institute for Computer Sciences and Technology in the National Bureau of Standards. This BBS provides information on the acquisition, management, and use of small computers.

- The Climate Assessment BBS, operated by the Climate Analysis Center of the National Weather Service. The BBS provides historical climate information. It is open to anyone who uses historical meteorological data.

- The East Coast Marine Users Bulletin Board, operated by the National Weather Service. The BBS provides marine weather and nautical information for coastal waterways, including data for bays and sounds, coastal waters, and offshore waters; tidal information; advisories on tropical storms; and weather, nautical, and fishing news. The BBS is geared towards commercial fishermen and other users of coastal waters in the mid-Atlantic, but it is open to the public.

Several government BBSes are listed in Appendix B, "BBS Numbers."

In addition to federal BBSes, city, county, and state offices often use BBSes to list job openings, solicit bids on projects, make announcements about new legislation, and even solicit opinions from citizens. Most cities, counties, and states have an ombudsman or some kind of central office that can tell you which office to call for the answer to a question. Start with those offices to find out if there are BBSes you can call. Also check with individual offices and agencies for BBS numbers. You may even be able to interest an office in setting up a BBS to provide information.

# BECOMING AN EXPERT

Applications for BBSes in business are limited only by your imagination. BBSes do best at distributing information that changes frequently and that must go to a number of people separated from the source of the information and each other.

Note that a BBS is not always the best solution for distributing information. Sometimes a paper routing system or an occasional conference call between offices will work better and more cheaply. If your only solution is a hammer, pretty soon every problem will start looking like a nail.

If you do set up a corporate BBS, make sure that its intended users understand how to use it. Offer to teach classes in basic telecommunications. Provide each office or department with adequate written documentation on how to log on to the BBS, use the BBS's features, and log off. Appoint someone in each office as a BBS resource to answer questions for other users who may be having problems. Also, appoint someone as sysop in the same office as the BBS.

Schools and colleges frequently have BBSes to help answer questions. School BBSes can contain course catalogs, scheduling information, class changes, cafeteria menus, and announcements about school events. BBS networks on specific education topics also help educators stay current in their field.

Finally, BBSes in government offices are an often-overlooked source of information on almost any topic. Government BBSes are particularly good for providing information that requires very large amounts of data to be gathered and collated, such as census or weather data. Information originally gathered for official government purposes can also be helpful to you, such as the government's recommendations on purchasing small computers. Although local and state government BBSes will probably not provide as much statistical information as federal BBSes, they will help you keep in touch with what is happening at the state and local levels and give you an opportunity to express your opinions.

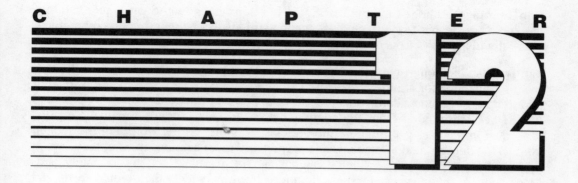

# EPILOGUE: THE FUTURE OF BBSING

T his chapter is comprised of quotes about the future of BBSes from computer experts who have been using, running, and designing bulletin board systems for many years.

**Tom Jennings,** author of the Fido BBS, says "I think it's going to get bigger and bigger, and more 'techie-toy' oriented. Someone will always be working on communications—I will anyway. Lots of people will."

**Randy Bush** is a long-time network user and system programmer. He is also the system administrator for a number of Unix machines and wrote the specification for (but "didn't design") the standards document for the FidoNet protocol. Randy's opinion is that BBSes are moving from the computer domain to the social domain. He says, "Information tends to get around pretty quickly. It's the written word, not the spoken word. That doesn't tend to make people sufficiently more cautious in what they say. It *is* a broadcast medium, and as such it can have an interesting effect; unfortunately, people on some of the more amateur nets do not realize how widely their words are spread or the effects of their inaccuracies. It has the same effect as CB radio.

"The thing that's happened with FidoNet over the past two years and is happening with Usenet is that the understanding necessary to bring a system on the net has been substantially reduced. This means that people who have no appreciation of the technology are getting on the net. But you don't have to understand how a telephone works to use it, or a fax to use it, and pretty soon you won't have to understand how a BBS works, either. It will have the same problems of anything used by normal people."

**Lisa Gronke,** another long-time Usenet user, said "It's a hard question because it depends a lot on what the telephone companies do. Some major change in telephone rates could have a major impact. Where I think it's going is that BBSes will become bigger and more professional, networked, powerful, financed somehow. There will also be a separate group of BBSes becoming more private: little ones that don't network but are maybe connected for mail, or are operating a point, and don't publish their phone numbers. It's very dependent on what the phone company does. If the phone company does manage to get through business rates for BBSes, that would have a major impact for BBS in that direction."

**Tim Pozar,** one of the authors of the UFGATE software for connecting FidoNet BBSes with the Usenet network, says that he wants to see communist countries get tied into international telecommunicating. He says, "[Telecommunicating] will promote the greater free flow of information so we can get our ideas over there...There are FidoNet nodes in Poland right now, and they're working on getting some into Russia." Tim adds that Usenet was also getting into Russia, but there are trade restrictions on Unix computers to Soviet-bloc countries, so they're concentrating on getting FidoNet nodes established and then using gateways to provide an uplink to Usenet."

**David Dodell,** FidoNet International Coordinator, is co-founder of the disabled conference on FidoNet. He also does a medical newsletter on FidoNet, BITNET, and INTERNET, as well as on some Usenet conferences, the purpose of which is to distribute medical information for free that would otherwise cost $30 an hour or more on a commerical information service. Dave says "BBSes that come up with just more games, more files, more word processors are not unique any more. The sysop must take the time to make the BBS unique." Dave's BBS, which specializes in distributing medical information and provides forums for disabled users, has about 600-700 active users.

Dave has several friends he got to know through amateur radio who are blind. He realized that amateur radio was very good for bringing down the prejudices. Dave feels that BBSing is very similar: everyone always starts off on an equal footing. When you are reading mail, it doesn't matter how long it took someone to type in a message. It is the content of the message that you judge them by. Moreover, Dave adds, BBSing opens the world to shut-ins, who can meet and exchange messages with dozens of people they would not otherwise have an opportunity to meet. He went on to say, "Computers are a tool. They are not an end in themselves. I've seen too many people wrapped in computers just for computers. They're a sophisticated tool.

"I correspond [via email] with a dentist in Argentina. I met him by accident on one of the nets. The uniqueness, the beauty, the simplicity with which I can send an electronic message to someone halfway around the world is wonderful. I'm still amazed with the idea.

"Almost everyone I know now has electronic mail addresses. Friends from college I haven't seen have in 15 years all have addresses. I can't think of the last time I sat down at a typewriter or a piece of paper and actually wrote someone a letter. You run into a lot of people who you've known for years."

**Phil Becker,** president of eSoft, Inc., and creator of The Bread Board System (TBBS) says that BBSes give the user a feeling of access to people. "If you send email to someone on a conference, they'll send you mail back usually. The only commonly accepted procedure is that if you send messages to someone, and he doesn't answer, he's ignoring you. There is a directness to this, until procedures for etiquette develop, that is unavoidable. This is not the technology, but the integration of it into the society. Voice mail and answering machines have their own etiquette, and there will be similar things developing [for BBSes]." Phil also says that messages on BBSes provide no cues to how a person feels about something, such as voice tone, inflection, even their breath rate. "Smiley faces and other things really help." But, he continued, the fact that it is so sterile lets everyone communicate on an equal footing.

"The future is that all of this [BBSes] will become very pedestrian technology. I think that BBSes are early technology, like buckboards. A Ferrari is pretty related to a buckboard, yet quite different. But I do think that BBSes have reached the point of technology where the limits are far more human than technological—that is, I think that people have to figure out how to fit them into their everyday life."

Phil also says, "BBSes on the hobbyist level are the ultimate information undergound. They probably forever undermine the ability of any government to censor information. It will probably make the common man feel more informed and more helpless at the same time."

Phil sees more businesses going online for their customers. "There are a number of businesses that this will fit into and others where it will not. I think you'll also see a lot of businesses getting an advantage in the market by learning how to use the technology. I think the technology is a tremendous enabler for increasing productivity. I'm constantly looking for how this product [TBBS] can be applied to this business or that business to see how they can get an edge. Usually if you find one, the edge is going to be huge. I think that businesses are just now realizing that this technology is available."

**Jim Harrer,** president of Mustang Software, Inc., says "I think that there'll be a day when there is a modem in every PC that's made, one way or another. As that happens, obviously there'll be thousands and thousands of more people coming to the BBS community. As far as BBS software goes, we're going to see the interfaces really polished up with BBSes. There will be more 'what-you-see-is-what-you-get,' more realtime applications, more pull-down applications. There seems to be a real push now for multi-tasking—being able to upload, and download, and enter a message at the same time. I think that in the next year or two, you'll see that the users won't just start a download and walk away; they'll start a download and then be more inclined to go into the message base [while the download is going]."

Jim is very excited about the connectivity that BBSes offer. "I estimate that conservatively, there are probably 10,000 BBSes in the U.S., and there are 300 users for each on the average. When you multiply it out, there are over three million people who are accessible via BBS today." He adds that more and more companies are going to take advantage of this connectivity by using BBSes for support and for letting the public know about their products.

Jim gave an example of how BBSes can be used for business. "Shareware authors can distribute a product and theoretically have it continue to be distributed from hand to hand. When we [Mustang Software] are looking to have our products distributed as shareware, we can today get our product seen by as many as three million people. Then it's just a percentage game to see how many people are willing to register your product. It's up to your product at that point. I feel that if the product is a serious effort and it offers something for the customer, they will register it. It's just a matter of making sure that your product is worth it and that [the customers] feel that it's worthy of the registration fee."

All of these views of the future have assumed that the technology and the social effects of BBSing will continue to evolve. BBSes in 1980 were mostly 300-baud, single-user systems designed largely for exchanging messages. By the end of the decade, thousands of BBSes were hooked up in a worldwide network that could automatically route messages and files to any other BBS in the network. Multi-user BBSes comprised a sizable portion of the public BBSes. Businesses also started using BBSes to gain a competitive edge. BBSes for customer support, remote order entry, and for exchanging mail between offices became an accepted business tool. BBSes in the 1990's will be able to take increasing advantage of new technology: software designed for multiple users, extended graphics capabilities, and fast modems (9600 baud and higher).

The social effects of BBSes are no less amazing. The connectivity and opportunities for exchanging ideas are mind-boggling. As a BBS user, you can directly reach as many people as are in Seattle, Miami, or Dallas. Furthermore, the speed with which you can transmit an idea and the number of people to whom you can communicate that idea are both increasing.

As a BBS user, you have a podium and a very large audience. What you say is up to you.

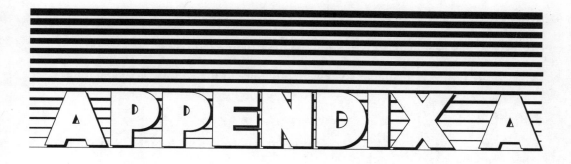

# APPENDIX A

# COMMUNICATIONS
# SOFTWARE

This appendix contains a representative sampling of communications packages for several types of computers. The emphasis is on software that is inexpensive, commonly available, and easy to use, with particular emphasis on public domain and shareware packages. Prices are subject to change without notice, so you may wish to phone or write to confirm.

# Amiga

*JRCOMM,* Jack Radigan, P.O. Box 698, Mays Landing, NJ 08330.

> JRCOMM is a popular shareware program for the Amiga, available for $30.

# APPLE II

*ModemWorks,* Morgan Davis Group, 10079 Nuerto Lane, Rancho San Diego, CA 92078-1736, 619-670-0563 (voice).

> ModemWorks is a commercial product, available for $59.95. You can download it from 619-670-5379 3/12/24/9600-8-N-1.

*Talk Is Cheap,* Quality Computers, 15102 Charlevoix, Grosse Point, MI, 800-443-6697 (voice) or 313-331-0941 (voice).

> Talk Is Cheap is available for $49.95.

# Atari ST

*Flash,* Antic Software, 544 2nd St., San Francisco, CA 94107, 415-957-0886 (voice).

> Flash is commercial software, costing $29.95 plus $3.50 shipping and handling.

# CoCo

*GregETerm, UltimaTerm,* and *MickeTerm* are popular CoCo Communication programs. Talk with your local CoCo users' grouot for more information and sources.

# Commodore 64 and 128

*ProTerm, CCGMS, Cesar's Term, DarkTerm,* and *MultiTerm* are Commodore communications programs available through Commodore magazines. Check with Commodore users' group for more information.

## Macintosh

*MockTerminal*, CE Software, P.O. Box 65580, West Des Moines, IA 50265, 515-224-1995 (voice) or 800-523-7638 (voice).

> MockTerminal is part of MockPackage Plus Utilities. This may not be as full-featured as some other communications programs for the Macintosh.

*Termworks*, James Rhodes, 401 Eastwood Place, Lufkin, TX 75901.

> Termworks is shareware, available for $20.

*White Knight*, Freesoft Co., 150 Hickory Drive, Beaver Falls, PA 15010, 412-846-2700 (voice).

> White Knight is the successor to Red Ryder, probably the most widely used of all Macintosh shareware communciations programs. White Knight can be had for $139 which includes a free subscription to the GEnie RoundTable for Freesoft products.

*ZTerm*, David P. Alverson, 5635 Cross Creek Court, Mason, OH 45040

> ZTerm is shareware written by David P. Alverson and is available for $40.

## MS-DOS

*BackComm 1.4*, RML Associates/BackComm Software, 991-C Lomas Santa Fe Drive, Suite 233, Solana Beach, CA 92075, 619-259-0119 (voice).

> BackComm 1.4 lets you download a file while working on something else at the same time. It is available for $149.

*PC-Talk III*, The Headlands Press, P.O. Box 862, Tiburon, CA 94920.

> PC-Talk III can be had for $35. Many shareware communications programs for MS-DOS computers have commands that are similar to PC-Talk III's, making it easy to switch from one communications program to another.

*Procomm 2.4.3*, DataStorm Technologies, Inc., P.O. Box 1471, Columbia, MO 65205, 314-443-3282 [443-DATA] (voice).

> Procomm 2.4.3 is one more good MS-DOS shareware communications program. For $50, you can currently get a registered copy of the software, support, and a manual. You can download Procomm 2.4.3 at 314-875-0503 3/12/24/9600-8-N-1.

*QMODEM SST 4.0b,* FORBIN Project, P.O. Box 702, Cedar Falls, IA 50613, 319-232-4515 (voice).

QMODEM SST 4.0b is shareware written by John Friel III and distributed by the FORBIN Project. You can download QMODEM through the FORBIN Project BBS at 319-233-6157 12/24/96/19200/38400-8-N-1. Write or call for prices and more information.

*Telix,* Exis Inc., P.O. Box 130, West Hill, Ontario, Canada M1E 4R4.

Telix is another good MS-DOS shareware communications program. You can download Telix through the Telix Support BBS, 416-284-0682.

# APPENDIX B

# BBS NUMBERS

This appendix lists BBS numbers and sources for BBS numbers. The list of BBS numbers is as up to date as possible, with emphasis on BBSes that are likely to be in existence for several years after publication of this book.

# BBS Numbers

These are numbers for various BBSes around the country, listed in order of area code. Many of these are the customer support BBSes for various BBS-related products. Remember that BBSes cease operations frequently. Please be considerate and do not phone a BBS number at odd hours until you have determined that the BBS is still in operation.

Eskimo North, 206-FOR-EVER, 3/12/2400-8-N-1, Seattle, WA. 206-361-8759 is 2400 baud.

> To get a phone list of BBSes, dial in and type *BBS* at the login prompt. This is a multi-user BBS that uses a Unix system with a multi-user room system.

The Library, 206-641-7978, 3/12/2400-8-N-1, Seattle, WA.

> The Library is an exceptionally fine multi-line BBS run by The Flying Kiwi using eSoft's TBBS software. This BBS is strongly recommended for people interested in a well-managed, consistent BBS.

TurboTech, 206-362-6828, 3/12/24/9600-8-N-1, Seattle, WA.

> Sysop: Ray Johnson. TurboTech is the home of the TurboCit BBS software. Try this out if you want to find out what room BBSes are like.

TBBS Net 104/23, 303-699-9248, 3/12/24/9600-8-N-1, Aurora, CO.

> Sysop: Phil Becker/eSoft, Inc. Home of The Bread Board System (TBBS) software.

ProComm Support BBS, 314-875-0503, 3/12/24/9600-8-N-1, Columbia, MO.

> Sysop: Thomas Smith/DataStorm Technologies, Inc. Home of the ProComm 2.4.3 and ProComm Plus communications programs.

Hayes Microcomputer Products, Inc., operates a customer service BBS at 800-874-2937 (800-USHAYES) and a BBS for the general public at 404-446-6336 (404-HIMODEM). Both are 3/12/24/9600-8-N-1.

The WELL (Whole Earth eLectronic Link), 415-332-6106, Sausalito, CA.

> Sysop: Whole Earth eLectronic Link. Very popular multiline BBS.

Fido Support BBS, 415-764-1629, 3/12/24/9600-8-N-1, San Francisco, CA.

> Sysop: Tom Jennings. Support BBS for Fido BBSes.

Telix Support BBS, 416-284-0682, West Hill, Ontario, Canada.

> Sysop: Colin Sampaleanu/Exis, Inc. Support BBS for Telix communications software.

Home of WILDCAT! BBS, 805-395-0650, Bakersfield, CA, 3/12/24/9600-8-N-1.

Sysop: Jim Harrer/Mustang Software. Support BBS for WILDCAT! BBSes.

## Government BBSes

Here are numbers for a few of the BBSes funded by your tax dollars. *Boardwatch Magazine* (listed below) has current numbers for other government BBSes.

The Economic Bulletin Board of the U.S. Department of Commerce, 202-377-3870, 3/12/2400-8-N-1.

Operated by the Office of Business Analysis. You can log on as a guest user to look around. Full membership is $25 a year and .10/minute. Besides being an interesting BBS, this board frequently has current lists of other federal BBSes. For more information, contact the sysop, Ken W. Rogers, at 202-377-1986 (voice).

Naval Observatory BBS, 202-653-1079, 3/12/2400-8-N-1, operated by the US Naval Observatory.

National Science Foundation BBS, 202-634-1764, 3/12/2400-8-N-1.

Results of scientific studies, National Science Foundation data and general information. For more information, call Geane Deans or Bill Phillips at 202-634-4250 (voice).

NASA Spacelink, 205-895-0028, 3/12/2400-8-N-1.

The NASA Spacelink data base is maintained by the Public Services and Education Branch of the Marshall Space Flight Center Public Affairs Office, with operational support provided by the Information Systems Office at the Marshall Center. Phone this BBS for information on NASA, the current space shuttle flights, and general information on spaceflight.

FCC BBS, 301-725-1072, 3/12/2400-8-N-1.

The Public Access Link for the Federal Communications Commission.

Fort Myer O Club BBS, 703-524-4159, 12/2400-8-N-1.

Operated by the Fort Myer Officers Club. This BBS is primarily for the members of the Military District of Washington Club System and military and civilians of the U.S. Army Military District of Washington, but other people who wish to exchange programs and information are also welcome. For more information, call John Bomberger at 703-524-4839 (voice).

# Magazines

*Boardwatch Magazine*, 5970 South Vivian St., Littleton, CO 80127, 303-973-6038 (voice).

> Jack Rickard in Denver, Colorado, publishes *Boardwatch Magazine*, a monthly magazine that focuses on BBSs and on-line information services. *Boardwatch Magazine* includes a list of Denver area and national BBSs. The writing is good and the articles are very informative. Subscription rates are currently $28/year or $3.95/issue. For more information or to order, call the Boardwatch Online Information Service at 303-973-422 12/2400-8-N-1.

*Computing Canada Online*, #703, 2 Lansing Sq., Willowdale, Ontario, Canada  M2J 5A1, 416-497-5263.

> *Computing Canada Online* can provide numbers for many Canadian BBSes.

*Computer Shopper*, One Park Avenue, New York, New York  10016, 800-274-6384 (voice).

> *Computer Shopper* is a monthly tabloid covering personal computing. It prints a list of BBS numbers from around the country in each issue.

*Infomat Online Weekly PC News Magazine,* The BBS Press Service in Topeka, Kansas, 913-478-9239 (voice.

> Infomat is an excellent online magazine. You can probably obtain the numbers of local BBSes that also carry *Infomat*.

# Other Sources

Check with local users' groups, computer stores, even software businesses. Most major metropolitan areas have at least 300 to 500 public BBSes. It won't take you long to find a few.

The International FidoNet Association, P.O. Box 41143, St. Louis, MO 63141, 314-576-4067 (voice), can provide you with a few numbers for local BBSes. You can then ask the local sysop if there is a general list of local BBS numbers. If nothing else, you can arrange to download the FidoNet nodelist. The nodelist is updated weekly and contains the numbers for all the BBSes participating in FidoNet around the world.

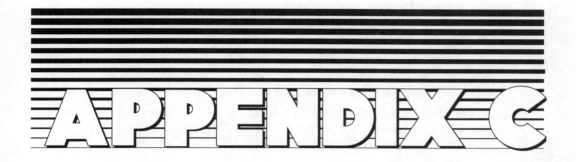

# BBS SOFTWARE

This appendix is for people planning to set up their own bulletin board system. It lists manufacturers and distributors for a number of popular BBS software packages.

**Fido**  Fido Software, P.O. Box 77731, San Francisco, CA  94107, 415-764-1688 (voice), 415-764-1629 (BBS).

**OPUS** is not currently being supported.  You can obtain a copy of the latest OPUS software from the sysop of an OPUS BBS.  Also check with the sysop for further information on OPUS suport and new releases.

People using or recommending OPUS for commercial purposes are required to send a $50 donation to the Shanti Project, an AIDS support group at 525 Howard St., San Francisco, CA 94105, 415-777-2273 (voice).

**PCBoard**  Clark Development Company, Inc., P.O. Box 571365, Salt Lake City, UT, 84157-1365, 801-261-1686 (voice), 801-261-8976 (BBS) and 801-261-8981 (BBS) 12/24/9600-8-N-1.  New orders for software can be placed by calling 800-356-1686 (voice).

**ProLine**  Morgan Davis Group, 10079 Nuerto Lane, Rancho San Diego, CA, 92078-1736.  619-670-0563 (voice) or 619-670-5379 (BBS) 3/12/24/9600-8-N-1. ProLine is a very good BBS for Apple II computers.

**RBBS-PC**  Distributed with *The Complete Electronic Bulletin Board Starter Kit,* Charles Bowen and David Peyton (New York: The Bantam Book Software Library, 1988).

**Second Sight**  (formerly known as Red Ryder Host), Freesoft Co., 150 Hickory Drive, Beaver Falls, PA  15010, 412-846-2700 (voice).

**TEAMate**  MMB Development Corporation, 1021 North Sepulveda Boulevard, Suite K, Manhattan Beach, CA, 90226, 213-545-1455 (voice), 213-545-0853 (1200-8-N-1), 213-545-9824 (2400-8-N-1).  TEAMate runs on UNIX computers.

**TBBS (The Bread Board System)**  eSoft, Inc., 15200 E. Girard Ave., Suite 2550, Aurora, CO  80014, 303-699-6565 (voice), 303-699-8222 BBS 3/12/24/9600-8-N-1.

**TurboCit**  Ray G. Johnson, P.O. Box 55904, Seattle, WA  98155.  $49.95 (Washington residents add 8.1% sales tax).

**WILDCAT!**  Mustang Software, Inc., 3125 19th St., Suite 162, Bakersfield, CA 93301, 805-395-0223 (voice), 805-395-0650 (BBS) 3/12/24/9600-8-N-1. Orders can by placed at 800-999-9619.

# TROUBLESHOOTING

C hapter 2 gave you a number of tips on how to solve some basic communications problems. If your modem has external lights, you can use them to gain a lot of information about the modem and the phone connection.

There are commonly eight indicator lights on a modem. These are usually labeled with the abbreviations HS, AA, CD, OH, RD, SD, TR, and MR (this order may differ slightly from modem to modem).

*HS* (High Speed)—This light simply says that your modem is operating at its top speed, such as 2400 bps on a 2400 bps modem. If you are running the modem at a lower speed, this light will be off.

*AA* (Auto-Answer)—This light will be on if you have set up your modem for auto-answer. When the phone rings, the light will turn off with each ring and then answer the phone after a predetermined number of rings. If the modem is not set to auto-answer, the light will be normally off and will only light up when the telephone line rings.

*CD* (Carrier Detect)—This light goes on when you connect with another modem. It will stay on until the modem can no longer hear the other modem, or the modem hangs up. The electronic circuitry that is connected to this light is also directly connected to the serial port of your computer. The circuit sends a signal to your computer that tells your communications software that the modem has connected with another modem.

*OH* (Off Hook)—This light goes on when the modem has picked up the telephone.

*RD* (Receive Data)—This light goes on whenever your modem passes data from the other modem to your computer.

*SD* (Send Data)—This light goes on whenever your computer passes data to your modem.

*TR* (Terminal Ready)—This light generally goes on when your commmunications program sends a DTR (Data Terminal Ready) signal to your modem. However, some modems leave this light on at all times. Check your modem manual for more information.

*MR* (Modem Ready)—This light indicates that the power to the modem is on. If you run self-tests using the modem's internal commands, the Modem Ready light may blink or turn off entirely during the test.

As was mentioned in Chapter 1, communications problems can be hard to trace because you have no way to see where a signal is going and what it is doing. Your modem's indicator lights solve this problem by displaying when and where communications signals are occurring. In the following figures, a bullet (•) is used to represent a steady light, an asterisk (*) represents a blinking light, and a small dot (·) is used to represent an unlit indicator.

For example, when your modem is sitting idle, you should probably see the front panel looking like this:

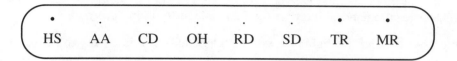

The HS light shows that the modem is set to run at its highest speed, and the TR and MR lights show that the modem is turned on and ready to receive commands from the communications software.

When you are connected but aren't sending or receiving data (such as when you're just looking at your screen), the modem should look like this:

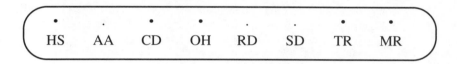

The CD and OH lights indicate that the modem has picked up the phone and is currently connected to another modem on the other end of the line.

When you are typing an entry or receiving data, you should see this:

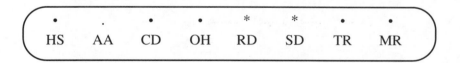

The Send Data and Receive Data lights will flicker as you send and receive data. You can see how this works by typing one character at a time on your keyboard and watching the RD and SD lights.

You can use the lights to diagnose problems in a number of ways. For example, if the BBS you are talking to suddenly stops transmitting and the Carrier Detect light has gone out, you know that the connection has been broken for some reason such as a power failure.

Similarly, if you are sending a file and start receiving transmission errors, the RD and SD lights may give you a clue as to what has happened. If the remote computer is not sending you blocks of data, the Receive Data light won't come on. You may also be able to find out more about the signals going through your modem by running tests or issuing specific commands. See your modem manual for more information.

Learning how to read the lights on your modem will provide you with a source of quick, easy-to-use information about your connection to another computer. You will rapidly find that you can interpret a row of indicator lights like a pro.

**access fee:** a fee charged for access to a BBS or for an increase in access privileges.

**access privileges:** the privileges—features, conferences, and files—a user is allowed to use on a BBS. Also known as access level.

**acoustically coupled:** a modem into which the handset of the telephone is placed. Tones are sent and received with a microphone and a speaker next to the handset.

**addressee:** the person to whom a message is addressed.

**adventure games:** games that describe action with text descriptions.

**ALL:** used as the addressee in a message header to show that anyone on the BBS can read the message.

**amateur radio:** two-radio transmission on a specific set of noncommercial shortwave radio frequencies.

**AMTOR:** short for <u>am</u>ateur <u>t</u>eleprinting <u>o</u>ver <u>r</u>adio.

**anonymous topics:** a topic that does not show who a message is from.

**anti-static wrapping:** special plastic and wrapping materials that don't generate or conduct static electricity. Most computer equipment is packed in anti-static wrapping

**ARC:** a common extension of an archived file.

**archive:** to compress a file in order to save space.

**archiving program:** a program that compresses a file (see compression program).

**ARPA-style address:** a UUCP/Usenet address with the general form username@domain. Also known as at-sign syntax.

**ARPANET:** Advanced Research Projects Agency Network. ARPANET is being replaced by the Defense Research Internet, commonly known as Internet.

**315**

# Glossary

**ASCII:** acronym for American Standard Code for Information Interchange.

**ASCII value:** a unique numeric value identifying every number, character, and symbol that appears on a computer screen.

**asynchronous:** a method of sending information via modem at random intervals, using start and stop bits to tell where one byte of information ends and the next begins.

**at-sign syntax:** another name for ARPA-style addresses.

**autoanswer:** short for automatic answering. The ability of a modem to answer incoming phone calls.

**autodial:** short for automatic dialing. The ability to have the modem dial a number by sending it a command from a communications program.

**automatic speed sensing:** the ability of a modem to detect another modem's speed automatically.

**automatic voice/data switching:** a modem feature that lets a user break into the middle of a data call and actually talk on the phone.

**backbone site:** in UUCP/Usenet, a computer that connects to many other computers in the local area as well as to other backbone sites in other areas.

**backing up:** making a copy of files and programs on a computer.

**bang:** a typesetting term referring to an exclamation point.

**bang path:** a type of UUCP/Usenet email address. Bang paths are complete routing paths separated by exclamation points.

**baud:** technically, how fast a modem can change its tone to indicate a bit. Commonly (and incorrectly) used as a synonym for bits per second.

**BBS:** acronym for Bulletin Board System.

**BBS policy:** the rules and regulations for using a BBS.

**beta test program:** a program that has been given to a few people for final testing before it is released to the general public. Beta test programs frequently do not have all the features of the finished product and are likely to contain bugs.

**binary file:** a file containing ASCII control characters as well as text.

**bit:** short for binary digit.

**BITNET:** a network for educators.

**bits per second:** how many bits a modem can transmit or receive. Commonly (and incorrectly) referred to as baud or baud rate.

**block:** a group of consecutive bytes in a file treated as a unit when uploading or downloading the file. Blocks are usually 128 or 1024 bytes long.

**body:** see message text.

**bps:** an acronym for bits per second.

**browsing:** looking through a BBS or an online information service to see what it has to offer. May also mean to scan messages in a topic to see the message headers.

**BT TYMNET:** a packet-switching network run by BT Tymnet, Inc.

**bug:** an error in a program. Errors in programs are called bugs because in 1946, a four-inch moth got into ENIAC, considered the first electronic computer (it used vacuum tubes instead of transistors or chips), and shorted out a circuit, preventing the computer from working correctly.

**bulletin board system:** a computer equipped with a modem and a program that lets people call the computer over a standard telephone line.

**bulletin menu:** a menu of the bulletins currently on a BBS.

**bulletproof:** slang term meaning "not prone to errors."

**byte:** seven or eight bits in a group to form a single character.

**call transfer service:** a method for extending a local calling area inexpensively. Also known as a local area extension or a phone linking service.

**callback:** a system for the BBS to phone you back at a specified number in order to immediately verify your registration information.

**cancel:** to abandon a message in progress without saving it.

**capture:** to save information appearing on the screen to a disk file or the printer.

**CD-ROM:** a data storage unit that uses a compact disk to store several hundred megabytes of data and files.

**character translation table:** see filter.

**chat:** to have a conversation with someone through the BBS. Also known as an exclusive chat.

**CheckFree Processing Center:** a check-free transaction service that lets a user pay bills electronically by debiting his or her checking account and crediting the payee's account.

**checksum:** the total ASCII values of all the characters in a block.

**Citizen's Band conference:** a common name for an area of an online information service devoted to chatting between many users.

**clean:** slang for a phone connection with no line noise.

**command:** a combination of keys, usually involving the [ALT] or [CTRL] keys, that tell the communications program to do something.

**communications parameters:** the bits per second; the number of start, stop, and data bits; and the parity.

**communications software:** a program or set of programs that allow a computer to talk to a modem.

# Glossary

**compression program:** a program that to archives, or compresses, files and then restores them to their original size. Compression programs (also known as archiving programs) are used to save space on a disk.

**conference:** a topic that frequently combines both messages and files. Can also mean a forum or round-table with multi-user chatting.

**connect time:** the time actually spent connected to an online information service.

**control characters:** the characters with ASCII values from 0 to 31. These characters don't normally show up on the screen but they do tell the computer to do something such as enter, backspace, or tab.

**copy protection:** any one of several methods of making a diskette or program uncopyable in order to prevent it being pirated.

**copyrighted program:** a program that is sold rather than distributed as shareware or public domain.

**crash:** of a BBS or a program, to shut down suddenly and unexpectedly, usually because of an equipment, software, or power failure.

**crasher:** someone who tries to crash a BBS.

**CRT:** acronym for cathode ray terminal. Also known as a terminal.

**customizing:** changing display screens, menus, or commands on a BBS. Customizing is almost always done by the sysop.

**cyclic redundancy check:** a more complex and more accurate type of error correction than a checksum.

**data bits:** the bits in a byte that hold the actual information.

**DB-25 connector:** a connector designed for 25 pins, 13 over and 12 under.

**default:** the predetermined settings or options.

**demodulate:** to translate modulated tones back into separate electrical pulses for each bit.

**dialing directory:** a list of frequently dialed phone numbers, together with specific communications parameters for each number.

**digitize:** to turn something (usually a sound) into a set of bits.

**DIP switches:** acronym for dual inline package. Very small switches you set with the tip of a pen or a screwdriver.

**direct-connect:** a modem that plugs in to the phone line directly. Almost all modems in use these days are direct-connect modems.

**direct mail:** mail sent directly from one BBS to another.

**display options:** user's preferences for how a BBS should be displayed.

**domain:** the formal name for a computer or group of computers that share a common purpose or function, even though they may not be in the same geographical area.

**door:** a program (usually a game) run through the BBS.

**dot command:** a command preceded by a period or "dot." Dot commands are used almost exclusively on room BBSes.

**download:** to receive a file from a BBS.

**Dragon Citadel:** a popular type of room BBS.

**echo:** a conference on a specific subject where echomail can be sent and received.

**echomail:** mail sent from one BBS to a number of other BBSes that are all connected to a network.

**email:** short for electronic mail. An exclusive message addressed to someone else. Also known as mail.

**even parity:** a standard for checking parity where the total number of binary "1" digits in a byte, including the parity bit, is always even.

**exclusive chat:** having a conversation with someone through the BBS.

**extended help:** in-depth help that covers a specific subject in greater detail than the standard help available.

**extension:** the characters in a filename after the period. The extension is usually used to identify the type of file, such as DOC for a document, COM or EXE for a program, and TXT for general text.

**external modem:** a modem that has a chassis and a power supply of its own.

**factory defaults:** the settings on a piece of hardware as it comes out of the box.

**FCC registration:** a certification by the Federal Communications Commission that a piece of equipment will not cause excessive amounts of static and that it can be hooked safely to telephone lines.

**female connector:** a connector that has sockets.

**Fido:** a type of linear BBS.

**FidoNet:** an international network of BBSes.

**file creation date:** the date a file was originally created. This may not be the same as the upload date.

**file request:** a request for a file sent to another BBS.

**file system:** the portion of a BBS devoted to files.

**file transfer prompt:** a prompt asking what default file transfer protocol should be used.

**filename prompt:** a prompt asking for the name of a file to upload or download.

**filter:** a feature in a communications program that automatically changes one character into another. Also known as a character translation table.

**flame:** a message that disagrees violently with someone else's point of view. Also known as flame mail.

**floor:** another name for a hallway.

# Glossary

**folders:** a way of categorizing messages used by WILDCAT!.

**forum:** a round-table discussion. May also be known as a conference.

**freeware:** see public domain.

**full duplex:** able to send and receive information at the same time.

**full-screen editor:** a message editor that lets you move the cursor around on the screen to make changes to message text, very much like a standard word processor.

**gateway:** a connection between two different networks by a BBS. The most common example is a gateway between FidoNet and UUCP/Usenet.

**global command:** a command that can be entered at any prompt that will always do the same thing.

**goto command:** a command on room BBSes that takes the user to another room.

**graphics mode:** a prompt asking whether you want your display in plain text, with ASCII graphics characters, or with color graphics.

**hacked program:** a program that has had copy protection removed.

**hacker:** someone who attepts to gain unauthoriaed access to a BBS.

**half duplex:** able to send and receive information, but not simultaneously.

**hallway:** a set of rooms in room BBSes.

**hardware:** computer equipment.

**Hayes-compatible:** identifies a modem as accepting a set of commands like those used in modems made by Hayes Microcomputer Products. Also commonly used to imply that a modem is "Bell 212-compatible"; that is, that it uses a certain set of tones for communications used by a particular type of Bell System modem.

**help:** information available online about using the BBS.

**hidden room:** a room that does not normally appear on the list of known rooms in a hallway.

**hot keys:** the ability to type a character and have the BBS perform the command without your having to press [ENTER].

**ignore page:** see page off.

**index:** a command for searching message headers for a word or phrase. Also known as topic search or text search.

**infection:** having a virus.

**information database:** a collection of specialized information or data that can be accessed with a computer.

**internal help file:** online help built into a modem. A user can ask the modem to display a list of its commands with a brief explanation.

**internal modem:** a modem designed to plug directly inside a computer. Almost always a printed circuit board without a chassis or power supply.

**Internet:** a number of individual networks that use the same protocols (known as TCP/IP protocol) for transferring messages and files. Also known as the Defense Research Internet.

**Kermit:** a transfer protocol that can be used to transfer files between almost any two computers.

**kill:** to delete a message from the BBS's hard disk.

**kilobyte:** 1024 bytes (1024 is 2 raised to the 10th power). Also used to mean 1000 bytes.

**length:** the size of a file in bytes. Usually part of the report from a compression program.

**line editor:** a message editor that lets a user make changes to individual lines of message text before saving the message.

**line noise:** static or extraneous sounds on a phone line that cause errors in data sent and received over the line.

**linear BBS:** a BBS that is organized hierarchically, like an organization chart.

**linefeed:** a control character that tells the computer whether or not to move the cursor down a line at the end of each line.

**lobby:** common name for the entry point to a room BBS.

**local area extension:** a method for extending the user's local calling area inexpensively. Also known as a phone linking service or a call transfer service.

**local echo:** another name for half duplex.

**log on:** to enter user ID and password on a BBS.

**logoff command:** the character or characters entered to log off of a BBS gracefully.

**logon procedure:** a set of steps for logging on to a BBS.

**logon script:** a script designed to automatically log on to a BBS.

**LORE:** short for line-oriented editor. LORE is a feature of OPUS.

**lowercase prompt:** a prompt asking whether the BBS is to display information in all uppercase (capital) letters or uppercase and lowercase letters.

**macro:** text assigned to a key on the keyboard (usually a function key).

**mail:** an exclusive message addressed to someone else. Also known as email.

**mail war:** a series or flames sent back and forth that invariably involve a number of people outside the scope of the original argument.

**main menu:** the starting point for almost everything on a BBS.

# Glossary

**male connector:** a connector that has pins.

**mall:** a name for a group of businesses from which goods and services can be bought by placing an order electronically. Used almost exclusively in online information services. Also known by a name such as Merchant's Corner.

**manual:** a written guide for using software.

**matrix:** another name for the network of BBSes. The term was originally used by William Gibson in his novel *Neuromancer* to describe a large, loosely connected network of computers.

**megabyte:** 1,048,576 bytes (1,048,576 is 2 raised to the 20th power). Also used to mean 1,000,000 bytes.

**memory resident program:** see RAM-resident program.

**menu:** a list of options appearing on the screen.

**Merchant's Corner:** see mall.

**message header:** information about the message, such as name of the person sending the message, the addressee, the date, the time, and the subject.

**message recipient prompt:** a prompt when entering a message asking to whom the message should go.

**message system:** the portion of a BBS devoted to messages.

**message text:** the actual information in the message. Also known as the body of the message.

**MILNET:** a network used almost exclusively by people involved in projects funded by the Department of Defense. Also part of Internet.

**modem:** short for modulator-demodulator. A modem translates the electrical impulses from one computer into tones and sends them over the phone line, where another modem translates the tones back into electrical impulses.

**modem port:** another name for a serial port.

**moderator:** a person who keeps the discussion in a conference alive and on the subject.

**modulate:** to translate bits into electrical pulses.

**multi-player games:** games that have several players playing against each other as well as against the computer.

**multi-user BBS:** any BBS than can have more that one user online at the same time.

**multi-user log:** a list of users on a multi-user BBS.

**multiple key command:** any command that requires several keystrokes, such as .EE or OPEN.

**name prompt:** a prompt that is asking specifically for your name.

**netmail:** short for networked mail. Electronic mail that is sent directly from one BBS to another.

**network:** a group of BBSes that can communicate with each other automatically. Networks are used to route netmail, echomail, programs, and other electronic information. In FidoNet, the term is also used to identify a relatively small geographical area, such as a single city or metropolitan area.

**networking:** exchanging mail and files with other BBSes.

**news:** echomail on UUCP/Usenet.

**newsgroups:** echomail conferences on UUCP/Usenet.

**node:** a BBS in a network. Also used to mean the individual phone lines on a multi-user BBS.

**noncommercial BBS:** a BBS run largely for the pleasure of having a BBS; a BBS that is not run for a specific business application.

**nondocument mode:** another name for a file stored as plain ASCII text.

**NSFnet:** the network for the National Science Foundation. Also part of Internet.

**null:** a delay the BBS sends to your computer to give it time to skip to the next line.

**nym:** slang term short for pseudonym. A nickname used on a BBS.

**odd parity:** a standard for checking parity where the total number of binary "1" digits in a byte, including the parity bit, is always odd.

**online:** to be connected to a BBS. Also, for something such as a file to be available on a BBS.

**online games:** a computer game that can be played through a BBS.

**online information services:** multi-user systems that provide a variety of services online.

**online publications:** newspapers and magazines that are distributed via BBS.

**online time:** the amount of time you can spend on a BBS in one session or one day. Also known as access time or connect time.

**OPed:** short for OPUS editor. OPed is a full-screen message editor used with OPUS.

**opening screen:** the first screen of information displayed by a BBS. The opening screen tells you such things as the name of the BBS, the phone number, the baud rates, hours of operation, and location.

**OPUS:** a type of linear BBS.

**OSCAR:** acronym for Orbiting Satellite Carrying Amateur Radio. Any of a number of satellites put in orbit for use by amateur radio operators.

**packet:** a chunk of data sent over a packet-switching network.

**packet radio:** a method of routing messages and files from one location to another in packets with short-wave radio.

# Glossary

**packet-switching network:** a network of high-speed modems and transmission lines that sends packets of data cheaply and effectively from place to place.

**page off:** a user option that prevents other users from paging.

**paging:** sending a one- or two-line private message to someone from within a forum.

**parallel port:** a connector on the back of a computer that sends and receives data a whole byte at a time.

**parity bit:** a bit added to a byte for the purpose of checking if the total number of binary "1" digits in the byte is odd or even.

**password:** a unique set of letters, numbers, and other characters used to log on to a BBS.

**PC Pursuit:** a packet-switching service for BBS users. PC Pursuit is part of SprintNet (former TeleNet).

**PCBOARD:** a type of linear BBS.

**phone linking service:** a method for extending a user's local calling area inexpensively. Also known as a local area extension or a call transfer service.

**picture files:** digitized pictures that are displayed on the screen of a computer.

**pirate software:** hacked programs, illegal copies of commercial software, or beta test programs.

**point:** a FidoNet address for a single user.

**policy:** a set of rules and guidelines that state how the sysop wants the BBS to run and the users' rights and responsibilities.

**port:** a connector on the back of a computer that sends and receives data. Ports can be serial or parallel.

**power flicker:** very short (usually less than a second) power outage, after which a computer may have to be restarted.

**prime time:** normal business hours; times of peak load on packet-switching networks and online information services.

**print-formatted command:** command to show what a message will look like when it is saved.

**private message:** a message that can be read only by the addressee, the sender, and the sysop.

**private message prompt:** a prompt when entering a message asking if the user wants to make the message private.

**prompt:** a set of characters on the screen that cue the user to enter information.

**protocol:** a specific set of rules for uploading and downloading information.

**public conference:** a round-table discussion, with chatting between several different users. Also known as a forum. The term *conference* may also be used to describe a message area.

**public domain programs:** programs that have been released for general, noncommercial distribution by their authors. Also known as freeware.

**pulse dialing:**  ability to generate electrical pulses like a rotary dial phone.

**RAM-resident program:**  a program that stays in memory.  Also known as a memory resident or TSR program.

**ratio:**  the amount of space (expressed as a percentage) saved by compressing a file.  Usually part of the report from a compression program.

**RBBS-PC:**  a type of linear BBS.

**read:**  to display a message's message header and message text.

**registration:**  entering new user information on a BBS.

**remote sysop:**  a user who has sysop privileges but logs on to the BBS over the phone lines instead of directly through the BBS computer.

**return receipt:**  an option when entering a message for showing when the message was read by the addressee.

**room:**  an area in a room BBS.

**room BBS:**  a BBS organized like a hallway with rooms coming off it.

**round-table:**  another name for a forum or a multi-user conference.

**RTTY:**  abbreviation for radio-teletype, the communications method used by Teletype machines.

**save:**  to enter the message on the BBS's hard disk and record it as part of the message file.

**scan:**  the display of message headers only to quickly see the messages' subjects, who they are from, and who they are addressed to.

**screen width:**  the width of the screen expressed as the number of characters that can appear from one side of the screen to another.  Most later model computer screens are 80 characters wide.

**script:**  a collection of commands, text, and instructions executed by the communications program.

**search:**  see topic search.

**serial port:**  a connector on the back of a computer that sends and receives data a bit at a time.

**Shanti Project:**  an AIDS support group at 525 Howard St., San Francisco, CA 94105, 415-777-2273 (voice).

**shareware:**  software that has been released for distribution and is licensed to users for a trial period.  If the user likes the software, it should be registered.

**shortwave BBS:**  a BBS that uses shortwave radio instead of phone lines.

**size:**  the size of a file after compression.  Usually part of the report from a compression program.

**smart menu:**  a menu that can accept and immediately act on a command before the menu is completely displayed on your screen.

# Glossary

**SprintNet:**  A packet switching Network owned by US Sprint Communications.

**squelch:**  to suppress messages from a specific user.

**start bit:**  a bit sent before a byte to let the modem know that it is about to receive a byte of information.

**starter kit:**  package offered by many online information services, containing things like introductory materials, registration information, manuals, and a certificate good for a certain amount of connect time.  Many starter kits also offer special communications software made specifically for use with the online information service.

**stop bit:**  one or more bits sent after a byte to let the modem know that there is no more data in the byte it just received.

**subject prompt:**  a prompt when entering a message for the subject of the message.

**submenu:**  a menu of commands for a specific area of the BBS, such as the message or the file system, that you get to from the main menu.

**synchronous:**  sending information via modem at timed intervals, thereby eliminating the need for start and stop bits.

**sysop:**  short for system operator, the person who runs a BBS.

**sysop unavailable message:**  a message saying that the sysop is not available for chatting.

**system failure:**  a computer error serious enough to require you to restart the computer.

**TBBS:**  acronym for The Bread Board System, a type of linear BBS.

**telecommunications:**  transmitting or receiving data in the form of electrical signals by wire, radio, or light beam.

**telecommuting:**  working at home and transferring information via a company BBS.

**Telenet:**  a packet-switching network run by General Telephone and Electric.  Now known as SprintNet and owned by US Sprint Communications.

**template:**  a pre-formatted file that is used in a spreadsheet or word processing program.  A template for a spreadsheet program might contain formulas and places for entering numbers that will then automatically compute some result.

**terminal:**  a keyboard and a display but no central processing unit (the part of the computer that "thinks").  Also known as a CRT.

**terminal emulation:**  the type of terminal commands the communications program can accept.

**test mode:**  a set of procedures built into a modem that let the modem check itself.

**text buffer:**  feature that automatically captures the information displayed on the screen and allows the information to be scrolled through at any time.

**text file:**  manuals, documentation, or stories written by computer users.

**text prompt:** a prompt after the various prompts for the message header indicating that you can enter the message text.

**thank you:** an often overlooked and underused form of praise.

**threading:** tracing a string of messages and replies through a message system, skipping over any intervening messages.

**time:** the amount of time one can spend on a BBS in one session or one day. Also known as online time or access time.

**time delay:** the amount of time it takes for a piece of echomail to reach all the other BBSes in an echo.

**tone dialing:** ability to generate actual tones like a Touch-Tone telephone.

**topic search:** a command for searching message headers for a word or phrase. Also known as index or text search.

**transfer errors:** an error that occurs when uploading or downloading a file where information is not received as it was sent.

**transfer protocol:** a set of rules for establishing communications between two computers.

**trojan horse:** a program designed specifically to cause damage to a computer by erasing or altering data. Trojan horses do not reproduce themselves, as do viruses.

**TSR program:** acronym for Terminate and Stay Resident program. See RAM-resident program.

**turbokeys:** RBBS-PC's version of hot keys.

**UFGATE:** software that allows BBSes in FidoNet to exchange mail with UUCP/Usenet.

**unformatted mode:** another name for a file stored as plain ASCII text.

**Unix:** a type of powerful operating system used on multi-user computers.

**upload:** to send a file from your computer to a BBS.

**upload date:** the date the file was uploaded to the BBS. This is not necessarily the same date as the file creation date.

**user ID:** a name or a set of characters used for identification on a BBS.

**userlog:** the list of current users on a BBS.

**username:** another name for user ID. A unique identifier for a particular user.

**utilities:** a type of general program that does something helpful for a computer, such as sort information or copy files. Also, a category of commands on a BBS that are used for setting up and maintaining your user options.

**UUCP:** Short for Unix-to-Unix-Copy.

# Glossary

**UUCP/Usenet:** a conferencing and news network based on Unix computers.

**UUENCODE:** a program that translates a program or other binary file into ASCII text so you can then send it over UUCP/Usenet as a message. A second program called UUDECODE translates the ASCII text back into a program.

**verified access:** BBS access that is granted after the sysop has phoned a new user to verify his or her identity.

**virus:** a program that is capable of reproducing and attaching itself to other programs. Viruses may be benign (causing no harm to a computer other than filling up the hard disk) or malignant (destroying data or programs).

**The WELL:** acronym for Whole Earth 'Lectronic Link. The WELL is a large, multi-user BBS that is a public access UUCP node.

**WILDCAT!:** a type of linear BBS.

**window room:** a room that connects to more than one hallway in a room BBS.

**write-protect:** to prevent someone from accidentally erasing or changing the information on a diskette by placing a small adhesive foil tab over a notch in the side of the diskette, or by flipping a little plastic tab on the diskette so that light can be seen through a hole in the diskette (the latter method is used for 3-1/2" diskettes). The computer checks the diskette to see if it is write-protected by shining a light at the write-protect spot and seeing whether or not it can see the light on the other side of the diskette.

**XMODEM:** the most popular transfer protocol. Sends a 128-byte block of information.

**XMODEM-CRC:** XMODEM that uses a cyclic redundancy check.

**Y connector:** a connector that lets two phone lines be pluggged into the same socket.

**YMODEM:** a transfer protocol that uses a 1024-byte block and that allows a user to send several files in a single transfer.

**ZIP:** a file extension used by a type of compression program.

**ZMODEM:** a transfer protocol with exceptionally good error correcting.

**zone mail hour:** a set time, usually in the middle of the night, when BBSes in the FidoNet is unavailable for calls from BBS users. During this time, the BBSes send and receive netmail, echomail, and files.

# BIBLIOGRAPHY

This is a bibliography of related books and magazines that may be of interest.

## General

Bowen, Charles and David Peyton. *The Complete Electronic Bulletin Board Starter Kit*. New York: The Bantam Book Software Library, 1988.

> The definitive book on RBBS-PC. Includes a copy of the RBBS-PC software. $39.95

Flock, Emil, Miriam Flock, and Howard Schulman. *The Shareware Book: Using PC-Write, PC-File III, PC-Talk III*. Berkeley, CA: Osborne/McGraw-Hill, 1987.

> Good guide to PC-Talk III. $14.95

Gliedman, John. *Tips and Techniques for Using Low-Cost & Public Domain Software*. New York: McGraw-Hill, 1989.

> An excellent book for anyone interested in public domain software and shareware. $24.95

Kelly, Kevin, ed. *SIGNAL: Communication Tools for the Information Age*. New York: Harmony Books, 1988.

> A "Whole Earth" book—bits and pieces about tools for communications. Includes some good references about data communications. $16.95

Landreth, Bill. *Out of the Inner Circle*. Redmond: Tempus Books. 1989.

> Should be required reading for everyone who wants to set up their own BBS. Discusses security from the point of view of someone who used to break it.

von Oech, Roger. *A Whack on the Side of the Head*. New York: Warner Books, Inc., 1983.

> A very good book that will help you become more creative. This is an excellent book to read before starting a BBS of your own. $10.95

Wallace, Jonathan D. *Syslaw: The Sysop's Legal Manual*. New York: LLM Press. 1990

> The author is a lawyer and a sysop for LLM (212-766-3788), a BBS for law-related material. LLM Press, 150 Broadway, Suite 607, New York, NY, 10038, 212-766 -3785 (voice). $25.

## Bibliography

### Amateur Radio

ARRL (American Radio Relay League), 225 Main St. Newington, CT, 06111, 203-666-1541.

Membership (which includes a subscription to *QST*, a monthly magazine devoted exclusively to ham radio) is $25 a year. Persons age 17 or under may qualify for special rates. Single copies of *QST* are $3.00. The ARRL also publishes a number of books about amateur radio—*The ARRL Handbook* (an annual), *Tune in the World with Ham Radio* (a beginner's introduction), *Help for New Hams,* and books on satellites, packet radio, and operating an amateur radio station, among others. You can also write the ARRL for information on local groups, swap meets and conventions, and licensing.

*Amateur Radio Supply,* 6213 13th S., Seattle, WA 98108, 206-767-3222.

Call for a catalog of amateur radio publications and products.

*CQ,* 76 North Broadway, Hicksville, NY 11801, 516-681-2922.

Monthly amateur radio magazine. $19.95 a year.

*Ham Radio*, Greenville, NH 03048, 800-289-0388

Monthly amateur radio magazine. $22.95 a year.

*73 for Radio Amateurs*, Peterborough, NH 03458, 800-289-0388.

Monthly amateur radio magazine. $19.97 a year.

### Online Information Services and Databases

Glosbrenner, Alfred. *Alfred Glosbrenner's Master Guide to CompuServe.* New York: Brady/Prentice Hall Press, 1987.

A good book for learning all about CompuServe. $19.95.

Glosbrenner, Alfred. *How to Look It Up Online.* New York: St. Martin's Press, 1987

A much-needed specialty book. $14.95

Banks, Michael A. *Delphi: The Official Guide.* New York: General Videotex Corporation, 1990.

Like the title says. The easiest way to order this is to phone Delphi at 800-544-4005. $19.95 plus $3.00 shipping and handling.

Banks, Michael A. *The Modem Reference.* New York: Brady Books/Simon & Schuster, 1990.

Another good book on using your modem. This one focuses more on online information services than BBSes. $21.95

Bowen, Charles and David Payton. *How to Get the Most Out of CompuServe.* New York: Bantam, 1989.

Another good book on CompuServe. $21.95

Lambert, Steve. *Online,* Bellevue: Microsoft Press, 1985.

A good look at seven major online information services. If it's out of print, see if you can find it at a used book store. $19.95

Newlin, Barbara. *Answers Online: Your Guide to Informational Databases.* Berkeley: Osborne/McGraw-Hill, 1985.

A good book for seeing what's out there in the world of information databases. $16.95

Soergel, Dagobert. *Organizing Information.* Orlando: Academic Press, Inc., 1985.

A very technical book on searching for information. Not a light read, but recommended for people who plan on doing a lot of work with information databases. $65.00

# INDEX

byte, 5, 6, 7, 10
bits in, 5, 20
definition of, 5

# C

C, 77
cable, modem, 20
cafeteria menus, 291, 293
CAIN on Delphi, 249
call signs, 221, 222
call transfer service, 204
call-waiting, 34
callback system on OPUS, 137-138
Caller's Guide, 127
calling a BBS, 23-40
calling history, 109
cancelling a call, 22
cancelling a download, 73-74
cancelling a message, 55
capital letters, 59
capturing
    bulletins, 36
    file directories, 80
    help, 37, 38
    information, 25, 39, 242
    messages, 61
    screens, 16-17, 24
carbon copies, 57, 158
card slots, 13
case sensitivity, 53, 257
catalog of files, 80, 84
categories of files, 69
CB radio, 2, 8, 220, 228, 296
CB simulator, BIX, 254
CBBS, 3
CBix, BIX, 254
CD-ROM drive on RBBS-PC, 116
CD-ROM 36, 105
censoring information, 298
census information, 264, 292, 293
Center for Seismic Studies, 215
Chamber of Commerce mailings, 276
character translation filter, 18
characters, displayed on screen, 27-28
charges, 229
charging for access, 228, 275, 277, 281
chat, exclusive, 88-89
chatting, 18, 85, 86-93, 104, 228, 281
    on business BBSes, 289
    cueing, 87
    etiquette, 102
    on packet radio, 224

on PCBoard, 149
on room BBSes, 201
with other users, 31, 86, 87-93, 142, 172, 227, 270
with the sysop, 119, 178
CheckFree Processing Center, 229
checking accounts, 229
checking parity, 7
checksum, 65, 73
chemical engineering databases, 264
Christensen, Ward, 3, 65
circuits in switching office, 34
CIS, 233, 234, 238
Citadel, 180
Citadel-86, 180
Citizen's Band conference, 228
citizen's band radio, 220, 296
Clark Development Corporation, 139
classified ads, 60, 264-265
clean circuits, 34
Climate Assessment BBS, 292
clipping services, 262, 263
closing a BBS, 281
closings in messages, 59
CMIC Electronic BBS, 292
college BBSes, 293
color graphics, 28
COM1, 21
COM2, 21
combination BBSes, 270
commands, 16, 17
    different, 51
    entering multiple, 51
    global, 178-179
    in linear BBSes, 105
    OPed, 132
    PCBoard, 142
    planning, 268
    room BBSes, 178-179
    single-key, 105
    two-character, 105
commercial BBSes, 271
commercial domain, 217
commercial fishing BBSes, 292
Commodore 64 computers, 2, 9, 28, 33, 77
communications parameters, 16, 21
    resetting, 33
    setting, 24
communications software, 11, 15-19, 28, 67, 231
    autodial, 32
    capturing screens with, 36, 39
    configuring, 21-22
    downloading with, 84, 199
    exiting, 39
    features in, 16-18
    for online information services, 230

help in, 17
IBM, 71
Macintosh, 71-72
screen capture, 24
scripts, 51
transfer protocols in, 64
using scripts for downloading, 74
ZMODEM in, 66
compact disks, 105, 116
compatibility problems, 18
complaints, 271
Complete Electronic Bulletin Board Starter Kit, The, 117
composing a message, 56, 60
compression, 64
compression programs, 77-79
CompuServe Information Service, 233, 234
CompuServe, 15, 233-239, 245, 264
    access time, 238
    address, 239
    broker's database, 239
    BYE command, 238
    changes, 235
    comments, 239
    company information, 239
    conferences, 235, 237, 238
    connecting, 234
    customer service numbers, 233
    demo account, 233-235
    demographic database, 239
    discounts, 239
    EAASY SABRE, 264
    Executive News Service, 239
    Executive Option, 238-239
    exempt activities, 238
    experimenting, 238
    financial reports, 239
    flight reservation databases, 264
    forecasting earnings, 239
    forums, 237, 238
    free activities, 238
    going to a forum, 238
    guided tour, 235
    history, 233
    host name, 234
    identifying securities, 239
    increasing online storage space, 239
    InfoPlex mail service, 233
    jumping to the demo menu, 235
    Last page! message, 235
    listing conference topics, 235, 237
    local access number, 233-235
    logging off, 238

# P

pacing the display, 49
packet radio, 221-223, 224, 225
packet-switching, 216
packet-switching networks, 204-208,
    221, 225, 231, 239, 246
    accessing, 205
packets, 205, 221
page identifiers, 235, 241, 232
page off, 88, 92
page on, 88
Page-Operator command on Fido,
    119
pages, 232
paging a user, 92
paging the sysop, 86, 119
paging, 88, 89-90, 91
paper routing system, 293
parallel ports, 9-10, 21
parity bit, 6
parity, 6-7, 22, 24, 33
party lines, 34
Pascal, 78
password-protecting messages on
    RBBS-PC, 113
passwords, 39, 102, 269, 284
patents, 262
path, routing, 216
pausing the display, 49, 107
    TBBS, 165
    TurboCit, 182
paying your bills online, 229
PC Magazine, 262
PC MagNet, 261-262
PC Pursuit, 205-206, 208
PC-SIG, 36
PC-SIG library on RBBS-PC, 116
PCBoard, 103, 139-150, 187, 208
    archiving, 149
    changing user information,
        142, 143
    chatting with other users, 142,
        149
    checking message areas, 140-
        141
    commands, 142
    conferences, 149, 150
    continuous display, 143
    customizing, 139
    default file transfer protocol,
        142
    doors, 149
    downloading a file, 140, 146-
        148
    entering messages, 144-145
    file areas, 147, 149
    file compression, 149
    file directories, 150

file menu, 146-148
file transfer protocols, 140, 142
forums, 149
graphics display mode, 142
group-only messages, 145
help, 145-146
listing file directories, 147
listing files, 147
logging off, 150
logging on, 139-142
logon screen, 139
main menu, 139, 142
message areas, 140-141
message header, 144
message text, 145
multi-user, 142, 149
new user procedure, 139-142
next message command, 144
online help, 139, 145-146, 150
opening a door, 142
page length, 142, 143
private messages, 145
public messages, 145
read command, 145-146
reading messages, 144
registering on, 139-142
replying to a message, 142
saving user settings, 142
setting page length, 142, 143
setting user options, 142-143
stacking commands, 150
transfer protocol, 142
uploading, 140, 147, 148-149
userlog, 139
viewing archived files, 147
viewing settings, 141
viewing user options, 141, 142
zippy directory scan, 150
PCMagnet
    password, 262
    user ID, 262
personal download, 74, 270, 284
personal information, 27, 60, 266,
    272
personal messages on echomail, 213
philosophy conference on The
    WELL, 256
phone bills, 212
phone cables, 20
phone company, 60, 282
phone equipment, old, 34
phone lines, 14, 272, 276
    party, 34
    sharing with a BBS, 271
phone linking service, 204
phone numbers, 16, 272, 276
phone service, 31, 271
    problems with, 12
phone services, 203, 204-208

pictures, 68
pirate software, 80, 84
plugging in the modem, 20
plus sign to switch rooms, 59, 189
points, 208, 209, 218
policy statement, 30, 106, 268, 272,
    273-274, 291
    reviewing, 268
    setting, 272-275
    TurboCit, 197
    writing, 268
political thought conference on The
    WELL, 256
political BBSes, 289
ports and modems, 9, 10
post office box, 271, 272
power supply, computer, 13
power supply, modem, 12, 13
power users, 282
previous message command
    Fido, 122
    WILDCAT!, 157
Print Formatted on TurboCit, 186
printed circuit boards, 13, 19
printer, problems with, 82
printing with online information ser-
    vices, 232
printing selected information, 266
privacy, ensuring, 26, 88
private BBSes, 281
private download, 74
private mail on a packet radio BBS,
    222
private messages, 49, 52, 56-57, 74,
    77, 274, 284
    echomail, 213
    Fido, 123-124
    PCBoard, 145
    PCBoard, 145
    sending, 92
    TurboCit, 191-193
    WILDCAT!, 156, 157-158
problem users, 75, 277, 278
problem-solving, 99
processing sales orders, business
    BBSes, 291
ProComm, 28
Prodigy, 261
ProDoor, 149
product support conferences, 229
professional organizations, 230
professors, 219
profiles, 89, 92
program manuals, 67, 68
programmers, 286
programs, 64, 67-68, 228
    anti-viral, 82
    backing up, 81
    compression, 77-79

converting to ASCII text, 218
copyrighted, 77
disappearing, 82
loading, 82
memory-resident, 82
public domain, 82
receiving, 63-84
running, 77, 82, 93
sending, 63-84
size of, 82
uploading, 77
virus, 80-83
protocols, 30, 64-67, 84, 269
   OPUS, 128, 136-137
   PCBoard, 140, 148, 149
   TBBS, 170
   WILDCAT!, 160
pseudonyms, 26, 39, 60, 88
public access UUCP nodes, 219, 261
public BBSes, 268, 271, 275
public conferences, 87
public domain BBSes, 127, 269
public domain programs, 67-68, 81, 82, 84, 278, 279
public messages, 52, 56, 274
   PCBoard, 145
   TurboCit, 193
   WILDCAT!, 156
public Usenet access, 256
publishers, business BBSes, 289
pull-down applications, 298

# Q

QMODEM, 28
questionnaires, 89, 92, 232, 269, 288, 289, 291
quitting a BBS, 35

# R

radio station BBSes, 289
radio transmission, 220
radioteletype, 221
RAM-resident programs, 18
RATES command, GEnie, 244
RBBS-PC, 103, 105-117, 208, 269
   @ command, 116
   bulletin menu, 109-110
   calling history on, 109
   CD-ROM drive on, 116
   default transfer protocol, 115
   default user options, 109
   doors, 116
   downloading files on, 114-115
   echomail, 117
   entering a file description, 115

entering messages, 112-113
expert mode, 116
file areas, 116
file menu on 117
file menu, 114
file transfer protocol, 107-108
help, 113-114
library command, 116
list files command, 114
logging off, 117
logging on, 106
main menu, 110-111
message editing, 113
message header, 113
multi-user, 116
netmail, 117
node, 109
password-protecting messages , 113
pausing, 107
PC-SIG library, 116
quit command, 117
quoting messages, 112
read message command, 111
reading messages, 111-112
registering as a new user, 106
replying to a message on, 112
setting display options on, 115
setting options on, 107-109
skipping messages on, 112
source code for, 106
stacking commands on, 116-117
stopping display on, 107
system information, 108-109
threading, 112
toggle command, 116
turbokeys, 108, 116
uploading files on, 115
user options, 109
utilities on, 115-116
utility menu on, 117
with single phone line, 109
Read By-User command, 200
read command
   PCBoard, 145-146
   TurboCit, 196
Read Directory command, 197
read message addressed to someone, 44
read message command, 44
   RBBS-PC, 111
   TurboCit, 185
read reply command, 58
Read Userlog command, 192
Read Verbose Directory command, 197
reading a file directory, 70
reading a long message, 47-48
reading a specific message, 47

reading backward, 44, 59
   Fido, 123
   OPUS, 131
   TurboCit, 185, 189
   WILDCAT!, 156
reading bulletins, 36, 110
reading forward, 44, 59
   Fido, 123
   OPUS, 131
   TurboCit, 185, 189
   WILDCAT!, 157
reading mail, 297
reading marked messages, 50
reading messages, 12, 31, 41-61, 43-51, 61
   Fido, 121-123
   OPUS, 130-131
   PCBoard, 144
   RBBS-PC, 111-112
   TBBS, 166-168
   TurboCit, 185, 189
   WILDCAT!, 156-157
reading replies, 58, 59
reading second half of a message, 48
real-estate agents, business BBSes, 290
real-estate appraisers, 286
reassigning BBS numbers, 281
receiving files, 12, 16, 63-84
receiving messages, 2
recovering operating expenses, 281
recreating directories, 83
recreating folders, 83
recreation conference on The WELL, 260
reformatting messages, 55
regional coordinators, 209
regions, 208, 209
registering shareware, 68
registration, automatic, 137-138
regulations, 262
Relaxed XMODEM, 65
relay stations, 222, 223, 224
remote order entry, 299
remote sites, 3
remote sysops, 56, 270
replacing text, 53
replies to a message, reading, 45, 46-47
replying to a message, 57-59, 213
   OPUS, 133-134
   PCBoard, 142
   RBBS-PC, 112
   TurboCit, 192-193
requesting a file, 213
requirements for logging on, 39
researching with information databases, 266
researching, online information services, 265

resorts, business BBSes, 288
restoring BBS files, 279
restricted access, 31
restricted functions, 35
restricting options, 284
restricting the BBS, 275
return receipt, 169, 193, 158
rights of users, 273, 274
room BBSes, 104, 177-202
    advantages of, 201
    appearance, 202
    bulletin menu, 183
    chatting, 201
    commands, 201
    description, 178-180
    design, 201
    differences from linear BBSes,
        178-179
    disadvantages, 201
    exploring, 178-180
    flexibility, 201
    floors, 180
    games, 201
    grouping information on, 180
    novice users, 201
    restricting access, 180
    security, 201
    structure, 178-180
    types, 180, 201
    writing, 201
room list, 184
rooms with unread messages, 188-189
rooms, 178-179
    creating, 201
    file, 184
    group only, 184
    hidden, 200, 201
    message-only, 184
    window, 179-180
root hallway, 191
round-table discussion, 88, 90-91
RoundTables, GEnie, 241, 243, 244
routed mail, 209-210
RTTY, 221
running a BBS, 268, 271, 282
running programs, 77

# S

Safety Catch, 264
satellite uplinks, 105
satellites, 220, 223-225
saving a file, 72
saving a message, 55-56
    OPUS, 133
    TurboCit, 183, 186
saving a reply, 58

saving money, 264-265
saving screens, 16
saving time, 75-77
scanning messages, 48-49, 52, 61
    TBBS, 168
    TurboCit, 200
school BBSes, 283, 291, 293
science fiction, 266
scientific databases, 264
screen capture, 16, 17, 24
screen display, setting, 27-28
screen width, 30, 130
screen, logon, 105
screen, splitting, 18
screening calls, 271
screening candidates, business
    BBSes, 288
scripts, 17, 51, 74, 231
scrolling, 16
SCSI drives, 81
search strategy, 230
search, topic, 50
security, 27, 102, 150, 232-233, 237,
    269, 277, 280
selling through a BBS, 60
selling through online information
    services, 264
serial port, 9, 12, 20, 21
    and modems, 10
    built-in, 13
serial-to-parallel conversion, 10
servicing field locations, business
    BBSes, 285
servicing your computer, 21
Shanti Project, 127
shareware BBSes, 269
shareware, 19, 67-68, 82, 84, 118,
    139, 150, 213, 298
shopping online, 228, 229, 232
shortwave BBSes, 203, 220-221,
    222, 223, 225
    logging on, 220
    monitoring, 220
    viewing, 220
shortwave satellite uplinks, 105
SideKick, 132
SIGs, 8
Silicon Valley, 261
Singer, Jon, 216, 217
single phone line, 109
single player games, 94
single-key commands, 105
single-player games, 96, 97, 98, 99,
    100
single-user BBSes, 223
single-user systems, 298-299
singles BBSes, 87, 102
size of programs, 82
skipping menus, 232

skipping messages, 47, 58
    RBBS-PC, 112
    TurboCit, 185
skipping paragraphs in messages,
    185
slots, 13
smart mailing programs, 216
smart menus, 174, 162
social science databases, 264
social conferences on The WELL,
    259
software companies, 214, 229, 290
software user groups, 285
software
    hacked, 80
    pirate, 80, 84
    setting up, 21-22
sound, 96, 97, 99
source code, 78, 106, 180
space shuttle, 220
spaces in echomail, 213
speaker volume, 20
speaker, 14, 25, 32
special education BBSes, 291, 293
special interest groups, 8, 230
SpecialNet, 291
specialty magazines, 281
speed of shortwave BBSes, 220-221
speed sensing, 14
speed, modem, 8, 11-12, 20, 25, 231,
    229
speeding up screen display, 29
spell-checking, 77
spikes, 33
splitting the screen, 18
sponsoring events, 277-278
spreadsheet, 18, 64, 67, 83, 93, 228,
    285, 290
SprintNet Data Network, 231, 239,
    246
squelching, 93
stacking commands, 51
    GEnie, 242
    online information services,
        231
    PCBoard, 150
    RBBS-PC, 116-117
STadel, 201
stamps, 281
start bits, 7, 16
starter kits, 230, 231, 233, 265
starting node, 216
state BBSes, 292, 293
static electricity, avoiding, 21
static, 12, 33, 79
status display lights, 12, 13, 14, 20,
    34-35
statutes, 262
stock market figures, 239, 251, 263

The WELL, 259
trade journals, 276
Trade Wars, 100
trademarks, 272
transceiver, 221
transfer errors, 64, 79-80
transfer messages, 209, 210, 212
transfer protocols, 16, 64-67, 79, 84,
    107-108, 269
    delays caused by, 70
    Fido, 126
    menu of, 72
    OPUS, 128, 136-137
    PCBoard, 140, 142, 148, 149
    RBBS-PC, 115
    TBBS, 170
    WILDCAT!, 160
transferring encrypted files, 284, 289
transferring files, 14
    access for, 31
    over FidoNet, 213
transferring information, 286
translating programs into ASCII text,
    219
translation filter, 18
transmission errors, 70, 92
transmission errors, reducing, 205
transmitting data, 205
transmitting on radio, 220
transportation costs, business BBSes,
    286
travel planning databases, 264
travel services, 228
trojan horses, 80, 81, 273
trouble connecting, 25
troubleshooting, iv
TRS-80, 162
truncating message lines, 53
TurboCit, 177, 180-201
    / command, 157
    ? command, 194
    bulletin menu, 183
    changing halls, 190-191
    changing rooms, 187-190
    changing tabs, 193
    directory rooms, 197-198
    dot commands, 187
    downloading a file, 197-199
    editing message text, 186
    Enter Configuration command,
        193
    Enter Exclusive command, 191
    Enter Old Message command,
        200
    entering messages, 185-186
    extended help, 196-197
    file rooms, 184
    full-screen editor, 186
    getting help, 194-197
    going to a specific room, 190

Goto command, 188, 189
group only rooms, 184
help, 194-197
hidden rooms, 200
interesting features, 199-200
Intro command, 197
Known Rooms command, 187
listing files, 197-198
listing help topics, 197
logging off, 200-201
logging on, 180-183
Login command, 181
logon screen, 180-183
mail, 183
message entry commands, 186
message header, 185, 192
minus sign, 189
new messages, 183, 188
passwords, 181, 182
pausing the display, 182
plus sign, 189
policies, 197
print formatted, 186
private messages, 191-193
public messages, 193
Read By-User command, 200
read backward command, 185,
    189
Read commands, 196
read forward command, 185,
    189
Read Directory command, 197
read message command, 185
Read Userlog command, 192
Read Verbose Directory com-
    mand, 197
reading backward , 185, 189
reading forward, 185, 189
reading messages, 185
reading new messages, 189
reading old messages, 185
replying to a message, 192-193
restricted access, 184
return receipt, 193
room list, 184
room names, 184
rooms with unread messages,
    188-189
root hallway, 191
saving a message, 183, 186
scanning messages, 200
see also room BBSes
sending mail, 191-193
seniors hallway, 184
setting display options, 182,
    183
setting options on, 193
skipping messages on, 185
skipping paragraphs in mes-
    sages, 185

stopping the display, 182
Terminate command, 200-201
turbokeys, 181
unread messages, 183
uploading files on, 199, 182
window rooms, 188, 189, 184
word count command, 186
wordwrap, 185-186
turbokeys, 108, 116, 152, 181
turning off the modem, 39
turning paging off, 92
two-character commands, 105
two-way radio transmission, 220
Tymnet, see BT Tymnet
TYMSHARE, Inc., 206
typesetters, business BBSes, 289
typing sticks, 200
typography, 216
typos, correcting in messages, 52-53

# U

U.S. Robotics, Inc., 271
UC Berkeley, 215
UFGATE, 215, 217, 219, 296
unformatted files, 64, 83
unformatted text, 76
universities, 214, 215, 219
Unix, 214, 215, 216, 259, 296
UPI on Delphi, 250
uplinks, satellite, 105, 224
upload date, 70
upload statistics, 270
uploading, 63, 74, 75-79, 213, 275
    and connect time, 274
    and paging, 92
    ASCII text, 126
    BIX, 253
    errors, 79
    Fido, 126
    infected software, 83
    messages, 56, 83
    OPUS, 137
    PCBoard, 140, 147, 148-149
    programs, 77
    programs from PC MagNet,
        261-262
    RBBS-PC, 115
    resumes, 288
    room BBSes, 178
    strategies, 84
    TBBS, 172
    TurboCit, 199
    via satellite, 223
    WILDCAT!, 160
uppercase letters, 28
US Sprint Communications Co., 205
USA Today Decisionline Update, 68,
    278